Protecting
Psychiatric Patients and Others
from the Assisted-Suicide
Movement

Protecting
Psychiatric Patients and Others
from the Assisted-Suicide
Movement

INSIGHTS AND STRATEGIES

Barbara A. Olevitch

Foreword by N. Gregory Hamilton, M.D.
Foreword by Albert Ellis

Westport, Connecticut
London

Library of Congress Cataloging-in-Publication Data

Olevitch, Barbara A.
  Protecting psychiatric patients and others from the assisted-suicide movement : insights and
  strategies / Barbara A. Olevitch ; foreword by N. Gregory Hamilton ; foreword by Albert Ellis.
    p. cm.
  Includes bibliographical references and index.
  ISBN 0–275–96957–6 (alk. paper)
    1. Mentally ill—Care. 2. Psychotherapy patients—Care. 3. Assisted suicide.
  4. Euthanasia. I. Title.
    RC454.4.O446 2002
    362.2—dc21   2002019624

British Library Cataloguing in Publication Data is available.

Library of Congress Catalog Card Number: 2002019624
ISBN: 0–275–96957–6

First published in 2002

Praeger Publishers, 88 Post Road West, Westport, CT 06881
An imprint of Greenwood Publishing Group, Inc.
www.praeger.com

Printed in the United States of America

The paper used in this book complies with the
Permanent Paper Standard issued by the National
Information Standards Organization (Z39.48–1984).

10 9 8 7 6 5 4 3 2 1

To the memory of my beloved father
Zangwill Rand

Contents

Acknowledgments

I would like to acknowledge with gratitude two individuals whose work provided the foundation for my thinking, and whom I have had the privilege to meet. I would like to thank Albert Ellis for developing his method of psychotherapy, and for communicating it so well in his workshops. His work has offered me much clarification about psychological misery and how to ease it. I would also like to thank Wesley J. Smith, whose clear vision of the ideas about death that are circulating in our society, and the effects of these ideas upon health care in America, gave me so much understanding, and whose writing style was an inspiration. I would like to thank Albert Ellis and N. Gregory Hamilton for writing the forewords for this book.

I would also like to thank those pioneers in the field—Herbert Hendin and Rita Marker—whose documentation of the problems of the assisted-suicide movement and whose insights are essential to everyone interested in this area.

I would also like to thank Rita Marker and the International Anti-Euthanasia Task Force for creating and maintaining their web site (www.internationaltask force.org) from which I obtained much valuable information and inspiration. Special thanks to Wesley J. Smith and Kathi Hamlon for answering my questions.

I would like to thank Mary Johnson and the staff of the library at the Missouri Institute of Mental Health for helping me so many times, and the staff of numerous other libraries—Olin Library, Bernard Becker Medical Library, and the Law Library at Washington University, the St. Louis County Library, University City Public Library, and the St. Louis Public Library—who helped me find pertinent materials.

I thank the many individuals who listened to me, encouraged me, told me stories about personal or professional experiences, answered questions, shared clippings, books, and tapes, or read earlier versions of this manuscript and gave me their reactions.

My thanks to Greenwood Publishing Group for giving me this opportunity and to the many fine editors I worked with—Nita Romer, Margaret Maybury, and Lindsay Claire. Special thanks to Debbie Carvalko, whose thoughtful selections of reviewers gave me valuable feedback, and whose understanding made even the final stages of writing into a very positive experience and to Douglas Williams, for his commitment and patience.

I gratefully acknowledge the community in which I live for impressing upon me a high standard for kindness to the handicapped, which I believe the helping professions should strive to match or exceed, and providing me with the enlightenment and the social support necessary to persist in writing on this difficult subject. I also thank the patients I treated in chronic-psychiatric facilities who showed me how people can live well in spite of multiple illnesses and problems.

I would like to express my gratitude to my family—to my parents for their example and their encouragement, to my husband, who besides being my beloved companion, helped me in innumerable ways in the writing of this book, for example, calling my attention to important materials, reading the chapters and giving his reactions, and helping me find the time to work, and to my son, who besides giving me great joy, helped me stay in touch with the lighter side of life as I worked on this serious subject.

I thank the advocates of physician-assisted suicide and those individuals who have publicized their own cases for calling our society's attention to the plight of sick individuals. If they succeed in prodding our society to take better care of the sick, they will have made an important contribution.

My subject is a controversial one. I hope that the flaws of my book will not serve as justification for ignoring the perspective that I offer.

My usual hope when I research a topic is that the research area will grow. In this case, I hope, instead, that the desire for assisted suicide will diminish and our research will be devoted to other more productive topics.

Foreword

N. Gregory Hamilton, M.D.

Joan Lucas, a 65-year-old woman, made a suicide attempt using sleeping pills she'd hoarded. Her adult children watched her as she lay on her bed throughout the day. They couldn't make up their minds what to do, according to the *Medford Mail Tribune* (June 25 and 26, 2000).

When Joan eventually awakened, instead of getting evaluation and treatment for her suicidal despair, her family called George Eighmey, executive director of Oregon's Compassion in Dying Federation, a politically active assisted-suicide group. Mr. Eighmey helped arrange Joan's assisted suicide in Oregon, where such a practice was legal at the time.

The doctor wouldn't reveal his name but told a news reporter he decided to get a mental health opinion, which is not required in Oregon, to cover himself. The psychologist he hand picked sent an MMPI to the patient, because Joan could not easily come into the office. Joan's family helped her fill out the paper-and-pencil test. Then, the psychologist cleared her for a second, more effective overdose. This one killed her.

Never before had families, friends, doctors, and mental health professionals had to struggle with such a dilemma—whether to evaluate and treat a desperate person or offer her legalized assisted suicide. Now, the struggle for assisted suicide continues—with profound implications for the health and safety of mentally ill individuals, as well as the physically ill, their families, and those who care for them. That's why *Protecting Psychiatric Patients and Others from the Assisted-Suicide Movement* is so important. This book is the first comprehensive discussion of assisted suicide from a purely psychiatric perspective. It is written to be understandable for patients, family members, and interested students, while also being thorough and scholarly enough to serve as an up-to-date resource for mental health professionals.

According to a well-known Oregon assisted-suicide guidebook, "If the mental health professional finds the patient competent, refusal of mental health treatment by the patient does not constitute a legal barrier to receiving a prescription for a lethal dose of medication" (Ganzini & Farrenkopf, 1998, p. 31). This opinion by Veterans Administration psychiatrist, Linda Ganzini, is in stark contrast to the 1996 Oregon Psychiatric Association report on the ethics of assisted suicide. The association determined that assisted-suicide referrals to mental health professionals are implicitly requests "for treatment, NOT just for an assessment of psychiatric diagnosis."

Not too long ago, every suicide threat was considered a cry for help. But now, debate over assisted suicide has set up two competing paradigms for responding to patients with suicidal feelings and impulses—evaluate and treat or provide a competency evaluation with little or no therapeutic intervention. Assisted-suicide and "rational suicide" activists are already demanding that mental health professionals shift from caring for vulnerable individuals to providing a gatekeeper function for assisted suicide. It's a bit shocking that with an issue of this magnitude, with its life and death implications for the mentally ill as well as the physically ill, there has been no previous comprehensive book addressed exclusively to the mental health implications of this looming paradigm shift in handling suicidal despair.

Dr. Barbara Olevitch doesn't hail from either the pro-assisted-suicide or the pro-life movements. She is a highly regarded psychologist who has spent most of her career helping individuals with chronic and serious mental illnesses recover feelings of being accepted as worthwhile human beings. Her first book, *Using Cognitive Approaches with the Seriously Mentally Ill: Dialogue Across the Barrier*, teaches therapists to assist vulnerable and marginalized patients in using cognitive skills to find hope and meaning in the midst of suffering. Interestingly, the seriously physically ill are now becoming marginalized like the mentally ill. Their suffering is beginning to share more fully the attributes of stigmatization, pessimism, and neglect once reserved for those considered psychologically disturbed.

It should come as no surprise that someone who has studied how to overcome despair in the chronically mentally ill has a great deal to offer professionals and the public concerning despondency in the physically ill. There is so much overlap between the two populations. The physically ill have extraordinarily high rates of depression and anxiety, as often as not overlooked by their primary care physicians. And the most severely affected mentally ill are clearly known to have complex biological illnesses, as well as the psychological, social, and spiritual struggles everyone shares.

Dr. Olevitch places the issue of assisted suicide within the context of suicide in general. She begins by addressing the long history of hopefulness and triumph in the field of suicide prevention. In doing so, she raises an important question. Would physician-assisted suicide lead to more suicides? Cogently, she observes, "The difference between the ordinary suicidal person and the terminally ill suicidal patient is the reaction he meets with in the therapist." This issue of therapist response is something that concerns all of us, clinicians and patients alike, because it is upon the caring of the caretaker that we all depend when suffering and vulnerable.

Dr. Olevitch goes on to consider whether or not physician-assisted suicide would inevitably lead to euthanasia. This very question was of prime importance to the U.S. Supreme Court in its 1997 determination that there is no constitutional right to assisted suicide. She reviews the fear of medical technology and how the assisted-suicide and the euthanasia movement has capitalized on that fear. She discusses the important role of shifting medical economics and HMOs in creating an environment favoring assisted suicide over medical care.

On a more hopeful note, Dr. Olevitch offers a fine chapter on how health professionals can establish a productive frame of reference for addressing psychological problems in the seriously ill. She describes what all patients and their family members should come to expect, even demand, as the appropriate response to distress in the face of medical catastrophe. In closing, she suggests practical steps health professionals, especially mental health professionals, can take to insure that all people have available to them an appropriate, considered, and professional response to the powerful emotions that arise when, in all likelihood, one is close to death. These are the very steps patients should encourage their doctors and other health care professionals to take as a matter of public health policy.

Not all patients, however, receive the good care and advocacy Dr. Olevitch recommends. Personally, I did not fully understand the implications of this fact until I learned that my former medical school classmate, Peter Reagan, rode his bicycle over to the house of a patient he called Helen and gave her a lethal overdose. Helen had recently been diagnosed as depressed and as having a serious medical illness. Instead of giving her effective treatment for her depression, Peter gave Helen a deadly drug. Would Helen have died by suicide if she had been given good treatment for depression along with good palliative care for her physical concerns? As I eventually described elsewhere, many possible approaches could have helped Helen with her depression, feelings of helplessness, and suicidality. But, these problems were never adequately treated, a fact which eventually led to Helen becoming the first publicly reported legalized assisted-suicide in America.

It's high time the psychiatric community raised the issues inherent in Helen's case, the Joan Lucas case, and others like them. It's high time the psychiatric issues, including a risk to the lives of the mentally ill, become included in the national debate over assisted suicide.

This is an important book. It's the first book to discuss thoroughly from a purely psychiatric viewpoint how the notion of offering assisted suicide as a response to distress among the seriously ill affects all of us—health professionals, doctors, clergy, psychologists, patients, families, anyone who cares about the seriously ill or who may become seriously ill themselves.

This is an important book. And it's a good read!

REFERENCE

Ganzini, L. & Farrenkopf, T. (1998). *Mental health consultation and referral," the Oregon Death with Dignity Act: A guidebook for health care providers.* Portland, OR: Oregon Health Sciences University.

Foreword

Albert Ellis

Although I do not agree with some of the points against physician-assisted suicide that are well-presented in Barbara Olevitch's book, I think she has comprehensively made her case against it, and that this book should be widely read. She gives nearly all the arguments that have been made by those who favor physician-assisted suicide and refutes their points of view with considerable data and with many relevant personal case histories.

Anyone who wants to become aware of both sides of this important question will find ample material in this well-written book. Both advocates and opponents of this issue can appreciably benefit from reading it.

Even more importantly, Barbara Olevitch includes in her book some important cognitive-behavioral methods of psychotherapy that can help alleviate the physical and mental suffering of many people who seriously consider getting physician-assisted suicide. With the help of these methods, they therefore may decide to continue living and leading a productive and enjoyable existence.

Olevitch carefully shows how many people who contemplate suicide, as well as others who are terminally ill or seriously disabled, can be helped to overcome their depressed condition. She optimistically indicates the possibilities and proven benefits of Rational Emotive Behavior Therapy (REBT) and Cognitive Behavior Therapy (CBT), and other forms of constructive therapy in helping disturbed and seriously handicapped people to make what I have called "a profound philosophical-emotional change."

The author presents real hope to these severe sufferers and to the mental health practitioners who can effectively treat them. Her book not only presents views against physician-assisted suicide, but also includes some excellent suggestions for alleviating much of the "necessity" for ending the life of severely ailing people.

Carefully read this unusual book and see how it can be useful to you, whether you are a physician, a mental health professional, or an unfortunate patient, or his or her relative.

Introduction

In November 1998, I read an article in *Psychiatric Services* that shocked me. Schoevers, Asmus, and Van Tilburg (1998, p. 1476) told the story of a 50-year-old physically healthy Dutch woman, who was grieving over the death of her sole surviving son. She died after taking lethal medication given to her by her doctor.

Before reading this article, I had been vaguely aware of the physician-assisted suicide movement and wary of how it might transform the practice of the mental health professions, but I had considered this an unlikely possibility. However this article jolted me into awareness.

At the time of Schoevers, Asmus, and Van Tilburg's article, the Dutch had not yet made physician-assisted suicide or euthanasia legal—this finally occurred on April 10, 2001 (Dutch upper house, 2001)—but they had a set of guidelines. If the physician followed the guidelines, he was not prosecuted.

I was surprised to find that these guidelines had already been extended to include psychiatric patients. The Dutch Board of Psychiatrists had already claimed in 1992 that "suffering from a mental illness is not essentially different from suffering from medical diseases" and that "psychopathology in itself does not automatically make a person incapable of having an autonomous wish to die." In 1997, a report was issued by the Royal Dutch Medical Association and the General Inspection of Mental Health extending the guidelines so that a Dutch psychiatric patient could request assistance with suicide (Schoevers, Asmus, & Van Tilburg, p. 1475). Schoevers, Asmus, and Van Tilburg, although they made many excellent and severely damaging criticisms of the current Dutch guidelines as being extremely problematic for psychiatric patients, seemed surprisingly hopeful about more detailed guidelines being developed by the Dutch Board of Psychiatrists (Schoevers, Asmus, & Van Tilburg, 1998, p. 1479).

My career as an inpatient clinical psychologist flashed before my eyes. I saw my patients as they had come into the hospital, sometimes overwrought, yelling and screaming, sometimes pale and sick-looking, withdrawn, confused, and depressed. Then I pictured them as they looked when the day finally came for them to be discharged, or as they looked when they came back to visit—walking with family, wearing new clothes, and smiling and chatting happily.

I remembered their life stories—often very much worse than the Dutch woman's. (Her case is discussed under the pseudonym "Netty Boomsma" by Hendin, 1997, pp. 60–71, 85–88, 103–105.) I remembered in particular, a woman in her 30s making an immense effort to express herself in spite of her incoherence and telling me that the custody arrangements for her children were such that she was not allowed to see them. I remembered wondering if there was anything that would relieve her suffering. But then I remembered her later. She came to show me a bright orange knitting project that she was working on. Her eyes were glowing. She was looking forward to finishing it, and she was going out on a trip to the museum.

I remembered a man who had lost two daughters in a car accident. I remembered how much better he felt when he left the hospital and how eager he was to encourage other people with problems by telling them how much he benefited from his treatment.

I imagined what it would be like if physician-assisted suicide were legal for psychiatric patients. I pictured a team deciding to assist a patient with suicide, and I pictured them taking the patient into a room and giving a fatal dose of medication. I pictured the patient lying there quietly, dead. Then I pictured the reactions of the other patients and the staff.

These images launched me into reading more about physician-assisted suicide, and I discovered that things were changing in the United States as well, not just in the Netherlands.

Shavelson (1995) tells the story of Kelly Niles, a quadriplegic in his thirties, who was distraught about romantic and social rejection. His attendants, his family, his therapist, and his spiritual advisor were all unsuccessful in consoling him.

In the last few decades, the mental health professions have greatly increased their ability to help people like Kelly. New cognitive behavioral techniques, which are largely unknown to the public, can be used for brief therapy, focused on immediate problems.

At the same time, we have, in the United States, a movement for assisted suicide. An evolving intellectual context is being created in which the desire to die—far from being perceived as a dangerous but reversible symptom—is seen instead as normal and rational. Those concerned about the suffering of people like Kelly—unaware that he could actually be helped—have tried to create the popular support and the legal infrastructure to help him to die.

Unfortunately, the rhetoric of the assisted-suicide movement reached Kelly's family before the news about new psychological techniques. Not knowing how to help Kelly, but finding the lingo of the assisted-suicide movement persuasive, his family and everyone around him—including a police officer, social worker, court investigator, and sheriff (Shavelson, 1995, p. 132)—allowed him to starve himself to death without intervening.

Before the assisted-suicide movement, the public's unawareness of the latest ways of helping emotional suffering was a troublesome problem, but now it has become urgent.

In this book, I hope to inform therapists and others about the rapid diffusion of the assisted-suicide ideology and encourage them to show our society how we can successfully help even seriously ill and handicapped people.

As this book goes to press, physician-assisted suicide is legal in only one state, Oregon. On November 6th, 2001, Attorney General John Ashcroft indicated that physician-assisted suicide was not a "legitimate medical purpose" and that therefore Oregon physicians using federally controlled substances for assisted suicide would be in violation of federal law (Meyer and Murphy, 2001, p. A10). Ashcroft's attempt to halt physician-assisted suicide in Oregon was not successful. On April 17, 2002, Judge Robert James ruled against him (Liptak, 2002). Further appeals are likely, and this issue will therefore once again become a topic of public discussion. Advocates of assisted suicide will be arguing that depriving Oregonians of the option of assisted suicide will do them "irreparable harm," (Class Action, 2001) and many Americans will be listening, including troubled individuals like Kelly Niles and his friends and family.

In the course of researching this book, I learned that assisted suicide poses even more threats to the psychiatric patient and to our society than I had imagined. Nevertheless, this is an optimistic book, because there is so much we can do to help patients and to reveal to our society the serious weaknesses in the arguments of assisted suicide advocates.

If we are well prepared to discuss the issue of assisted suicide, we may greatly improve the quality of our national discussion. Wesley J. Smith (1997) reports that early polls in California and Washington indicated support for physician-assisted suicide, but as the public learned more about the issues, support declined and the proposals were voted down (p. 116). This same pattern was followed more recently in Maine (Smith, 2000).

The purpose of Part I is to assess the extent of the threat of physician-assisted suicide and euthanasia. In Chapter 1, I will begin with a discussion of how the legitimization or legalization of assisted suicide might affect the suicide rate. I will discuss the many ways that our society tries to discourage and prevent suicides and the extent to which we are successful in these efforts even with the terminally ill. I will discuss what might happen if certain potential suicide victims were, instead, given technical help, favorable publicity, and social support for carrying out their suicide plans.

In Chapter 2, I will address the question of whether physician-assisted suicide would lead to euthanasia. I shall argue, first of all, that it is too late for physician-assisted suicide to lead to euthanasia. I shall show, using data and cases from both Holland and the United States, that the deliberate ending of one person's life by another is already occurring, that it is sometimes involuntary, and that it is indeed a possible threat to psychiatric patients. I shall explain how the introduction of physician-assisted suicide could cause even more patients' lives to be ended. I shall show, furthermore, that there are so many cases that bridge the gaps between physician-assisted suicide, voluntary euthanasia, nonvoluntary euthanasia, and involuntary euthanasia, that it would be extremely naive to believe that we could devise guidelines ingenious enough to allow one while preventing the other.

In Chapter 3, I will give background information that will help the reader understand how we came to the situation described in Chapter 2, where lives are being ended by medical decisions which would not have been permitted a few decades ago. I will review the case of Karen Ann Quinlan, the important case in which it was decided that it would not be homicide if Karen Ann's doctors removed her respirator. In discussing the case, I will highlight how the social turmoil of the 70s and the public's developing fears of medical technology influenced the way in which this important decision was written and interpreted.

In Chapter 4, I will discuss some of the prominent activists promoting physician-assisted suicide and euthanasia and their conferences, accomplishments, and legal and social agenda. I will discuss both the highly well-known people who have promoted physician-assisted suicide such as Kevorkian, and the much less well-known people who have promoted euthanasia, such as the expert witnesses in court cases and the bioethicists who are crafting hospital policies. I will show how the changes in medical ethics are threatening not just psychiatric patients and other vulnerable handicapped individuals, but actually anyone who has a life-threatening illness.

Interestingly enough, advocates of physician-assisted suicide and euthanasia consider themselves to be level-headed realists and accuse those who are worried about the slippery slope of having exaggerated fears. What is ironic is that advocates of physician-assisted suicide and euthanasia also base their arguments on certain fears. These fears are not presented as possible dangers; instead, it is simply assumed that unless we make drastic changes in our ethics, we are seriously threatened. Advocates of physician-assisted suicide claim that modern medical advances make it likely that the agony of dying will be protracted for more people and that the finances of managed health care make it impossible to carry out the kinds of effective palliative care that would make these patients more comfortable. Singer (1994, p. 28), for example, makes reference to the "ghastly prospect" that our hospitals could fill up with unconscious bodies. They fear that traditional Judeo-Christian ethics are too inflexible, and that patients will increasingly be caught between the zeal of modern medicine and the inflexibility of ancient ethics in some sort of a twilight world of either pain or unconsciousness while our financial resources are pointlessly drained.

The purpose of Part II of the book is to address these issues and to develop a more realistic and a more optimistic way of viewing our future.

In Chapter 5, I will discuss the way in which the topic of financing has intruded into discussion of health care over the last few decades, and analyze whether some of the fears about the economy of health care are justified.

Just as I argued in Part I that psychiatric patients are uniquely vulnerable to the dangers of physician-assisted suicide and euthanasia, and that they deserve and need our protection, I will argue in Part II that the mental health professions are uniquely qualified to protect not only psychiatric patients but our entire culture from this intrusion.

First of all, I believe that we are in a unique position to prevent the desire for physician-assisted suicide. I shall argue in Chapter 6 that the current inability of people to deal with being handicapped and the inability of others to be sufficiently supportive is a consequence of the vision of mental health held by our culture and that the mental health professions are in a unique position to influence this vision.

I will discuss the popular conception of psychotherapy and how this conception has led to our culture being very pessimistic about meeting everyone's psychological needs. I will also discuss how a cognitive-behavioral approach to psychotherapy provides a comprehensive, optimistic way of conceptualizing psychological problems that will meet the needs of the sick and handicapped.

I will discuss in more detail the ideology of the developing subculture that holds suicide or even euthanasia to be a desirable way of ending life and what concepts we have in the field of mental health that could counteract this cultural trend. Our general culture has a very poor opinion of the ordinary person's ability to overcome handicaps. It also has a very inflated idea of the ability of professionals, managers, and committees to make life-and-death decisions. We cannot go along with either one of these.

Second, I shall argue that we are in a unique position to prevent the availability of physician-assisted suicide. Whenever advocates of physician-assisted suicide discuss the future guidelines that they believe will make this practice safe, they often refer to psychiatric or psychological evaluation as a safeguard. In Chapter 7, I shall argue that decisions about physician-assisted suicide are truly beyond our mental health expertise, and that we could very justifiably refuse as a group to cooperate with these consultations. I shall argue that without our agreement to participate in these consultations, it would be much harder for euthanasia activists to influence the public.

We can also further the field of health psychology. The problems that give rise to the demand for physician-assisted suicide are problems at the interface between psychiatry and medicine. Physical illnesses bring about psychological anguish, and psychological problems bring about lack of understanding and lack of compliance with medical treatment. In Chapter 9, I will discuss the difficulties that patients have in understanding medical treatments and the kinds of labor-intensive efforts that would be necessary to ensure that patient informed consent is truly informed.

In Chapter 10, I will discuss an area in which the contribution of the mental health professions to medicine is critically needed. Any contribution that we could make to helping with the terrifying psychiatric symptoms that afflict large numbers of intensive-care patients would help tremendously with the problems that are leading to the demand for physicians to deliberately end patients' lives. I shall also argue that as medicine adopts palliative care as a goal, we should also commit ourselves to this goal in mental health facilities. By doing so, we would be able to treat many patients who currently cause turmoil in medical facilities.

In Chapter 11, I will discuss the difficulties of persuading people to oppose physician-assisted suicide and highlight some of the arguments that may be successful.

There is no logical reason that the practice of physician-assisted suicide should come up within the mental health professions at this time. It is not founded on scientific discoveries or on theoretical work. As we shall see, it is based on misconceptions that can be corrected and on fears that can be reassured. In the past, the establishment of the mental health professions was successful in leading the general society to a more accurate and optimistic view of psychiatric patients. In spite of the fact that people in the general culture regarded patients as "possessed" and kept them in chains, their problems were eventually recognized as amenable to scientific discovery and curative interventions.

The current time may also be a time in which we have to follow the logic of our mental health professions rather than following popular trends. We have developed many promising techniques of dealing with suicidality, with serious mental illness, and with adjustment to incapacitating physical illness. These techniques are all underutilized. Our public hospitals that house our most seriously mentally ill have been withered by a period of discouragement and cost containment and are currently only for patients who are dangerous to themselves and others. If we also give up the principle of protecting these patients' lives, what would we have left?

What about all the patients who still want to be protected from their suicidal impulses? Where would they be able to go? In whom could they safely confide?

In the last two centuries, we have had unbelievable medical advances, and there are undoubtedly more to come, perhaps soon. To commit ourselves to the fullest possible efforts in medical research and to sustaining and comforting the handicapped and including them in our society as contributing members is a great intellectual, moral, and practical challenge that could revitalize our culture.

REFERENCES

Class action supplemental memorandum of points and authorities in support of the state of Oregon's motion for preliminary injunction. (2001, Nov. 20). Case No. CV-01–1647 Jo, U.S. District Court, District of Oregon. www.compassionindying.org.

Dutch upper house backs aided suicide. (2001, Apr. 11). *The New York Times*, p. A3.

Hendin, H. (1997). *Seduced by death: Doctors, patients, and the Dutch cure*. New York: W.W. Norton.

Kleinfeld, A. Is assisted suicide a right?: A review of legal history. 8th Annual Conference of the Institute for Jewish Medical Ethics, 1997.

Liptak, A. (2002, Apr. 18). Judge blocks U.S. bid to ban suicide law. *The New York Times*, p. A16.

Meyer, J. & Murphy, K. (2001, Nov. 7). Ashcroft targets assisted suicide law in Oregon. *St. Louis Post-Dispatch*, A1, A10.

Schoevers R.A., Asmus F.P., & Van Tilburg, W. (1998). Physician-assisted suicide in psychiatry: Developments in the Netherlands. *Psychiatric Services, 49*, 1475–1480.

Shavelson, L. (1995). *A chosen death: The dying confront assisted suicide*. New York: Simon & Schuster.

Singer, P. (1994). *Rethinking life and death: The collapse of our traditional ethics*. New York: St. Martin's Press.

Smith, W.J. (1997). *Forced exit: The slippery slope from assisted suicide to legalized murder*. New York: Times Books.

Smith, W.J. (2000, Dec. 18) Dead wrong, but still kicking: The physician-assisted suicide movement loses again. *The Weekly Standard*, 21–22.

PART I

Do Psychiatric Patients Need Protection from Physician-Assisted Suicide and Euthanasia?

CHAPTER 1

Would Physician-Assisted Suicide
Lead to More Suicides?

Advocates of physician-assisted suicide have focused attention on a very small group of competent, terminally ill patients in uncontrollable pain. Efforts by many to improve the quality of pain management will hopefully shrink the size of this group still further.

The question we will be primarily concerned with in this chapter is what would be the effect of the availability of physician-assisted suicide on the frequency of suicide in other groups, for example, terminally ill patients who are not in pain, patients with nonterminal diseases, or psychiatric patients?

Unfortunately, it is naive of advocates of physician-assisted suicide to think that guidelines will be able to create a special permission for certain patients while continuing to provide the same suicide prevention as usual for others. The availability and the sanction of physician-assisted suicide would forever change the relationship between any suicidal person and his helpers. It would alter the family and friends' reactions to the suicidal person as well as the nature of any psychotherapy that he might undertake.

If many of our efforts to prevent suicide are currently successful, what would happen if these efforts were weakened, or even, in some cases, reversed? What would happen if, in some cases, we were to provide technical help and social support for suicide?

Thoughts of suicide are not at all uncommon. As cited by Goldman and Beardslee (1999) in a recent review, it has been estimated that 10–15% of all teenagers have contemplated suicide (p. 442).

Currently in our society we make many efforts to prevent suicidal thoughts from developing into suicide attempts. Society's preventive measures are based on a commonsense model of suicidal ideation. Society recognizes that (1) the would-be suicide is undergoing emotional stress, (2) his judgment is temporarily impaired, (3) he has the potential to recover from the stress and impairment and to continue living.

Young people growing up in our society are taught many concepts that would prevent suicide in themselves and others. They are taught to be part of a community and to reach out and give extra emotional support to the bereaved, to the sick, and to the recently divorced. From their families and friends and their school and their religious communities, they learn many commonsense ways of dealing with emotions and conflict and loss. They are encouraged to turn to others for support when they are under stress. Those to whom they turn may not be skilled in counseling but they uniformly encourage them to go on living.

If his own social network fails to provide the potential suicide with enough support to go on living, he can call a telephone hotline manned by volunteers, seek psychiatric treatment, seek professional psychotherapy, or go to the emergency room of a psychiatric hospital. The encouragement or psychiatric treatment that he receives may refresh him so that he recalls and finds meaning in the kinds of stress-management he used to do before. Or, he might learn from those helping him some entirely new stress-management concepts that give him extra support. If he was hampered in his reasoning by psychiatric symptoms, as the vast majority of suicidal people are, no matter what their age group, he might receive medication or other treatments to help him with his depression or other symptoms, thus alleviating the threat of an impulsive suicide based on poor reasoning.

In the meantime, during the time that it takes for these sources of help to become effective, he is sustained in several ways. First of all, the concept that his judgment is temporarily impaired is explained to him. He is told in a tactful reassuring way that he is depressed and that depression is treatable and that he will feel differently after a short period of time. Second, he receives emotional support both from his family and friends and from mental health professionals. Third, he is also protected by being physically restrained from committing suicide in a variety of ways. He must evade family and friends who would try to prevent the suicide. If he tries to jump from a high place and is discovered, the police will be called. He cannot easily buy the kind of drugs that would be most preferable for suicide. Convenient firearms are also difficult to obtain in many places. He may be hospitalized and observed carefully or even physically restrained if necessary.

There is a lot of evidence that these general strategies followed by society are effective. The number of completed suicides, approximately 30,000 per year in the United States (U.S. Census Bureau, 2000, Table No. 138, p. 99), is much smaller than the number of people who contemplate suicide. To some extent, the continued lives of the people who were at risk for suicide but didn't commit suicide may be due to the outpouring of encouragement, counseling, the medical treatment of depression and other psychiatric disorders, and the protective laws that society enforces.

Those who have been interested in preventing suicide have not had difficulty in finding people to work with. Colt (1991) tells the story of Harry Marsh Warren, a 39-year-old Baptist minister who started the Save-a-Life League in 1906. He put an "ad in the newspaper urging anyone considering suicide to call" (p. 287). Within a week, 11 people called.

Colt writes (p. 287), "all of them admitted they had decided to kill themselves, yet all were eager to pour out their despair. Warren listened. All eleven eventually abandoned their plans for suicide." The Save-a-Life League spread to 35 cities and received 2000 letters a year asking for help (p. 288).

A similar example given by Colt was the story of Chad Varah, an Anglican minister, who put an ad in the newspaper in 1953 inviting suicidal people to call or visit. His organization, called the Samaritans, soon attracted so many people that they needed more and more volunteers. Today there are branches of the Samaritans in 24 countries with 180 branches in Britain. The organization has 22,000 volunteers handling 2 million calls per year (Colt, p. 289).

Jacobson (1999) points out that suicidality is the most common precipitant for psychiatric inpatient admissions. He writes that various surveys indicate that it accounts for 60–75% of child, adolescent, and adult patient admissions (p. 383).

Research indicates that even small interventions make a big difference with people with suicidal ideation. A study of a large population of elderly individuals enrolled in a tele-help service showed that telephone contact at home reduced the suicide rate to one seventh of the expected rate (De Leo, Carollo, & Dello Buono, 1995).

Evidence exists that preventive efforts could go a lot further than they ordinarily do. Clarke, Hawkins, Murphy, Sheeber, Lewinsohn, and Seeley (1995) found that group sessions teaching cognitive self-help techniques to adolescents who had been identified as demoralized, reduced the number of cases of depression. Isometsa, Henriksson, Aro, Heikkinen, Kuoppasalmi, and Lonnqvist (1994) found, in a study of psychological autopsies of suicide victims with depression, that less than half were receiving any form of psychiatric treatment. Only 3% were receiving adequate doses of antidepressant medication, only 7% had weekly psychotherapy, and only 3% had been treated with electroconvulsive shock therapy.

Although suicidal thoughts usually do not lead to suicide attempts, suicide attempts are unfortunately not uncommon either. For example, Goldman and Beardslee (1999) include in a recent review that although the suicide rate for adolescents is 13.8 per 100,000, attempts are a far more common 5% (p. 442).

Slaby and Garfinkel (1994) emphasize that 5000 youths under 25 kill themselves every year, including 2000 teenagers and that for every completed suicide, 300–350 attempts are made (p. 3).

National data on injury-related emergency department visits indicates that in 1996, 166,000 intentional self-inflicted poisonings were treated in the United States (McCaig & Stussman, 1997, p. 11).

Like those with suicidal thoughts, suicide attempters also respond to societal efforts to prevent suicide. Jacobson (1999, p. 403) discusses a study of over 1500 suicide attempters (Nordstrom, Samuelsson, & Asberg, 1995) in which it was concluded that the long-term suicide mortality for these attempters was somewhere between 6% and 11%. Only 6% had confirmed suicide deaths. Altogether, 11% had died (some died of drug overdoses which were not classified as suicide).

This is good evidence that some factors, whether it be the reassurance, attention, therapy, medication, treatment—or even just the delay caused by these efforts—are helping these would-be suicides to change their minds about suicide.

Besides offering the suicidal individual reassurance, medication, therapy, or hospitalization to prolong his or her life and to provide relief for his or her symptoms, we also make public health efforts to prevent suicide by restricting dangerous firearms and medications. Seiden (Colt, 1991, p. 335) calls this kind of very effective public health intervention "environmental risk reduction."

Seiden took part in the controversy over whether to put up a barricade on the Golden Gate bridge. By 1990, there were "885 confirmed deaths" by suicide from this bridge (Colt, 1991, p. 334). When the question came up of whether a barrier should be erected, making it more difficult to jump from the bridge, some were of the opinion that a barrier would not save lives because people wishing to kill themselves could and would simply find another way to do it.

According to Seiden, there are many famous sites where a number of suicides take place, for example, the Eiffel Tower, the Arroyo Seco Bridge of Pasadena, California, the Empire State building, and the Mount Mihara volcano on the Japanese island of Shima. At these sites, barriers have been put up to prevent suicides (Seiden, 1978, p. 204).

Seiden was in favor of putting up a barrier (Colt, 1991, p. 333) and did an ingenious study to investigate whether indeed, people who could not jump off the bridge would simply find another suicide method. He followed up people who had tried to jump off the bridge and found that after 26 years, the vast majority of the Golden Gate Bridge attempters—94%—were either still alive or had died from natural causes (Seiden, 1978).

Seiden's conclusion is that people can be saved from suicide by making it less convenient. His hypothesis was supported by the suicide note left by one man who jumped from the bridge. "Why do you make it so easy?" he wrote (Colt, 1991, p. 334).

Perhaps the most famous example of environmental risk reduction is the effect of cooking gas detoxification in Great Britain. When the cooking gas was switched from coke gas to a much less toxic natural gas, the number of English suicides by gas dropped from 2368 to 11. However, the rates of other kinds of suicide did not go up. Instead the overall suicide rate dropped by one third (Colt, 1991, p. 335).

The removal of coke gas from their homes saved lives. People who might have gassed themselves instead went on living—they were not serious enough about suicide to go to the trouble of seeking another method.

Other evidence for the efficacy of environmental risk reduction can be found from data on the restriction of barbiturates. Apparently, restrictions on barbiturates reduced the number of suicides from barbiturates without increasing other methods (Colt, 1991, p. 335). Also, states with stricter gun control had lower suicide rates (Colt, 1991, p. 336). For example, in Washington D.C., a gun-licensing law was followed by an abrupt decline in suicides by firearms (Loftin, McDowall, Wiersma, and Cottey, 1991).

Our successes in restoring the lives of people who might have committed suicide are not restricted to those who do not have a terminal, painful illness. Even with terminal patients in pain, there are reports of success, and as we examine the conceptual basis of mental health treatment, we will see why we should conclude that this is the outcome to strive for, even if we cannot always achieve it.

Advocates of physician-assisted suicide make the assumption that there is a clear dividing line between ordinary suicides and those who wish to die because of a terminal painful illness.

They believe that physician-assisted suicide can be safely allowed for the terminally ill without causing damage to uninvolved parties.

Opponents of physician-assisted suicide have questioned the clarity of this dividing line. They have pointed out how the meaning of words like *terminal* can be very unclear (Marker & Smith, 1996, pp. 90–94). Some people take the word "terminal" to mean that the person will die in a few days or a few weeks. Others use it to refer to a person who will die eventually from the disorder even if it takes years. Some would allow the word "terminal" to be used even for a condition that would only produce death eventually if it were not treated. Some have even used "terminal" to refer to chronic debilitating conditions that do not cause death at all but last until death occurs.

From a mental health perspective, we can challenge the assumption of a clear dividing line. Even more profoundly we must ask whether there is a dividing line at all. Advocates admit that for some people, or for some situations, suicide is inappropriate, and that in such cases mental health experts can be called in to provide treatment. They believe however, that in other cases, suicide may be appropriate, and mental health treatment is not. This attempt to draw a line, beyond which mental health treatment is inappropriate. It is also based upon a profound misunderstanding of the kind of expertise that mental health experts possess. It is based on a mistaken idea of what our profession can do and what it can't.

It is worth examining for a moment the logic of those who believe that a dividing line exists. In the popular mind, there is an imaginary standard of the proper emotional reaction for any given situation. According to this concept, a person needs mental health treatment if he reacts to minor problems as if they were major problems.

This popular concept of mental health treatment leaves no room for improvement if the current problem is indeed a serious problem. What could be more serious than having a fatal, painful illness?

In fact, however, there is no such thing as the "measurement scale" of emotions that laypersons imagine. Mental health workers' experiences tell them not what people should be feeling but just how wide the range of subjective emotional reactions can be.

Dr. Albert Ellis, founder of Rational Emotive Therapy, explains this principle to patients in the form of a simple A-B-C formula, where A stands for *Activating Event*, B stands for *Belief*, and C stands for emotional *Consequence*. Ellis explains that it is not the outside activating event, but, instead, your *belief* about the event that triggers your emotional response (Ellis, 1997, pp. 10–14; Ellis and Harper, 1997, pp. 14, 31).

Although Ellis has given this principle its clearest expression, the principle is implicit in any kind of psychotherapy or psychiatric treatment. The entire efficacy of psychotherapy or even medical psychiatric treatment is derived from this principle. The unique subjectivity of psychological experience is what gives treatment its power to influence well-being. By creating an experience or by changing the psychophysiological state of the patient, we create the opportunity for him to experience the very same world in a more favorable way.

Ellis points out in many of his workshops that much human misery is caused not by problems but what he calls "the problem about the problem." People are upset, to be sure, about their handicaps and their pains and their illnesses, but the truly paralyzing emotions—depression and anger—begin when, for some reason—either because of physiologically induced depression or because it is their habit to do so or because of a lack of skilled emotional support—they draw incapacitating conclusions about their problems.

When people are given skilled emotional support and have an opportunity to express their thoughts about their problems, often they arrive at a much more benign view of the situation that even enables them to make progress with the actual problem. Often, no matter how bad the problem, the emotional pain suffered from the depression and anger about the problem was worse than that from the problem itself.

This shift in thinking explains the efficacy of suicide prevention efforts. No one can be counseled or watched 24 hours a day. Eventually the unsuccessful suicide attempter has a chance to try again. But most of the time, they don't try again, because by that time the world appears different to them.

The mental health professional does not have a measurement standard of what the "proper" emotions are. Instead, he or she has an intimate acquaintance with certain kinds of states of mind or mental traps that people fall into that keep them from readjusting on their own. Biologically oriented psychiatrists try to improve the patient's biochemical abnormalities. Psychodynamic therapists work with her defenses. Rational-emotive behavior therapists work with his irrational beliefs. Cognitive therapists work with her automatic thoughts. Whatever the theoretical orientation, good mental health treatment helps people who are in unproductive states of mind such as depressed ruminations.

The important relationship between a patient's subjective view and his emotional reaction remains the same even when the patient has a terminal illness. Just because the patient's situation is serious does not mean that there is an objective standard of what his emotions should be. His emotions are still derived, as they always were, from his own psychophysiological state and his own beliefs and mental reactions.

Dr. Herbert Hendin, world-famous authority on suicide and executive director of the American Suicide Foundation, who visited the Netherlands to investigate their end-of-life practices, wrote in his book *Seduced by Death: Doctors, Patients, and the Dutch Cure* (1997), "The uninitiated are apt to assume that seriously or terminally ill people who wish to end their lives are different from those who are otherwise suicidal" (p. 22). He goes on to explain, "the first reaction of many patients to the knowledge of serious illness and possible death is anxiety, depression, and a wish to die. Such patients are not significantly different from patients who react to other crises with the desire to end the crisis by ending their lives" (p. 22).

Hendin (1997) gives an example of a terminally ill patient for whom a change of psychological focus meant a great deal. Tim was a young executive whose first reaction to his terminal diagnosis was a desire for suicide (p. 21). Hendin felt that the patient's anticipation of sickness was distracting him from his "fear of death itself." Once he engaged his patient in a discussion of death, Tim was able to accept his situation and make good use of his remaining time (p. 22).

Dr. Abraham Twerski (1987, pp. 1–4) describes his work with a man named Morris, who was "in his fifties" (p. 1) and who had a recurrence of cancer after surgery. He was in a great deal of pain and had become depressed. Walking was difficult. He no longer went to his business or to community meetings and sometimes "needed a wheel chair" even in the house (p. 2).

Twerski was trying to work with Morris by putting him in "a hypnotic trance" to produce pain relief. During their work, he suggested to Morris "that he allow himself to go back in time and recall some pleasant experiences" (p. 2). Morris enjoyed these sessions. He would recall long bike rides that he used to take when he was a child. Dr. Twerski didn't quite realize how effective these sessions were until he talked to Morris's wife. She said he had been back to the office and was going to his synagogue again and looking forward to the sessions (p. 3). He "died peacefully" and was "active almost to the end" and "hardly ever complained of pain" (p. 4).

Twerski speculates that "what keeps most of us going is the anticipation of the future. . . . What, then, happens to a person when he realizes that . . . for him, there is no future? . . . When a person feels this way, any physical pain he suffers must be magnified a thousand fold" (p. 4).

Twerski concludes that "within our billions of brain cells are the memories of virtually everything we have ever experienced. If only we could find the key to those files and retrieve those memories! Morris found that key. He knew that all he had to do was to recline in an easy chair, let himself drift into a trance, and set the clock back to some enjoyable experience which he could relive. He actually looked forward to getting up in the morning, because it meant that he had a full day to relive several more enjoyable episodes" (p. 4).

Ellis and Abrams (1994) have written a book to help the terminally ill: *How to Cope with a Fatal Illness: The Rational Management of Death and Dying.* Ellis and Abrams point out that it is not true that everyone with a fatal illness experiences emotional anguish. They report that "some people, the minute they hear that they have only a limited time to live, even if that limit is diagnosed at five to ten years, immediately make themselves completely miserable, stop themselves from having any—yes, *any*—enjoyment, and think only about the horror of it all until they finally pass away" (1994, p. 2). On the other hand, "the majority of death-notified individuals sometimes suffer emotionally and sometimes do not; often they are depressed or panicked and just as often are calm and light-hearted. Sometimes they are inert and ineffective and at other times they are active and productive" (p. 2).

They continue, "Similarly, the relatives and close friends of fatally afflicted people can feel almost any emotion, ranging from complete horror and constant anguish to calmness, acceptance, and sometimes real companionship and enjoyment of many fine hours with their about-to-die intimates" (p. 2).

Even in patients with a very severe problem, a significant amount of their misery comes from what Ellis calls "the problem about the problem."

Ellis and Abrams give a fascinating example from one of their Rational Emotive Behavior Therapy groups of AIDS patients. A patient, Gustavo, reported that he needed prolonged infusions of a drug through a catheter permanently and visibly implanted in his chest. His reaction to this was to say "I don't think so" (p. 186). He said he had done everything he had wanted to do and he didn't want to suffer. He was planning to kill himself. A few questions from Abrams clarified that the man was not currently suffering. He wanted to die only because he feared he might suffer later.

One of the other group members, Mark, who already had such a catheter, contributed that he too had anticipated that it would be horrible but that, in actuality, it was not. He said, "It was uncomfortable at the beach, but other than that I rarely think of it" (p. 186).

The group actively encouraged Gustavo not to harm himself and this swayed him to agree to go on living (p. 187).

The difference between the ordinary suicidal person and the terminally ill suicidal patient lies not so much in whether they have the inner capacity for improvement in their outlook. This is always present. As long as a person is alive and conscious, they have a myriad of ways of looking at the same situation.

The difference between the ordinary suicidal person and the terminally ill suicidal patient is the reaction he meets with in the therapist. For the ordinary suicidal person, the therapist meets his suicidal ideation with confidence and hope and commitment and persistence. Because of the therapist's hope, he conveys to the patient a conceptual frame of reference that gives the patient hope also. He explains to the patient that his thoughts are part of a depressed state of mind and that this state will pass. He questions the assumptions underlying the patient's suicidal conclusions. He conveys the willingness to work with the patient over a period of time.

Unfortunately, with the terminally ill patient, the therapist does not have the sense of an indefinite period of time. The therapist does not have the confidence that if he cannot help the patient find a more positive outlook at first, he will be able to keep trying until he is successful. He and his patient have a deadline. The patient's health is deteriorating.

However, though there is less time to work with the terminal patient, the terminal patient may be able to compress his or her therapy into a shorter time period. In therapy with the ordinary patient, as the patient accepts the idea of psychotherapy, he still clings to the idea that some problems are bad enough to justify the depression that he feels. In cognitive therapy at least, this issue often comes up explicitly. The patient will ask, what if he were suffering from a fatal illness or some such disastrous scenario? The therapist who is successful in conveying a strong positive outlook will have to help the patient to see that he could even encounter this disaster without being depressed. This graduated approach to learning how to deal with more and more difficult examples of stressful situations is not an option for the terminal patient. He is forced to face the ultimate right away. He cannot keep raising new problems of ever-increasing intensity to test the therapist's theory. So the therapist has less time to work but has fewer distractions. The patient is more serious.

Many books have been written about how a major illness taught the writers valuable psychological lessons about what was most important in their lives. Somehow they learned from the restrictions imposed by their illness that all of those life activities that they thought critical were not really critical at all. They felt liberated by the strictures of their illness to experience things that they had had no time for when they were well. The therapist who understands the subjectivity of emotions can indeed feel hopeful about a good therapeutic outcome even in a terminal patient. The experienced therapist knows that human emotions do not correspond exactly to any objective standard of the patient's situation. The same situation strikes each person differently at different moments. As the person in therapy turns the situation around in her mind, she often sees how her emotions are being affected by certain aspects of the situation rather than the entire situation, and then she can find constructive ways of dealing with her emotions.

If indeed our encouragement, our arguments, our therapy, our medication, and our preventive efforts are successful in reinspiring people to go on living— even suicidal people with terminal illnesses—what would be the effect of our weakening these efforts? What if, when a suicidal person first approaches his friends and family, instead of an outpouring of support and encouragement to go on living he instead encounters quite a few individuals who explicitly support him in his belief that suicide might be appropriate? What if, instead of meeting with a mental health professional who patiently listens to his suicidal conclusions but gently implies that his assumptions are depressed exaggerations and points him in a hopeful direction, he meets, instead, a therapist who agrees that suicide is a reasonable option?

The patient, in coming to the mental health expert, only very partially understands the potential of therapy for restoring his full mental and emotional capacity, whatever that capacity is. He has in mind, instead, the popular conception that there exists some sort of scientific scale of the appropriate reactions to various situations. He is seeking the therapist's expert objective judgment about his potential for living. If the therapist does not convey hopefulness, he takes this as an expert judgment that his life is indeed so terrible that hopelessness is in fact the appropriate reaction. In the past, in the mental health field, we used to say that a patient lacked "insight" if he didn't realize his conclusions were being influenced by his mental state. Now we truly have a situation where both the patient and the therapist may lack insight!

Hendin believes that in the Netherlands, therapists are indeed assisting suicides that could have been prevented. He says that the Dutch guidelines have not offered protection to those who could have overcome their suffering. He describes patients whose deaths were assisted: "a healthy but grief-stricken social worker" and "A man in his early forties who is HIV-positive but who has no symptoms and may not develop them for years" (p. 23).

Hendin points out that if assisted suicide had been legal, his patient, Tim, who was mentioned earlier, would have qualified (p. 22). He could have been referred to two doctors who believed in assisted suicide, one for a first opinion and one for a second opinion (p. 23). Hendin's conclusion is that he might have died "in an unrecognized state of terror" (p. 23).

We have been discussing two opposite ways of conceptualizing the emotions of the terminally ill suicidal patient. The first way is to see his emotions—just as in every other patient—as depending upon his own unique but ever-changing view of his situation. The second way is to see his emotions as somehow being objectively determined by the situation in which he finds himself.

The rational-emotive or cognitive behavioral view of psychotherapy highlights with great clarity the basic principle shared by all psychotherapies: that the patient's beliefs are critical for his improvement.

To pretend to have an objective scale of emotions would be to renounce the most basic principle of mental health treatment. If we buckle in to political pressure and pretend to have an objective scale of emotions as applied to the situation of the terminally ill, how could we justify not having such a scale for other situations as well? How could we rule out the complaints of other suffering groups that their pain is just as bad, if not worse, than the terminally ill? After all, a terminally ill person faces only a short period of pain whereas a younger person who is suffering for some reason—real or imagined—may face a longer lifetime of suffering (Hendin, 1997, p. 48).

To give up on comforting the terminally ill is to overthrow the principle of subjectivity which, once understood, gives so much comfort to people in psychological pain. To save the pain of some patients, we would be leaving open the psychological wounds of a much greater number.

Given the reality that emotions are so subjective that some people derive more suffering from a minor problem than others do from a painful, fatal illness, any attempt to establish a profession that can assist people to make decisions about suicide would be doomed from the start. Suppose, for example, this profession attempted to set up objective criteria allowing physician-assisted suicide in certain situations, for example, for certain diseases. There would be legitimate pressure from suffering people with all kinds of other conditions who felt that they were suffering as much. If, on the other hand, criteria were adopted which focused on the amount of pain instead of on the objective situation, it is clear than anybody could receive physician-assisted suicide for any reason whatsoever.

Schoevers, Asmus, and Van Tilburg (1998, pp. 1477–1478) have pointed out that when a patient fails to improve, a change of strategy, medication, physician, or treatment setting can make a difference.

Robert Dale Jones expressed this eloquently:

In the normal course of . . . practice we all run into cases of depressed patients who, for reasons that may not be apparent to us, can't seem to improve. If these patients request physician-assisted suicide, should we go along with it? I think not. I recall the case of a severely depressed man who simply continued to be severely and dangerously depressed despite everything I could recommend to him. He was transferred to another psychiatrists's care, and to my amazement he made a quick and complete recovery. (Jones, 1997, p. 28)

Schoevers, Asmus, and Van Tilburg (1998) have also pointed out that countertransference reactions would make the judgment of a therapist about a patient's wish for death particularly subject to errors. A therapist with negative feelings toward a patient or a therapist empathizing with a wish to die might err in the direction of approving suicide. They point out that "mere consultation with a colleague" would be "insufficient" to correct this (pp. 1478–1479).

Jack Kevorkian's patients are good examples of the sorts of people who would be dying in much greater numbers if physician-assisted suicide were legal. Out of Kevorkian's first 93 victims, only 27 were determined by autopsy to be terminal, that is, to have less than six months to live (Kaplan, O'Dell, Drogovic, McKeon, Bentley, & Telmet, 2000). Kevorkian's cases are examples of how suicides can be encouraged when the therapist accepts and sanctions the patients' view about the worthlessness of their lives.

Advocates of physician-assisted suicide might try to argue that Kevorkian was so unusual a person, with such strange motivation, that the horrible things that happened under his care would not characterize physician-assisted suicide and are therefore not fair cases to bring up in the debate. I do not agree with this argument. Unfortunately, when we decide upon the safety of any kind of policy, we cannot simply confine ourselves to imagining what fine guidelines we will develop in the future and how perfectly they will be carried out by the most highly qualified practitioners of the most excellent character. We must, instead, imagine a wide range of practitioners. Unfortunately, many of them will be terrible.

In ordinary medicine, bad practitioners do not survive in the market, because people seek out practitioners according to their success record. But in the field of medical suicide assistance, the selection will be in the opposite direction. Suicidal people with impaired judgment who don't comprehend the value of their own lives and who cannot recognize the value of good treatment will seek out the practitioner who imposes the fewest restrictions.

We must consider Kevorkian's cases because if physician-assisted suicide is legalized, it is inconceivable that there will be no others like him. He managed to single-handedly raise the suicide rate by over 130 people within a few years. Even if there were only a few Kevorkians, thousands would die unnecessarily. Unfortunately, as people in the mental health professions know, there is no shortage of the kinds of patients who travelled to Michigan to seek out his services.

Judith Curren was a 42-year-old nurse with two small daughters, who sought out Dr. Kevorkian (Clash in Detroit, 1996). Like many chronic psychiatric patients, she had an assortment of psychological, physical, and situational problems, each of which is difficult to assess because of the presence of all the others.

When working with such patients, instead of succumbing to hopelessness because of their multiple problems, it is important to demonstrate to them that when they focus on one problem and make some progress, they do indeed experience some improvement in their mood even though the other problems still exist.

Ms. Curren had one major problem that needed immediate attention: Her husband had been charged with assaulting her, and the police were called to her home on several occasions to break up fights (Clash in Detroit, 1996). Dr. Kevorkian said that he asked Ms. Curren and her husband, a psychiatrist, if they had domestic problems, but they told him they did not (Lessenberry, 1996, p. 6). Kevorkian's lawyer, Geoffrey Fieger, said that their domestic difficulties had "no relevance" to the case, and that Dr. Curren had not been convicted of anything (Question of family violence, 1996, p. 25). Clearly, either way, these reports of domestic assaults complicate the case. If Dr. Curren was assaulting his wife, he was clearly lowering her quality of life. If he was not, her complaints to the police would be a sign of greatly impaired judgment.

Ms. Curren reportedly complained of having chronic fatigue syndrome and fibromyalgia. Kevorkian's attorney claimed that she also had "funguses that attacked the brain" (Clash in Detroit, 1996, p. A13). Dr. Dragovic, the county medical examiner who performed the autopsy, believed that her fatigue could more probably be attributed to the fact that she was "grossly overweight" (p. A13).

Clearly, the extent to which these reported and disputed chronic medical problems contributed to her despair could not be determined without some assessment of Curren's daily situation. Her case clearly illustrates the danger that assisted-suicide advocates could help people commit suicide without a full evaluation.

The case of Rebecca Badger is another example of a case that revealed to many people the superficiality of Kevorkian's evaluations. Rebecca Badger, like Judith Curren, had a combination of psychiatric symptoms and physical complaints. She believed she was suffering from multiple sclerosis (MS). She used a wheelchair and claimed loss of bladder and bowel control and excruciating pain. After her autopsy, L.J. Dragovic said, "I can show you every slice from her brain and spinal cord, and she doesn't have a bit of MS. She looked robust, fairly healthy. Everything else is in order. Except she's dead" (Leiby, 1996, p. A1).

Her own doctor, Meyer-Mitchell, reported that Badger had a history of childhood sexual abuse, chemical dependency, and alcoholism (p. A12). She had been despondent about the breakup of her second marriage. She had refused antidepressants and was displeased with a psychiatric consultation. Moreover, she was angry about her health coverage. According to Wesley J. Smith, she had given a taped television interview "only days before her death" in which she revealed she had lost her private health coverage, and complained about five-hour waits to see a doctor. She said if someone could relieve her pain, she wouldn't want to die (Smith, 1997, p. 149). Smith points out that there is no indication that Kevorkian made any attempt to refer her for specialized pain treatment (p. 205).

Each of these cases is complex. These women had multiple problems, both somatic and psychological. It is hard to believe that they could not have benefited considerably from expert medical and psychiatric consultation and reevaluation, medication, psychotherapy, and good palliative care. Even advocates of assisted suicide consider their suicides highly questionable.

Besides practitioners like Kevorkian, there will be the normal practitioners, who, when they carry out well-defined procedures, make mistakes only very rarely. However, as we have discussed, there are insuperable theoretical obstacles inherent in the development of criteria for suicide assistance. The pressures and the complexities of this poorly conceived enterprise of evaluating suicide requests will unfortunately provide the occasion for many of these otherwise well-functioning practitioners to make fatal errors.

Moreover, if ordinary practitioners joined in this enterprise, clients wouldn't be limited to the unusual few who would travel cross-country to meet with a pioneer operating illegally and in isolation. A much larger pool of possible clients—ordinary conventional people with a mixture of psychiatric and physical symptoms—might be tempted to seek help of this kind.

Now we come to a critical question. What if preventive efforts are not merely omitted; what if they are actually reversed? Does the suggestibility of the would-be suicide—terminal or nonterminal—leave them vulnerable to influence in the opposite direction? Can they be influenced in the direction of killing themselves? Hendin writes that patients requesting help with suicide are often ambivalent, and their eventual decision may reflect their interaction with "family, friends, and doctor" (Hendin, 1997, pp. 156–157).

In the past, when cultural attitudes toward suicide were very negative, most people who contemplated suicide, if they were influenced, were influenced in the direction of remaining alive. Now, unfortunately, we face a situation in which large numbers of suggestible people contemplating suicide may meet, instead, with influences in the opposite direction. What if, instead of hearing consistent encouragement to go on living, the patient is exposed to a new ideology in which suicide is portrayed as an attractive alternative?

Hamilton, Edwards, Boehnlein, and Hamilton (1998) discuss the powerful effects of subtle influences in the direction of suicide from those individuals that the patient relies on, such as family members asking repeatedly if a patient's pain was "too much" (p. 62–63). Unfortunately, persuasion in the direction of suicide is no longer restricted to subtle influences. Hendin calls our attention to findings that in the Netherlands, physicians don't wait for patient requests; they actively suggest physician-assisted suicide and euthanasia for their patients (1997, pp. 52).

Wesley J. Smith (1997), in the introduction to his book *Forced Exit: The Slippery Slope from Assisted Suicide to Legalized Murder*, describes how he became inspired to become "an anti-euthanasia activist." He describes how he, along with the other close friends of a woman named Frances, "worried about her" because of her frequent talk about suicide. They wondered "where on earth she had come up with the idea that self-destruction was a positive thing. Who had coined all of the euphemisms for self-destruction that sprinkled her vocabulary, such as 'deliverance' and 'final passage'?" (p. xiii). After her death, Smith found a copy of the *Hemlock Quarterly* in her files, dog-eared and highlighted in yellow (p. xvi). The method of suicide described in the *Hemlock Quarterly*— the drugs and the "plastic bag"—was the same method Frances had used (p. xviii). Smith was "sickened" by the glowing descriptions of "peaceful" suicides attended by "loving" families who found it a rewarding experience (pp. xvi–xvii).

He writes, "Frances's death was not noble and uplifting as she had fantasized. . . . None of her friends appreciated the morbid experience of receiving photocopies of her suicide letter in the mail after she was gone, and most of us felt angry, betrayed, and empty in the wake of her self-destruction" (pp. xv–xvi).

The Hemlock Society and other similar organizations who help people interested in assisted suicide can, in some cases, be the Samaritans in reverse. They provide a new ideology to replace the old. They provide technical assistance and social support for carrying out suicide plans.

How effective are these organizations in "liberating" people from their difficulties? Given the large number of suicide attempters relative to the number of suicide completers, how many more people would commit suicide if they were given technical help and social support?

Even just the written instructions in *Final Exit*, the suicide manual written by Derek Humphry, the director of the Hemlock society, seems to have had at least some effect. Marzuk, Hirsch, Leon, Stajic, Hartwell, and Portera (1993) report that asphyxiations by plastic bag went up 313% in New York in the year after the book's publication. In 15 cases of asphyxiation or poisoning either the book itself was found at the scene or a suicide note patterned after the prototype in the book was found. Of these 15 cases, 6 were free of medical disease and 5 of the others had diseases which are not ordinarily precipitants of suicide— uterine fibroids, diabetes, arthritis. Marzuk, Tardiff, and Leon (1994) report that the number of suicides by poisoning and asphyxiation, the methods recommended by Humphry, rose significantly nationwide. Asphyxiations rose by 30.8% and self-inflicted fatal poisonings by 5.4%. In both the New York study and the nationwide study, there was no significant decrease in the use of other methods and the overall suicide rate did not increase significantly between the year before and the year after publication of the book. It is hard to estimate how many of the more than 500,000 people (Shavelson, 1995, p. 11) who bought the book filed away the suicide information for future use. It is also hard to estimate how many of those who successfully completed their suicide with the plastic bag might have failed to complete their suicide if they hadn't read Humphry's instructions.

A comparative study of adolescent suicide completers and suicide attempters in Oregon in 1988 showed that the "strongest predictor of outcome" was the method selected (Andrus, Fleming, Heumann, Wassell, Hopkins, & Gordon, 1991, p. 1069). Successful suicides used either firearms or hanging. Unsuccessful suicides used medications. This is consistent with national data on methods of suicide, which shows that for 1996 and 1997, for example, 58% of suicide deaths were by means of handguns or other firearms (U.S. Census Bureau, 2000, Table No. 138, p. 99).

The attempter for whom medication has a strong appeal has so far been handicapped in her ability to complete a suicide. Probably most people do not realize how difficult it is to kill yourself with over-the-counter medications. This lack of knowledge may save many lives, because after an ineffective attempt, the family and friends have a chance to persuade the patient to accept psychiatric treatment, and most patients succeed in remaining alive without further attempts. There is a danger that the increasing availability of technical know-how about suicide would remove this opportunity by making first attempts more successful. There were 166,000 intentional self-inflicted poisonings treated in hospital emergency rooms in 1996 (McCaig & Stussman, 1997, p. 11), and, in the same year, only 5080 successful suicides from poisoning by drugs, other solids, liquids, and gases (U.S. Census Bureau, 2000, Table No. 137, p. 98). This data at least suggests the possibility that with better information, more of these suicide attempts might be lethal.

Rose and Rosow (1973) studied over 400,000 death certificates in California over a three-year period. In an analysis separating professional and technical workers, the suicide rates for chemists were the highest in the professional category. Pharmacists headed the list for the technical category (Table 3, p. 802). This might be suggestive evidence that those with knowledge of how to use poisons are more successful at suicide. They report, moreover, that physicians used drugs, poisons, or gases for 73% of their suicides, whereas, for the general population, this percentage was only 39% (Table 10, p. 804). Although this is not conclusive evidence that technical suicide assistance would raise the suicide rate, it is certainly suggestive.

If physician-assisted suicide were legal, besides the availability of technical help, there would be another factor that might increase the suicide rate. Under cultural conditions where the idea of suicide is validated rather than automatically discouraged, there is more potential for individuals to make decisions to commit suicide. A large pool of individuals exist who have psychiatric symptoms and have thought about suicide who might be influenced by everything they see and hear about suicide.

There is a phenomenon known as a "suicide cluster," where a much larger number of people than expected commit suicide in a certain locality within a short period of time, often using similar methods. The suicide of the first individual is thought to give sanction to the idea of suicide, making it easier for the next potential suicider to carry out his plans. Many such incidents have been documented among adolescents. For example, in 1983 in Plano, Texas, a sunbelt city with a population of 90,000, 8 suicides occurred within 15 months, and in Clear Lake City, Texas, 6 teenage suicides occurred between August and October, 1984 (Doan & Peterson, 1984). Beginning in 1974, there were 8 suicides on an Indian reservation in 12 months. Psychological autopsies revealed that almost all suffered from family discord, alcohol abuse, and isolation (Ward & Fox, 1977).

These clusters often begin with the accidental death or suicide of one teenager, followed by the suicides of their close friends, and then the suicides of others. Mental health authorities in these localities often are swamped with calls from other teenagers who believe themselves to be suicidal as well (Gelman & Gangelhoff, 1983).

These clusters are often mentioned as an adolescent phenomenon. However, they are not confined to adolescents. For example, 82 people, most of whom were mentally disturbed, burned themselves in England and Wales between October 1978 and October 1979 following a widely publicized political suicide (Ashton & Donnan, 1981). In Oregon between June 1976 and July 1977, 8 physicians who were put on probation killed themselves and two more made serious attempts (Crawshaw, Bruce, Eraker, Greenbaum, Lindemann, & Schmidt, 1980).

Gould, Wallenstein, Kleinman, O'Carroll, and Mercy (1990) did statistical work identifying suicide clusters. They reported that suicide clusters occur primarily among teenagers and young adults but do occur occasionally at other ages. They reported a cluster for 55 to 64 year olds. Had their criterion for statistical significance been slightly less stringent (had they used a p less than .025 criterion instead of p less than .01), two other clusters in their data would have been reported as significant—one involving 55 to 64 year olds and one involving 65 to 74 year olds.

Phillips and Cartensen (1988) have done research indicating that even just television or news coverage of a suicide by a famous person can cause an increase in the suicide rate.

It matters little for the point that we are pursuing whether these clusters are interpreted as contagion or as the effect of similar circumstances impinging on large numbers of vulnerable individuals. In either case, these clusters indicate the potential for rises in the suicide rate.

The aged and the seriously handicapped, although they are not as emotionally labile as adolescents, have some circumstances in common with adolescents. Adolescents have not yet taken on the responsibilities of marriage, jobs, and parenthood, all of which occupy a person and give them a sense of purpose during their adult years. Many aged or seriously disabled people resemble adolescents in that they have given up many of their day-to-day responsibilities and find themselves once more preoccupied with their own comfort.

Adolescents do not feel themselves to be the masters of their own situation. They are subject to the authority of their parents and their school rules. Having not yet diverged into their own individual unique lives, they feel very similar to one another. When one of them commits suicide because of a situation, the others identify very strongly with him and feel that they too could have done this. Aged or seriously disabled people may also perceive themselves as very much alike. They have difficulty pursuing many of the interests that made them each unique and are, instead, subject in common to the symptoms and problems of their illnesses, which they eagerly gather information about. They are also subject to the rules and regulations of their health insurance plans.

The elderly have a higher suicide rate than other age groups (Steffens & Blazer, 1999, p. 451) and it is rising (Elderly's suicide rate, 1996, p. A14). Haas and Hendin (1983) suggest "careful scrutiny of the underlying causes of suicide among older people" (p. 153). They point out that, although the suicide rate of all birth cohorts increases as they age, certain birth cohorts with an especially high suicide rate will be aging in the first few decades of the 21st century.

Even among the elderly, those who commit suicide have a high incidence of psychiatric disorder (see, for example, Carney, Rich, Burke, & Fowler, 1994). As reported by Moscicki (1999) in a recent review on the epidemiology of suicide, "Psychological autopsy studies have consistently found that over 90%

of all completed suicides in all age groups are associated with psychopathology," particularly mood disorders and alcoholism (p. 45).

If physician-assisted suicide were legal, there might well be suicide clusters among older or seriously disabled people. There might from time to time be highly publicized suicide stories about older people with certain diseases. These might perhaps be celebrities that many older people had admired in their youth. Readers of the stories might have the same disease or think that they do. There could be rises in the suicide rate in reaction to these stories or in reaction to unfavorable changes in health coverage.

One could perhaps conclude that within the AIDS community, there is a continuous process like a suicide cluster. In the Remmelink Report, an investigation of physician-assisted suicide and euthanasia in Holland in 1990–1991, AIDS patients were handled as a separate group. Their rate of assisted suicide and euthanasia was estimated at 10–20% (van der Maas, van Delden, & Pijneborg, 1992, p. 172). Colt reports that AIDS patients are "sixty-six times more likely" to commit suicide than the general population (Colt, 1991, p. 260). Colt cites a quotation by Randy Shilts that AIDS patients exchange suicide prescriptions like "housewives swap recipes for chocolate-chip cookies" (p. 260).

It is clear that this group experiences the highest possible set of stresses with the least support—since the disorder itself often causes the fatally afflicted to be bereaved of their significant others and friends. Shavelson, however, points out an additional aspect of the high suicide rate among AIDS sufferers. He wrote, "Isolated by a society that had rejected them . . . assisted suicide for people with AIDS became an acceptable norm and an act that was not legally prosecuted" (1995, p. 46).

If physician-assisted suicide becomes an acceptable conventional solution to the problem of fatal diseases, and legal restrictions no longer play a part in assisted-suicide decisions, we may wonder whether the suicide rate for certain other fatal conditions could possibly approach the suicide rate for AIDS.

Advocates of physician-assisted suicide have so far claimed that the numbers of terminally ill people who chose physician-assisted suicide in Oregon were small. In 1998, 16 patients died after obtaining lethal prescriptions. In 1999, 27 died in this manner. In 2000, another 27 died following the provisions of the Death with Dignity act.

Sullivan, Hedberg, and Hopkins (2001) compare the number of physician-assisted suicides to the number of deaths in Oregon. For example, they state, "The 27 patients who ingested lethal medications in 2000 represent an estimated rate of 9 per 10,000 deaths in Oregon" (p. 605).

In asking the question whether these numbers are small or large, we have to think about what to compare them to. For purposes of our analysis here, what we really want to know is how they compare to other suicides. For the living population, the suicide rate in Oregon in 1999 was 15.1 per 100,000 (Oregon Vital Statistics, 1999, Table 6–3).

Sullivan, Hedberg, and Hopkins (2001) assembled a cohort of Oregon residents who died of similar diseases to those who had selected physician-assisted suicide. In 1999, this cohort comprised 6981 people. If we add the 27 who selected lethal prescriptions, the total number of people dying from these diseases was 7008. Out of 7008 people with these same kinds of diseases, 27 opted for physician-assisted suicide. This rate is equivalent to 385 per 100,000. This suggests that in Oregon, those dying of terminal diseases select physician-assisted suicide 25 times as often as members of the general population select suicide.

Another comparison that indicates that these numbers should not be considered small is a comparison based upon the attraction of suicidal people to certain methods of suicide. What if, instead of comparing the number who died from physician-assisted suicide to the number of people living or dying in the state of Oregon, we, instead, compare it to the number who committed suicide using medication?

Using Oregon statistics for the leading causes of death in 1999, the last year for which the final statistics are currently available (Oregon Vital Statistics, 1999, Table 6–30), we see that 87 women and 412 men committed suicide. Of those who committed suicide, 21 women and 27 men used medication. These statistics do not include physician-assisted suicides. Looking at the statistics for physician-assisted suicide for Oregon in 1999 (Sullivan, Hedberg, & Hopkins, 2001), we find that 16 men and 11 women died from prescribed lethal medication.

Using these statistics, we can see that if physician-assisted deaths are counted with unassisted suicides, the rate of suicide using medication as a method was increased by 52% for women and 59% for men.

From the point of view of prevention, we must be aware of the possibility that the climate of opinion may affect suicide choices in the general population. Wesley J. Smith alerts us to the possibility that changes in the climate of opinion regarding suicide may have a negative impact upon teenagers who consider suicide. Smith writes, "Oregon voters legalized physician-assisted suicide, but when newspapers run headlines about the state's soaring suicide rate among adolescents, nobody connects the dots" (1999).

Questions about specific effects upon the suicide rate are easier to raise than to answer, but nevertheless they should be raised because they highlight the need for preventive efforts which, fortunately, are already going on in Oregon.

Each state has unique demographic features—such as the ratio of men and women, the proportion of racial groups, the number of migrants from other areas, socioeconomic level, divorce rate, and prevalence of alcoholism—that play a role in determining the average suicide rate.

The suicide rate in Oregon has been high for a long time. A report put out by the Health Division of the Oregon Department of Human Resources includes the information that "During nine of the past ten years, Oregon's suicide rate has exceeded the nation's by at least 25%" and also that "The Oregon suicide rate has increased 28% since 1960 compared to 13% for the U.S." (Suicide and Suicidal Thoughts, 1997, p. 11).

The complex causal interplay between demographic features of the state, the climate of opinion, and the legalization does not have to be fully understood, however, for us to draw the conclusion that cultural influences within a subscribed geographic area can indeed boost the suicide rate, and that these same kinds of cultural influences can be generated in other states as well. If legalization occurs, the cultural influences that may have been previously confined to certain subcultures or certain regions may become more universal. At the very least, if physician-assisted suicide were legal, I would predict that we would lose thousands of people like Judith Curren and Rebecca Badger, that is, many of our suggestible psychiatric patients suffering from chronic medical conditions. These people would identify with role models of physician-assisted suicide patients. Their chronic medical condition would provide the justification for granting their request.

It is possible that physician-assisted suicide would become something of an attraction, like the Golden Gate Bridge. It is possible that, for a patient with psychological suffering, the affirming decision of the physician could be interpreted as a validation of his complaints. It could be perceived as a soothing indictment of all of those people who had hurt or abused him. It could be experienced as an honor to have one's pain measured and declared intolerable. The highly publicized physician-assisted suicide of a charismatic person with multiple problems could lead to a wave of requests and do-it-yourself suicides.

No one can truly provide accurate quantitative estimates of the size of the rise in the suicide rate that would occur if physician-assisted suicide were legalized and accepted in our culture, but it is clear that the suicide rate would rise. Herbert Hendin (1997) writes, "we will lose more lives to suicide (although we will call the deaths by a different name) than can be saved by the efforts of the American Suicide Foundation and all the other institutions working to prevent suicide in this country" (p. 223).

As our society considers physician-assisted suicide, there have been a growing number of underground but highly publicized family-assisted, friend-assisted, and organization-assisted suicides (see Jamison, 1995; Shavelson, 1995).

Besides estimating the increased suicide rate, we can ask, as well, about the hidden psychological toll of destigmatizing suicide. Would people who are currently not even experiencing suicidal ideation begin to experience it?

A person who enters into the suicidal dilemma assumes a crippling psychological burden. Each negative experience becomes not just an unpleasant event but also a trigger for a comprehensive assessment of his future pains and pleasures. If physician-assisted suicide were legalized, many ill people who have never before contemplated suicide might enter into this painful psychological exercise.

Advocates of managed dying are fond of pointing out that the best method of avoiding medical problems is prevention. If more people ate healthy food and exercised, there would be a reduced demand for heart transplants.

The method of prevention can also be exercised in the legal-moral realm. To help prevent many extra suicides and extra Kevorkians and extra arguments about guidelines, and extra psychological anguish and much cultural turmoil, there is something our society can do—avoid the legalization and the legitimization of assisted suicide.

REFERENCES

Andrus, J.K., Fleming, D.W., Heumann, M.A., Wassell, J.T., Hopkins, D.D., & Gordon, J. (1991). Surveillance of attempted suicide among adolescents in Oregon, 1988. *American Journal of Public Health, 81*, 1067–1069.

Ashton, J.R., & Donnan, S. (1981). Suicide by burning as an epidemic phenomenon: An analysis of 82 deaths and inquests in England and Wales in 1978–1979. *Psychological Medicine, 11*, 735–739.

Blazer, D.G. (1991). Suicide risk factors in the elderly: An epidemiological study. *Journal of Geriatric Psychiatry, 24*, 175–190.

Carney S.S. Rich G.L. Burke P.A. & Fowler R.C. (1994). Suicide over 60: The San Diego study. *Journal of the American Geriatrics Society, 42*, 174–180.

Clarke, G.N., Hawkins, W., Murphy, M., Sheeber, L.B., Lewinsohn, P.M., & Seeley, J.R. (1995). Targeted prevention of unipolar depressive disorder in an at-risk sample of high school adolescents: A randomized trial of a group cognitive intervention. *Journal of the American Academy of Child and Adolescent Psychiatry, 34*, 312–321.

Clash in Detroit over how ill a Kevorkian client really was. (1996, Aug. 20). *The New York Times*, p. A13.

Colt G.H. (1991). *The enigma of suicide.* New York: Simon & Schuster.

Crawshaw, R., Bruce, J.A., Eraker, P.L., Greenbaum, M., Lindemann, J.E., & Schmidt, D.E. (1980). An epidemic of suicide among physicians on probation. *Journal of the American Medical Association, 243*, 1915–1917.

De Leo, D., Carollo, G., & Dello Buono, M.L. (1995). Lower suicide rates associated with a tele-help/tele-check service for the elderly at home. *American Journal of Psychiatry, 152*, 632–634.

Doan, M., & Peterson, S. (1984, Nov. 12). As "cluster suicides" take toll of teenagers. *Newsweek*, pp. 49–50.

Elderly's suicide rate is up 9% over 12 years. (1996, Jan. 12). *The New York Times*, p. A14.

Ellis, A. (1997). *Anger: How to live with and without it.* New York: Citadel Press.

Ellis, A., & Abrams, M. (1994). *How to cope with a fatal illness: The rational management of death and dying.* New York: Barricade Books.

Ellis, A., & Harper, R.A. (1997). *A guide to rational living.* North Hollywood, CA: Wilshire Book Company.

Gelman, D., & Gangelhoff, B.K. (1983, Aug. 12). Teen-age suicide in the Sun Belt. *Newsweek*, pp. 70, 72, 74.

Goldman, S., & Beardslee, W.R. (1999). Suicide in children and adolescents. In D.G.

Jacobs (Ed.), *The Harvard Medical School guide to suicide assessment and intervention* (pp. 417–442). San Francisco: Jossey-Bass.

Gould, M.S., Wallenstein, S., Kleinman, M.H., O'Carroll, P., & Mercy, P. (1990). Suicide clusters: An examination of age-specific effects. *American Journal of Public Health, 80,* 211–212.

Haas, A.P., & Hendin, H. (1983). Suicide among older people: Projections for the future. *Suicide and Life-Threatening Behavior, 13* (3), 147–154.

Hamilton, N.G., Edwards, P.J., Boehnlein, J.K., & Hamilton, C.A. (1998). The doctor-patient relationship and assisted suicide: A contribution from dynamic psychiatry. *American Journal of Forensic Psychiatry, 19*(2), 59–75.

Hendin, H. (1997). *Seduced by death: Doctors, patients and the Dutch cure.* New York: W.W. Norton.

Isometsa, E.T., Henriksson, M.M., Aro, H.M., Heikkinen, M.E., Kuoppasalmi, K.I., & Lonnqvist, J.K. (1994). Suicide in major depression. *American Journal of Psychiatry, 151,* 530–536.

Jacobson, G. (1999). The inpatient management of suicidality. In D.G. Jacobs (Ed.), *The Harvard Medical School guide to suicide assessment and intervention* (pp. 383–405). San Francisco: Jossey-Bass.

Jamison, S. (1995). *Final acts of love: Families, friends, and assisted dying.* New York: G.P. Putnam's Sons.

Jones, R.D. (1997, Apr. 4). Assisted suicide. *Psychiatric News,* p. 28.

Kaplan, J.K., O'Dell, J.C., Dragovic, L.J., McKeon, M.C., Bentley, E., & Telmet, K.L. (2000). An update on the Kevorkian-Reding 93 physician-assisted deaths in Michigan: Is Kevorkian a savior, serial-killer or suicidal martyr? In K.J. Kaplan (Ed.)., *Right to die versus sacredness of life* (pp. 209–229). Amityville, NY: Baywood Publishing.

Leiby, R. (1996, Jul. 29). Just how sick was Rebecca Badger?: Jack Kevorkian helped end her life, and that's when the questions began. *The Washington Post,* pp. A1, A12.

Lessenberry, J. (1996, Aug. 17). Kevorkian goes from making waves to making barely a ripple. *The New York Times,* p. 6.

Loftin, C., McDowall, D., Wiersema, B., & Cottey, T.J. (1991). Effects of restrictive licensing of handguns on homicide and suicide in the District of Columbia. *New England Journal of Medicine, 325,* 1615–1620.

Marker, R.L., & Smith, W.J. (1996). The art of verbal engineering. *Duquesne Law Review, 35*(1), 81–107.

Marzuk, P.M. Hirsch, C.S., Leon, A.C., Stajic, M., Hartwell, N., & Portera, L. (1993). Increase in suicide by asphyxiation in New York City after the publication of *Final Exit. New England Journal of Medicine, 329,* 1508–1510.

Marzuk, P.M., Tardiff, K., & Leon, A.C. (1994). Increase in fatal suicidal poisonings and suffocations in the year *Final Exit* was published: A national study. *American Journal of Psychiatry, 151,* 1813–1814.

McCaig, L.F., & Stussman, B.J. (1997, December 17). National hospital ambulatory medical care survey: 1996 emergency department summary. *Advance Data,* No. 293. From Vital and Health Statistics of the Centers for Disease Control and Prevention, National Center for Health Statistics.

Moscicki, E.K. (1999). Epidemiology of suicide. In D.G. Jacobs (Ed.), *The Harvard*

Medical School guide to suicide assessment and intervention (pp. 40–51). San Francisco: Jossey-Bass.

Nordstrom, P., Samuelsson, M., & Asberg, M. (1995). Survival analysis of suicide risk after attempted suicide. *Acta Psychiatrica Scandinavica, 91,* 336–340.

Oregon Vital Statistics, Annual Report, Volume 2. (1999). Oregon Health Division, Center for Health Statistics (and Vital Records).

Phillips, D.P., & Cartensen, L.L. (1988). The effect of suicide stories on various demographic groups, 1968–1985. *Suicide and Life-Threatening Behavior, 18,* 100–114.

Question of family violence arises in a Kevorkian suicide case. (1996, Aug. 18). *The New York Times,* p. 25.

Rose, K.D., & Rosow, I. (1973). Physicians who kill themselves. *Archives of General Psychiatry, 29,* 800–805.

Schoevers, R.A., Asmus, F.P., & Van Tilburg, W. (1998). Physician-assisted suicide in psychiatry: Developments in the Netherlands. *Psychiatric Services, 49,* 1475–1480.

Seiden R.H. (1978). Where are they now? A follow-up study of suicide attempters from the Golden Gate Bridge. *Suicide and Life-Threatening Behavior, 8*(4), 203–216.

Shavelson, L. (1995). *A chosen death: The dying confront assisted suicide.* New York: Simon & Schuster.

Slaby A.E., & Garfinkel, L.F. (1994). *No one saw my pain: Why teens kill themselves.* New York: W.W. Norton & Company.

Smith, W.J. (1997). *Forced exit: The slippery slope from assisted suicide to legalized murder.* New York: Times Books.

Smith, W.J. (1999, Aug. 3). Don't rationalize suicide. *The Wall Street Journal,* p. A22.

Steffens, D.C., & Blazer, D.G. (1999). Suicide in the elderly. In D.G. Jacobs (Ed.), *The Harvard Medical School guide to suicide assessment and intervention* (pp. 443–462). San Francisco: Jossey-Bass Publishers.

Suicide and suicidal thoughts by Oregonians. (1997, Nov.). Oregon Department of Human Resources, Health Division.

Sullivan, A.D., Hedberg, K., & Hopkins, D. (2001). Legalized physician-assisted suicide in Oregon, 1998–2000. *New England Journal of Medicine, 344,* 605–607.

Twerski, A.J. (1987). *Generation to generation: Personal recollections of a Chassidic legacy.* New York: Traditional Press.

U.S. Census Bureau, *Statistical abstract of the United States: 2000,* 120th edition. Washington, D.C.

van der Maas, P.J., van Delden, J.J.M., & Pijneborg, L. (1992). Euthanasia and other medical decisions concerning the end of life. *Health Policy, 22*(1+2).

Ward, J.A., & Fox, J. (1977). A suicide epidemic on an Indian reserve. *Canadian Psychiatric Association Journal, 22,* 423–426.

CHAPTER 2

Would Physician-Assisted Suicide Lead to Euthanasia?

There has been considerable controversy about the question of whether physician-assisted suicide would lead to euthanasia.

Before defining the differences between physician-assisted suicide and euthanasia and categorizing different kinds of euthanasia so that the reader will be equipped to analyze the issues that he or she encounters in such discussions, I want to first give the reader some perspective on this whole question that I believe will make these discussions more fruitful.

Many opponents of physician-assisted suicide are against physician-assisted suicide because they are concerned about euthanasia. When advocates of physician-assisted suicide say "physician-assisted suicide will not lead to euthanasia," opponents might be mistakenly reassured because they interpret this statement to mean, "there will not be euthanasia." However, if we examine what is really happening both in the Netherlands and here in the United States, a different meaning to the statement "physician-assisted suicide will not lead to euthanasia" emerges.

Unfortunately, as will become clear in this chapter, many kinds of medical decisions that could easily be called *euthanasia* are already going on. It is too late to worry that physician-assisted suicide will lead to euthanasia, even in the United States.

Nevertheless, as I hope to show in this chapter, it is still important for opponents of euthanasia to oppose physician-assisted suicide. Blocking physician-assisted suicide would not be sufficient to eliminate the deliberate ending of life, but it would contain it. If physician-assisted suicide were to be legalized, it would greatly expand the number of patients whose lives could be deliberately ended. Currently in the United States, the deliberate ending of life is a legal possibility only for patients who are dependent upon respirators or other medical treatments or feeding tubes that can be withdrawn. If physician-assisted suicide is legalized and lethal medications or injections become one of the medical profession's legitimate tools, then a vastly wider range of patients could have their lives ended deliberately, including psychiatric patients.

When we try to determine if psychiatric patients are at risk because of physician-assisted suicide, we cannot restrict our attention to developing rules to be used by the mental health profession in evaluating assisted suicide requests. The reason for this is that psychiatric patients do not only consult mental health professionals. They frequently bring even their psychiatric problems to other physicians as well. Not only that, but they also, like the general population, are stricken with other medical problems and are treated in regular medical facilities.

I will now focus briefly on some statistics from the Netherlands as evidence for what I have just stated about the threat to psychiatric patients from euthanasia.

A special study on physician-assisted suicide for psychiatric patients in the Netherlands was carried out in 1996 and published in 1997 (Groenewoud et al., 1997). On the basis of the reports of a sample of 552 psychiatrists, it was estimated that physician-assisted suicide in psychiatric practice occurred approximately two to five times annually. Eleven cases were described, of which only three had been previously reported as unnatural deaths.

However, the assisted deaths of 13 additional psychiatric patients were reported in the study as well. These were patients whose medical specialist or general practitioner had consulted a psychiatrist before going ahead with physician-assisted suicide. Seven of these patients had a somatic disease as well as a psychiatric condition, but none of them requested physician-assisted suicide just because of the somatic disease (Table 5, p. 1799).

Let us now turn to the Remmelink Report, the statistics published by the government of Holland in 1990–1991 regarding the frequency of physician-assisted suicide and euthanasia in general medical practice (van der Maas, van Delden, & Pijneborg, 1992). If we examine this report carefully, we find that psychiatric patients showed up in several separate contexts.

Psychiatric patients were considered to be such a small percentage of the cases that, instead of being part of the main analysis, they were handled separately with other special groups. Twelve experts were selected covering four separate areas—newborn babies, older children, psychiatric patients, and AIDS patients. These experts gave their impressions. For psychiatry, these experts estimated that the number of cases of physician-assisted suicide were 10 or fewer per year (p. 172.)

If, however, we search for psychiatric patients not just in the special section on psychiatric patients, but also in the regular study data, we find that there are additional deaths of psychiatric patients recorded.

The Remmelink Report is organized according to certain categories. "Physician-assisted suicide" and "euthanasia" refer, according to the Dutch, to the administration of lethal substances. In physician-assisted suicide, the patient self-administers the substances. In the case of euthanasia, this is administered by the doctor to a patient who requested it. In these categories, there are very few psychiatric patients.

Other categories of the Remmelink data are as follows. Administration of a lethal substance to a patient without the patient's permission is not called "euthanasia." It is called, instead "life-terminating acts without explicit request" (LAWER). Withdrawal of life-sustaining treatment or lethal overdoses of pain medication are called "medical decisions at the end of life" (MDELs).

There was a study of death certificates between August and November, 1990. Let us examine the statistics for "medical decisions concerning the end of life" (MDELs). A patient was scored as positive for MDEL if his or her death was hastened by a medical decision. There were several categories that were added together as MDELs (Van der Maas, Van Delden, & Pijneborg, 1992, p. 116). Withholding or withdrawing a treatment or intensifying the alleviation of pain were counted as MDELs in several different kinds of circumstances—whether the hastening of the end of life was simply taken into account, whether the purpose was partly to induce death, or whether the purpose was explicitly to induce death.

The overall percentage of patients in the death certificate study who had MDELs was 39% (Table 13.8, p. 258). Data is given about the frequency of MDELs for groups of patients categorized according to cause of death. As we might expect, the cause of death showing the highest percentage of MDELs was cancer. For patients dying of cancer, 59% had MDELs (Table 13.8, p. 258). This is not surprising, because the whole justification of MDELs is to help patients avoid the kind of protracted, painful dying process that is associated with cancer.

What is surprising, however, is that the next highest percentage of MDELs is for "mental disorders." Of those patients dying of mental disorders, 52% had MDELs (Table 13.8, p. 258). According to Dr. van der Maas (1999), the first author of the study, the category "mental disorders" refers mainly to patients with dementia—geropsychiatric cases in nursing homes.

Patients dying of mental disorders accounted for .9% of the 128,786 deaths in the Netherlands in 1990 (van der Maas, van Delden, & Pijneborg, 1992, Tables 13.8 and F.8, p. 258), or 1159 patients. Taking 52% of these, we can calculate that the lives of 603 patients dying of mental disorders were shortened by medical decisions in 1990.

Patients dying of mental disorders are overrepresented among the patients with MDELs compared to patients with other causes of death. Although only .9% of the annual deaths in the Netherlands are for mental disorders, 1.2% of the MDEL actions listed in the death certificate study and 2% of the MDEL actions listed in a prospective study are for mental disorders (Tables 13.8 and F.8, p. 258).

Patients with mental disorders are also overrepresented among those who died because of "life-terminating acts without explicit request" (LAWER). According to the Remmelink Report, 1040 patients in the Netherlands died in this manner in 1990 (Shapiro & Bowermaster, 1994). Although mental disorders accounted for only 1% of the deaths in the Netherlands in 1990, patients dying of mental disorders constituted 3% of those terminated without explicit request (van der Maas, van Delden, & Pijneborg, 1992, Table 6.3, p. 60), or 31 patients.

If we turn to the statistics on patients who were dying of medical disorders rather than mental disorders, we can find evidence of even larger numbers of patients with dementia who died from medical decisions at the end of life (MDELs) without having the opportunity to discuss these with their doctor.

In the general medical population, 54% of the time medical decisions at the end of life were not discussed with the patient (Table 13.3, p. 131). The physicians' reasons for not discussing these decisions with the patient are tabulated in the Remmelink Report. "Dementia" was selected as the reason for not discussing MDELs with the patient for 31% of a sample of 465 (144 patients) in the prospective study and 27% of a sample of 1201 (324 patients) in the death certificate study (Tables F.6 and 13.6, p. 256).

There were 8500 deaths studied in the death certificate study (p. 15). Using the estimate that 324 patients out of 8500 in the death certificate study were patients whose doctors didn't consult with them about MDELs because of their dementia, and applying the proportion of 324/8500 to the number of deaths in the Netherlands in 1990, which was 128,786, we can estimate that there may have been approximately 4909 patients in 1990 in the Netherlands whose doctors ended their lives without discussing it with them because they had symptoms of dementia.

The disproportionate vulnerability of psychiatric patients to end of life decisions and to "life-termination without explicit request" occurred in spite of the fact that the Dutch are being particularly careful to scrutinize the requests of psychiatric patients for physician-assisted suicide and voluntary euthanasia.

A Dutch psychiatrist, Chabot, was reprimanded for his actions in the case of a 50-year-old woman for whom he prescribed lethal medication (Hendin, 1997, pp. 103–104).

When Dutch psychiatric patients explicitly ask for physician-assisted suicide or give specific instructions for voluntary euthanasia, they are turned down more often than patients in other categories. They constitute 14% of the patients whose requests for physician-assisted suicide or voluntary euthanasia were refused (van der Maas, van Delden, & Pijneborg, 1992, Table 5.17, p. 53). This indicates some caution on the part of the Dutch medical profession when psychiatric patients make explicit requests. However, when psychiatric patients are in situations where their medical treatments or life supports are being considered, their difficulties in communication render them more vulnerable to "termination of life without explicit request" or to "medical decisions at the end of life" that are "not discussed."

Let us keep in mind, then, as we consider the relationship between physician-assisted suicide and euthanasia, that psychiatric patients are threatened by both, but especially by euthanasia. Although only a handful of requests for assisted suicide or voluntary euthanasia were granted for psychiatric patients in the Netherlands, thousands of patients with symptoms of dementia suffering from medical disorders had their lives terminated early without having the opportunity to discuss this issue with their physician.

This issue is by no means unique to the Netherlands. It was recently reported in the *London Times* that nurses had reported to police that patients at a psychogeriatric ward were being dehydrated (Horsnell & Foster, 1999). According to Wesley J. Smith, in recent decades, as professional guidelines have changed, court decisions have made it possible to dehydrate patients at "hospitals and nursing homes" throughout the United States (Smith, 1997, p. 48).

There was once a "moral consensus" that food and fluids were given for the "duration" of the "natural lives" of seriously impaired people who could no longer swallow their own food (p. 44). But in March, 1986, according to Smith, the "first concrete step was taken to legitimize the intentional dehydration of unconscious, nonterminally ill patients" (p. 44). The "American Medical Association Council on Ethical and Judicial Affairs" issued an opinion stating that although a physician " 'should never intentionally cause death'," it was "ethical to terminate life-support treatment" if the patient's coma is " 'beyond doubt irreversible'." In this opinion, it was also explicitly stated that "Life-prolonging medical treatment includes medication and artifically or technologically supplied respiration, nutrition and hydration" (p. 45).

According to Smith, once this policy was in place, "the issue was ripe for adjudication" (p. 45). Only a "year after" this opinion, "in May, 1987," the parents of Nancy Beth Cruzan, the victim of a car accident, after "consulting with the Society for the Right to Die" (p. 46), filed their famous lawsuit "to force hospital employees . . . to remove their daughter's food and fluids" (p. 46)

There is disagreement about the condition of Nancy Beth Cruzan as she lay in her bed. Some reported that she "smiled at amusing stories" and "cried when visitors left" (p. 45). Some felt that she was completely unconscious (p. 45). No one claimed that she was in intolerable pain or that she was dying. They claimed only that she would have wanted to die under such circumstances.

The case reached the U.S. Supreme Court. The reason this case was particularly difficult was that the medical facility wasn't being asked, as in the case of Karen Ann Quinlan, to discontinue her respirator. Nancy Beth Cruzan was not dependent upon a respirator. Nancy Beth Cruzan could breathe on her own. Her vital organs were functioning well. Like many hospital patients, she received her food and fluids through a tube. After her accident, she had been able to eat and drink, but tube feeding had been instituted for the convenience of the medical staff (p. 45). The medical facility was being asked to discontinue her food and fluids.

Prior to the Cruzan case, it was acceptable to refuse medical treatment even if death was expected to be the consequence. However, food and fluids were not considered to be part of medical treatment. They were considered to be part of what was called "humane care" (p. 42)

The local court ordered the hospital to discontinue food and fluids. The "Missouri Department of Health appealed" to the Missouri Supreme Court. The Missouri Supreme Court overturned the local court. Their opinion stated, "This is not a case in which we are asked to let someone die. . . . This is a case in which we are asked to allow the medical profession to make someone die by starvation and dehydration" (p. 46). The Missouri Supreme Court found that the parents hadn't adequately proven that Nancy Beth Cruzan would have wanted to die. The U.S. Supreme Court ruled that it was perfectly constitutional for the state of Missouri to set strict criteria for what would constitute sufficient proof of a desire to refuse medical treatment.

The U.S. Supreme Court decision was not the end of the Cruzan case, however. Afterward the Cruzans "went back" to the local court again with a new report of another conversation in which Nancy Beth Cruzan had said that she "would not want to live in a coma." The local judge found this convincing. "There was no appeal" this time, and she was dehydrated until she died (p. 47).

According to Wesley Smith, "Since Nancy Cruzan's death, the starving and dehydration of cognitively disabled patients has become almost routine in hospitals and nursing homes all around the country" (p. 48). Soon, it became possible to withdraw food and fluids even from patients who were not permanently unconscious. In 1994, the American Medical Association Council on Ethics and Judicial Affairs once again revised their policy. Instead of requiring that the patient be permanently unconscious to permit withdrawing food and fluids, they stated, instead, "Even if the patient is not terminally ill or permanently unconscious, it is not unethical to discontinue all means of life-sustaining medical treatment [including food and fluids] in accordance with a proper substituted judgment or best interests analysis" (pp. 49–50). As we shall see, this kind of policy change enabled guardians to make choices to end the lives of conscious patients.

I have examined some statistics about euthanasia. I will now turn to some individual cases. I hope to show that there are so many cases that bridge the conceptual gaps between physician-assisted suicide and voluntary, nonvoluntary, and involuntary euthanasia that, in practice, these cannot be kept apart. There are also so many pressures in our society for various kinds of equality that it would be virtually impossible to restrict physician-assisted suicide to certain kinds of patients. Soon after Oregon passed a law allowing physicians to prescribe lethal medication, it was characterized as unfair to those who were unable to self-administer the medication (Oregon's second, 2000, p. 4).

Let us now turn to some definitions that will be useful in this conceptual analysis. If the patient takes a pill prescribed for him by a doctor or pushes the button of a suicide machine to bring about his own death, it will be called *physician-assisted suicide*. If the patient makes a clear request for a certain person, for example his doctor, to carry out a certain procedure that results in death at a certain time, it will be called *voluntary euthanasia*. When someone other than the patient decides to end a life and then does so, it will be called *nonvoluntary euthanasia*. If the patient would actually have opposed the procedure, it will be called *involuntary euthanasia*.

A few examples will illustrate the kinds of complications that make it difficult in actual practice to distinguish between physician-assisted suicide and voluntary, nonvoluntary, and involuntary euthanasia.

If we are intellectually honest, we will admit at the outset that it is extremely difficult to tell the difference between nonvoluntary and involuntary euthanasia. If a doctor thinks that a patient is in intolerable pain and decides that the patient has had enough, without consulting the patient, then, since the patient dies and and cannot be asked, it is impossible to know his feelings about the subject. Hendin (1997) suggests that "nonvoluntary euthanasia" of "competent patients" who could have been asked but were not asked should always be called "involuntary euthanasia" (p. 230 n. 23).

Nonvoluntary euthanasia is not a rare occurrence. As we have noted previously, according to the Remmelink Report, 1040 patients were given lethal injections without their request. An additional 4941 were overdosed on pain medication without their request (Shapiro & Bowermaster, 1994). Of these 5981 cases of nonvoluntary euthanasia using medication, how many may have been involuntary?

Chochinov et al. (1995) found, however, that only 8.5% of a sample of 200 terminally ill patients reported a serious and pervasive desire to die and that this 8.5% had a much higher rate of depressive syndromes than the rest of the sample. Also, some decreased their desire to die within a few weeks. Using Chochinov et al.'s 8.5% ratio as a means of estimating how many of these 5981 cases might have had a serious and pervasive desire to die, the result would be only 508. That suggests that as many as 5473 patients may have had their lives ended by involuntary euthanasia using medication.

Once nonvoluntary euthanasia is allowed, there are numerous ways in which involuntary euthanasia can occur. First, of course, it can happen by mistake. If informal communication is considered sufficient for the physician to make a decision about euthanasia, the patient's communication may be misinterpreted by the doctor. Reitsema (1997) wrote a heart-rending editorial in the *St. Louis Post-Dispatch* about the death of her grandfather. He was a rather cheerful nursing home patient in Holland whose wife and family visited daily. He enjoyed many pastimes such as a "chess club," concerts, and writing "newsy letters." On her last visit before leaving for the States, the author of the editorial noticed that he had deteriorated remarkably. He was "terribly thirsty" and "very sleepy." A few days later, a nurse stopped her aunt from giving him water, and the family found out that the doctor had given orders for "all food and water" to be withheld. The doctor refused to consult with them about the patient, who died a few days later.

"A week before his death" he had had a biopsy on a "bump on his gum." Because his "blood thinners" had been stopped to prepare for the biopsy, he developed some pain in his leg. He asked the doctor for "help" with the "pain in his leg." The doctor interpreted his request for "help" as a request to die, and he ordered morphine and the withholding of food and fluids without talking any further with her grandfather or with anyone in the family.

Advocates of physician-assisted suicide with whom I have discussed this story invariably react to it as a terrible departure from the purpose of physician-assisted suicide. However, given the difficulties of doctor-patient communication, and given that the medical profession realizes how critical it is to improve, it is inconceivable that misunderstandings of this nature would not occur if euthanasia is allowed. A recent study found that the patient's complete agenda was only solicited in 28% of a sample of interviews with physicians (Marvel, Epstein, Flowers, & Beckman, 1999).

When the results of research on new medications are considered by the Food and Drug administration's advisory committees, the benefits of a medication are weighed against the risks. Shouldn't new policies have to undergo the same kind of analysis? Isn't a policy unsafe if it results in a certain number of inevitable accidents that could have been avoided if the policy was discarded?

Second, even if the doctor does comprehend the patient's communication, the doctor may sincerely believe that he can judge what is in the best interest of the patient. Hendin (1997, p. 79) gives an example of a nun whose physician ended her life against her wishes. She did not want to be killed for religious reasons, but he decided that she was in too much pain and did it anyway.

Colen, a *Washington Post* reporter who wrote a book about the Karen Ann Quinlan case, found some other interesting examples of doctors who made life-or-death decisions on behalf of the patient. Colen's bias in most of his book, which was written at the time of the Quinlan case, seems to be against the use of medical equipment for prolonging the lives of patients with dire conditions that would have, a few years earlier, resulted in death. For example, in the preface, he refers to the "fact that Karen Ann's physicians insisted upon making her a prisoner of medical technology" (Colen, 1976, p. 11). Later in the book, he compares modern doctors to Mary Shelley's Dr. Frankenstein:

Like Victor Frankenstein, these physicians have only the best of intentions. But also like Victor Frankenstein, they sometimes create monsters. Theirs are not the sort of Late Show monsters who run amok, killing children and terrifying villagers. But they are, nevertheless, monsters who by their very existence destroy families and ruin lives. (p. 69)

In spite of his bias against the use of medical technology for saving these kinds of patients, Colen seemed shocked when he encountered doctors who were not doubtful about their ability to make appropriate life-or-death decisions on behalf of their patients. Such doctors were rare during the time when Colen wrote his book. During the court proceedings regarding the Karen Ann Quinlan case, her neurologist testified that he could not find a case in medical tradition as a precedent that would allow him to go along with the Quinlan's wishes to disconnect their daughter from her respirator (p. 85). Nevertheless Colen succeeded in finding such examples. He had previously, in 1974, interviewed the clinical director of the Maryland Institute of Emergency Medicine, the Shock Trauma Unit. He was told about cases of quadriplegics who were paralyzed from the neck down but who could see, hear, and think. The physicians at the unit had disconnected four such patients from their respirators in the previous year. Colen asked the doctors pointedly how many of the four had expressed a desire to die. The answer was "two." Of the others, they said, "two became very introverted" and "they didn't necessarily have to communicate it verbally . . . it's obvious. They withdraw into themselves" (p. 93). Colen pursued the point further. The doctors clarified that they did have verbal communication with these quadriplegics but didn't ask them if they wanted to die. One doctor said, "it would be inhumane to force this question. . . . Everyone dearly loves life." Another said, "I . . . would find it almost at odds with my ethics as a doctor, certainly with my Hippocratic oath, to approach a patient and take away all hope of life" (p. 94).

Rita Marker, the head of the International Anti-Euthanasia Task Force, has written an eloquent description of a pro-euthanasia conference that she attended in 1984 (Marker, 1993, pp. 50–57). Everyone waited eagerly for a keynote address by Dr. Christian Barnard, the medical pioneer of heart transplants. He began as they expected, but somewhere in the middle of his speech, the audience realized that he was veering off in a different direction than they had anticipated. To their horror, instead of extolling patient autonomy, he voiced his belief that the timing of euthanasia should be the physician's decision.

Third, involuntary euthanasia can happen because the decision-maker has a preexisting bias toward believing that the patient would want to die.

Wesley J. Smith gives an example of an appointed guardian who made this assumption. Joseph Shaaf was appointed to be the guardian of Ronald Comeau, because his family didn't come to the hospital at first (Smith, 1997, pp. 52–53). Shaaf succeeded in getting a judge's order to remove the ventilator from Comeau. Instead of dying, he improved. The speech therapist wrote that he seemed to recognize his "favorite nurses" and that he had given her a "big smile" when she said she came just "to talk" (p. 53). Shaaf, however, told Smith, "I thought that if it were me there, lying helpless in a bed, I hope to God that someone would help me move on from my misery to whatever comes next," (Smith, 1997, p. 54).

Not content with having removed the ventilator, Shaaf tried to have Comeau's food and fluids disconnected, and he almost succeeded. In spite of the speech therapist's comments and in spite of the neurologist's report that "it is difficult to support withdrawing nutrition in a patient who is demonstrating some neurological function" (p. 54), Shaaf and the ethics committee succeeded in getting a judge's order to discontinue nutrition (p. 55). Comeau would have died if not for the intervention of a minister, Reverend Mike McHugh. McHugh "issued a press release" (p. 56), and an attorney helped him get a temporary stay of the order to remove food and fluids, but he would have been unable to accomplish anything at the next hearing because he had no standing in the case. However, he succeeded in finding the patient's father who had not understood the situation and who didn't want his son to die (p. 57). More family members soon came as well. In the presence of his family, Comeau showed very positive emotions. He clearly was very responsive. His family was shocked that he had almost been allowed to die (p. 58). Although he is still handicapped, Comeau can now "communicate quite well" using "one syllable words," and his "reading comprehension is good." He can draw with an Etch-a-Sketch, "use the television remote control, and . . . push himself in a wheelchair" (p. 59).

For incompetent patients, the concept of substituted judgment blurs the distinction between voluntary euthanasia and nonvoluntary euthanasia. Because the guardian regards his job as representing the patient's true wishes rather than instituting his own wishes, it seems to everyone involved as if this is a case of voluntary euthanasia, when in fact it is nonvoluntary or possibly involuntary.

These examples show, I believe, that by virtue of the nature of incompetence, it is impossible to draw a clear line between voluntary, nonvoluntary, and involuntary euthanasia. By allowing any of these, we are, in theory, leaving open the possibility that a certain number of cases of involuntary euthanasia will occur.

The status quo right now in the United States is that there are cases where people have almost succeeded or succeeded in terminating the lives of *conscious* patients who were capable of improvement and some cognitive activities and social interaction and who were not in unbearable pain and had *not* left living will instructions to discontinue life supports. Smith (pp. 38–64) discusses a number of such cases in which family members or guardians sought to have the patient's food and fluids removed. For example, Robert Wendland (pp. 39–42), the victim of a car accident, was in a coma for 16 months and then woke up. After a while, he was able to drive through the hospital on a "motorized wheelchair," and although he did not speak, he responded correctly to requests for "colored pegs" (p. 40) and could use "yes" or "no" indicators (p. 42). He showed his emotions by kissing his mother's hand (p. 40). In spite of these signs of consciousness and interactivity, his wife sought to have his food and fluids discontinued because she believed he would not have wanted to live this way. His mother fought to prevent his death. This case reached the California Supreme Court. Dr. Vincent Fortanasce, a neurologist, said that the ruling in this case "could affect hundreds of thousands of brain-injured people who need feeding tubes to survive" (Ressner, 2001). Robert Wendland died of pneumonia on July 17, 2001 (Saunders, 2001). After his death, the court ruled that his wife had failed to provide "clear and convincing" evidence of his wish to disconnect his feeding tube (Conservatorship of the person of Robert Wendland, 2001). The fact that this litigation continued for many years and reached the California Supreme Court in spite of the fact that Wendland was conscious and engaging in recreational activities is a clear illustration of how advocates of managed dying are trying to allow surrogates to withdraw life supports from people with higher and higher levels of functioning.

Michael Martin is another patient with limited cognitive abilities. He narrowly escaped the fate of dehydration. Even though he could spell words on the blackboard, shake his head "yes or "no" in response to questions, spell "My name is Mike" by pointing to letters, and smile when reassured that he could stay in treatment, his wife was seeking to end his life by dehydration. His life was in danger when, in spite of evidence that he was currently happy and wanted to live, the judge relied on testimony regarding a private conversation in which he was alleged to have said that he would not want to live incapacitated. Finally his life was saved when the Michigan Supreme Court ruled that the testimony about his conversational statements was uncorroborated and not sufficient (Smith, 1997, pp. 60–64).

Michael Martin's wife has made public appearances and spoken about her opinions on his case. She told the audience at a "Families on the Frontier of Dying" conference in Philadelphia: "He's in well enough health, thanks to the feeding tube, he could outlive us all. And for what? Because his mother and sister aren't willing to let him go. . . . He does nothing but smile. . . . Patients like this can smile and nod their head. . . . They could be the organ donors who are so desperately needed" (Martin, 1998).

Christine Busalacchi wasn't as lucky as Michael Martin. In spite of the fact that she could push buttons to call the nurses and could obey simple requests, her family's lawsuit to have her dehydrated was successful (Smith, 1997, pp. 48–49).

Hugh Finn, 44, died on October 9, 1998, after his feeding tube had been removed. He had been left permanently brain damaged after a car accident. Virginia law allows the withholding of food and fluids from patients in a persistent vegetative state (PVS). The court battle about Finn's case centered on whether he was or was not a PVS patient. His wife wanted his feeding tube removed, but when the nurse from the State Department Medical Assistance Services visited him, she reported that he said "Hi" to her and used his hand to smooth his hair (Molotsky, 1998). Governor James S. Gilmore 3d ordered that an appeal be taken to the State Supreme Court, but it could not save Hugh Finn (Virginia's top court, 1998).

Nancy Ellen Jobes also died after her feeding tube was removed, in spite of testimony from Dr. Maurice Victor, a professor of Neurology at Case Western Reserve and also Dr. Allan Ropper, an associate professor of neurology at Harvard Medical School that that she could see, hear, and respond to commands. Dr. Ropper explained that she may have appeared to be unaware at times because of the high levels of medication that she was given. The administration at the nursing home refused to carry out the court order to dehydrate her, and she was transferred elsewhere. The administrator of the nursing home took out an ad in the newspaper, begging the community for help. He listed the physical effects of dehydration and stated that "to ask our hospitals and health care institutions to become exterminating grounds is the greatest insult to the medical profession" (Marker, 1993, pp. 89–93).

Having discussed how it is hard to draw a line between voluntary, nonvoluntary, and involuntary euthanasia, especially when the patient is incompetent, we are now in a position to take another look at the question of physician-assisted suicide as it is usually presented to the public. The advocates of physician-assisted suicide usually present a model case of a competent patient in unbearable pain who is terminally ill and who is making a clear request to die at that time.

This model case may sometimes occur but, in actual practice, by the time death approaches, many people are no longer legally competent. They may be sedated, incoherent, emotionally labile, unconscious, unresponsive, or seemingly aware but unable to communicate. Because of this fact of human biology or human psychology, the ideal of a patient autonomously and competently planning physician-assisted suicide or voluntary euthanasia is often impractical and burdened with ethical complications. The patient can do their planning while they're competent, but often they don't want to die at that time, but later. Their idea of what they will experience later is really just speculation. Once the competent patient becomes incompetent, and the doctor is contemplating euthanasia on the basis of the patient's formerly expressed wish, is this truly voluntary? Very often, when a person experiences a change in medical status like Wendland, Comeau, Martin, or Bussalacchi, they may adapt psychologically and become content with their new level of abilities. Perhaps their level of discomfort is not as bad as they had anticipated. Can it be called voluntary euthanasia if we end the life of this new person on the advice of the old person? But yet the new person is not considered competent enough to be asked.

Smith (1997, pp. 216–218) gives an example of a woman who died against her will because of instructions that she had given her brother in the past. Marjorie Nighbert had given her brother the authority to make her health care decisions, and she had once told him verbally that she wouldn't want a feeding tube. After having a stroke, she was in rehabilitation and was having difficulty learning to eat and drink, and the doctors inserted a feeding tube. Her brother, remembering their conversation, asked the doctors to stop the food and fluids and they did so. Twenty days later, she still hadn't died, because she kept asking the nurses to feed her and give her drinks and they were doing so against the doctor's order. In spite of this clear evidence that she no longer agreed with her advance directives, the guardian and the judge couldn't find a way to allow her to reverse her previous instructions and she was allowed to die of starvation and dehydration.

Unfortunately cases where even the boundary between physician-assisted suicide and euthanasia is blurred are all too common. Hendin discusses a fascinating case of this type that was reported in the *New York Times Magazine* in 1993 (Hendin, 1997, pp. 35–42). A woman, who is called Louise, had been diagnosed with a "degenerative neurological disease" (p. 35). She discussed with her doctor that she wanted to "end it" (p. 36) before she had to go to a medical facility. The doctor contacted a suicide-advocacy organization headed by Ralph Mero to advise Louise and give her support (p. 37). A journalist, Lisa Belkin, was going to cover the story.

After making these plans, Louise hesitated. The journalist told her that the doctor thought if she didn't end her life soon, she might lose her opportunity (p. 38). Her mother confirmed this. Louise said, "I . . . feel as if everyone is . . . pressuring me" (p. 39).

Hendin concludes, "The patient who wants to live until the end but senses his family cannot tolerate watching him die is familiar to those who care for people who are terminally ill. Once those close to the patient decide to assist in the suicide, their desire to have it over with can make the pressure put on the patient many times greater. . . . the fact that she took the lethal medication herself—offered no protection to Louise. It is hard to see how her doctor, Mero, her mother, her friend, and the reporter could have done more to rush her toward death" (p. 42).

Dutch government guidelines for physician-assisted suicide state that the desire to die must be voluntary (Schoevers, Asmus, & Van Tilburg, 1998, p. 1476). Schoevers, Asmus, and Van Tilburg correctly point out that the wish to die arises in a social context that is difficult to separate from the patient's wish. In practice, families have a major role in euthanasia decisions in Holland. Hendin (1996) wrote that a 1983 study showed that more euthanasia requests in the Netherlands came from families than from patients. According to Hendin, Dutch doctors "invariably support the relatives" desire to be free of the burden of caring for the patient (p. A25).

Wesley J. Smith describes a case in which the boundary between physician-assisted suicide and euthanasia was even more clearly violated (Smith, 1997, pp. 18–19). This case had been described by Lonny Shavelson in his book, *A Chosen Death*. Gene, a depressed alcoholic widower arranges with "Sarah" from the Hemlock Society—not her real name—for help with suicide. "Sarah" prepared some medicine for him and placed "a plastic bag over his head." Suddenly, he said, "I'm cold," and struggled to take the bag off his head, but she held him down and tightened it. Smith doesn't even call this "euthanasia." He calls it, quite simply, "murder" (p. 19).

Unfortunately, similar accounts are not difficult to find. Even during the recent few years that material about such cases has been published, there have appeared several well-known cases in which someone who attempted to commit suicide did not die immediately and would not have died at all if not for the actions of somebody standing by. For example, Ann Humphry, cofounder of the Hemlock

Society (Marker, 1993, p. 44) and first editor of the Hemlock Quarterly (p. 45) and wife of Derek Humphry, the author of the suicide manual, *Final Exit* (1991), reportedly smothered her mother with a plastic laundry bag because her mother's breathing became agitated after taking lethal medications (Marker, 1993, p. 72). In a recent case, a 43-year-old man with amyotrophic lateral sclerosis (ALS), who had received his lethal medication by Federal Express, had trouble self-administering the medication and needed help from his brother-in-law (Oregon's second, 2000, p. 4).

This pattern often recurs because many patients don't really want to die unless their pain becomes unbearable. Usually it does not become unbearable when they can still swallow the medications on their own. Aside from a few patients like Janet Adkins, who went to Kevorkian long before her Alzheimer's disease caused her any serious problems (Smith, 1997, p. 24), even advocates of suicide indicate they want to stay alive as long as they can. When they anticipate that they will no longer be able to communicate their wishes, they are in terrible fear that their pain will become unbearable later on. According to the account described above, they attempt suicide under pressure even if they are still ambivalent, and sometimes somebody helps them finish it.

Joan Lucas's suicide in Oregon also followed this pattern of committing suicide under pressure. She wrote to her doctor: "I feel the ability to swallow can go at any time. I do not want to take the chance of waiting until it's too late. I do not want to be on a feeding tube or a resuscitator or be paralyzed with absolutely no control over my body. . . . Please let me have this prescription as soon as possible. I don't have any time to waste" (Kettler, 2000, p. 8A).

Even a physician's prescription is no guarantee that death will be painless. According to an editorial from the *Oregonian* (Death without dignity, 1997), the Oregon legislation permitting physician-assisted suicide allows doctors to give lethal prescriptions, but they fail 25% of the time, causing "vomiting, convulsions, brain impairment, kidney damage, comas, and lingering deaths" (p. E4). The editor expains that this is why euthanasia is used much more frequently than physician-assisted suicide in Holland. According to the various estimates provided by van der Maas et al. (1996, p. 1701, Table 1), in both 1990 and 1995, there were probably at least 5 times as many cases of voluntary euthanasia for every case of physician-assisted suicide and possibly as much as 12 times as many. The ending of life by large doses of opioids was between 37 and 95 times more common than physician-assisted suicide.

Advocates of euthanasia who have personal experiences helping with suicides know about these kinds of problems, of course. But when Oregon voters were considering Measure 16, Oregon's act legalizing physician-assisted suicide, physician-assisted suicide was nevertheless presented to the Oregon voters as if it were a trouble-free way to die. Rita Marker describes in a pamphlet how a 60-second television commercial was the centerpiece of the campaign. In the commercial, a woman described how her 25-year-old daughter, dying of painful bone cancer, slipped peacefully away after taking lethal pills. However, Marker points out, the story wasn't true. In actuality, the woman, a former nurse, was worried that the pills weren't working and gave her daughter a lethal injection (Marker, 2000, pp. 5–6).

These kinds of accounts have been published and available over a long period of time, but now, we no longer need to rely on this kind of information to establish the point that people attempting physician-assisted suicide often need expert help to complete the job.

In February 2000, the *New England Journal of Medicine* published an article (Groenewoud et al., 2000) with quantitative data bearing upon this issue. There had been hints in the 1992 report from the Netherlands of technical problems with physician-assisted suicide. Only 83% of the physician respondents characterized the performance of their euthanasia or physician-assisted suicide cases as technically satisfactory (van der Maas, van Delden, & Pijneborg, 1992, p. 46). Also, it was mentioned that physician-assisted suicide cases in which the physician also administered lethal medicine were classified as euthanasia (p. 179). Groenewoud et al. (2000), using data from 1990–1991 and 1995–1996, separated categories of patients that had been combined in previous reports and revealed that in 18% of the 114 cases where physician-assisted suicide was intended, the physician intervened and did something further to produce death.

It is unfortunately clear how euthanasia activists react to this kind of information about the limitations of physician-assisted suicide. Rather than suggesting that physician-assisted suicide should be curtailed, they, instead, press for active euthanasia.

In the same issue as Groenewoud et al.'s paper, the *New England Journal of Medicine* published an editorial by Sherwin Nuland (Nuland, 2000). Nuland characterizes Groenewoud et al.'s findings as shocking and concludes from them that it may be time for physicians to rethink their reluctance to participate in euthanasia.

Let us now evaluate again the idea that physician-assisted suicide is an entirely self-contained step in the direction of more compassion for competent, terminal patients in unbearable pain, and that clear guidelines will prevent this from leading to euthanasia.

For those who were unaware of the technical problems that occur when someone tries to wait as long as possible to swallow his own lethal medications before becoming incompetent, this might have been plausible. For those who were unaware of the deaths from dehydration that have been occurring the last few decades in our hospitals and nursing homes, this might have been plausible. For those who were unaware of the presence of a large core of euthanasia enthusiasts who intend to push for euthanasia as soon as the limitations of physician-assisted suicide become more widely known, this might have been plausible. However, given the facts, it is not plausible.

Given the current situation, which is that patients who are not terminal and not in unbearable pain and not unconscious but who are dependent upon feeding tubes are candidates for euthanasia on the basis of isolated, hypothetical conversational remarks about dying under certain circumstances that they made earlier in their lives, how can we protect psychiatric patients, who have often spoken, and written, and acted upon suicidal ideas and plans and whose verbally expressed thoughts and feelings are recorded voluminously in their psychiatric records?

If lethal medication were legalized for physician-assisted suicide, why would it not be used in hospitals and nursing homes instead of dehydration? And if it were used, what would protect large numbers of patients who are cognitively disabled like Wendland and Comeau, but who, unlike Wendland and Comeau, are not dependent upon feeding tubes?

Psychiatric patients currently have three layers of protection. The first is the long-standing legal practice of regarding lethal medical intervention, that is, physician-administered poison, as homicide. The second is the climate of opinion in society and medicine regarding the value of life and the assumption that people, even severely handicapped or sick people, wish to live. The third is the idea that when people are insane, their wishes to commit suicide are temporary and should not be taken seriously. If euthanasia activists succeed in challenging the first two principles, the third principle will also lose its protective power. The idea of protecting the insane may not be compelling to those who don't believe that people want to live.

If any of these protections change, we cannot simply write careful guidelines and wait for our patients to make formal suicide requests. They often put themselves in life-threatening situations and need medical intervention to be saved. Their situations often seem pitiful, and the doctors responsible for resuscitating them may not believe resuscitation is in their best interest. If the climate of opinion in medicine changes, so that any evidence that the patient would not wish to be resuscitated is weighed heavily, there is a risk that some of our future patients may perish at home or in the emergency medical facility and never arrive safely at the psychiatric ward at all.

REFERENCES

Chochinov, H.M., Wilson, K.G., Enns, M., Mowchun, N., Lander, S., Levitt, M. & Clinch, J.J. (1995). Desire for death in the terminally ill. *American Journal of Psychiatry, 152*(8), 1185–1191.

Colen, B.D. (1976). *Karen Ann Quinlan: Dying in the age of eternal life.* New York: Nash.

Conservatorship of the person of Robert Wendland, Supreme Court of California, August 9, 2001, 28 P. 3d 151.

Death without dignity. (1997, May 11). *The Oregonian*, E4.

Groenewoud, J.H., van der Heide, A. Onwuteaka-Philipsen, B.D. Willems, D.L., van der Maas, P.J., & van der Wal, G. (2000). Clinical problems with the performance of euthanasia and physician-assisted suicide in the Netherlands. *New England Journal of Medicine, 342,* 551–556.

Groenewoud, J.H., van der Maas, P.J., van der Wal, G, Hengeveld, M.W., Tholen, A.J., Schudel, W.J., & Van der Heide, A. (1997). Physician-assisted death in psychiatric practice in the Netherlands. *New England Journal of Medicine, 336* (25), 1795–1801.

Hendin, H. (1996, Mar. 21). Dying of resentment. *The New York Times*, Op-Ed, p. A25.

Hendin, H. (1997). *Seduced by death: Doctors, patients, and the Dutch cure.* New York: W.W. Norton.

Horsnell, H., & Foster, P. (1999, Jan. 6). Euthanasia claims sow doubt in families' minds. *The Times* (London), p. 9.

Humphry, D. (1991). *Final exit: The practicalities of self-deliverance and assisted suicide for the dying* Eugene, OR: Hemlock Society.

Kettler, B. (2000, June 25). A death in the family: "We knew she would do it." *Sunday Mail Tribune* (Medford, OR), pp. 1A, 8A.

Marker, R. (1993). *Deadly compassion: The death of Ann Humphry and the truth about euthanasia.* New York: William Morrow and Company.

Marker R. (2000). *Assisted suicide: The debate in the States.* Steubenville, Ohio: International Anti-Euthanasia Task Force.

Martin, M. (1998). How do families cope? Families on the Frontier of Dying conference. Philadelphia, May 21.

Marvel, M.K., Epstein, R.M., Flowers, K., & Beckman, H.B. (1999). Soliciting the patient's agenda: have we improved? *Journal of the American Medical Association, 281*(3), 283–287.

Molotsky, I. (1998, Oct. 2). Wife wins right-to-die case; Then a governor challenges it. *The New York Times*, p. A26.

Nuland, S.B. (2000). Physician-assisted suicide and euthanasia in practice. *New England Journal of Medicine, 342*(8), 583–584.

Oregon's second assisted-suicide report: Not the whole story. (2000). *IAETF Update,* No. 1, 1–5.

Reitsema, E.M. (1997, Nov. 30). Grandpa is dead—a victim of Dutch euthanasia. *St. Louis Post-Dispatch*, p. B3.

Ressner, J. (2001, Mar. 26). When a coma isn't one. *Time*, p. 62.

Saunders, D.J. (2001, Jul. 24). If disabled means expendable. *San Francisco Chronicle*, p. A19.

Schoevers R.A. Asmus E.P. Van Tilburg, W. (1998). Physician-assisted suicide in psychiatry: Developments in the Netherlands. *Psychiatric Services, 49,* 1475–1480.

Shapiro, J., & Bowermaster, D. (1994, Apr. 25) Death on trial. *U.S. News and World Report*, p. 36.

Shavelson, L. (1995). *A chosen death: The dying confront assisted suicide.* New York: Simon and Schuster.

Smith, W.J. (1997). *Forced exit: The slippery slope from assisted suicide to legalized murder.* New York: Times Books.

van der Maas, P.J. (1999). Personal communication, May 6.

van der Maas, P.J., van Delden, J.J.M., & Pijneborg, L. (1992). Euthanasia and other medical decisions concerning the end of life: An investigation performed upon request of the Commission of Inquiry into the medical practice concerning euthanasia. *Health Policy*, Vol. 22 (1+2) pp. vii–262.

van der Maas, P.J., van der Wal, G., Haverkate, I., De Graaff, C.L.M., Kester, J.G.C., Onwuteaka-Philipsen, B.D., Van der Heide, A., Bosma, J.M., & Willems, D.L.

(1996). Euthanasia, physician-assisted suicide, and other medical practices involving the end of life in the Netherlands, 1990–1995. *New England Journal of
Medicine, 335* (22), Table 1, p. 1701.

Virginia's top court rejects appeal in right-to-die case. (1998, Oct. 3). *The New York
Times*, p. A13.

CHAPTER 3

The Beginnings of the Fear of Medical Technology

The tragedy of the Karen Ann Quinlan case is well known, but the strange paradox of the case is not. Although Paul Armstrong, the attorney for the Quinlans, asserted dramatically the helplessness of Karen Ann Quinlan in the face of her hospital's refusal to disconnect her respirator, he also—and this seems like a contradiction—won the case by suggesting that removing respirators was already a common medical practice.

If indeed, removing respirators was already a common practice, why were the Quinlans having such difficulty? Moreover, if removing respirators was a common practice, why was the public so interested in the case?

If, however, disconnecting respirators was not a common practice, why was everyone so ready to accept the argument that it was?

The Karen Ann Quinlan case was not just a decision about Karen Ann's respirator. It was a public relations triumph for the champions of managed dying. By studying the events and the ideas surrounding this case, which took place in the social turmoil and confusion of the 1970s, we can understand more about the profound transformations taking place in American attitudes toward medical care.

On April 15, 1975, Karen Ann Quinlan was hospitalized in an unconscious state. Her friends had called the police because she was having difficulty breathing. No definite reason for her collapse was ever established. She and her friends had been drinking, but her symptoms seemed to be excessive for the amount that they thought she had consumed. Later tests showed traces of aspirin,

Valium, barbiturates, and also quinine, which is found when people have been consuming mixed drinks, in her body, but none of these traces were present at a toxic level (Quinlan & Quinlan, 1977, p. 187).

She lay still for several days in a coma, and then began to appear awake but remained unaware of her surroundings. She moved her head and opened her eyes, but showed no recognition of anybody (pp. 23–24). A tracheotomy was performed to insert a respirator tube (p. 19). As time passed, her joints began to bend into a rigid position. Her knees were drawn up towards her chest. Her wrists were bent as well (p. 24). Her head often moved from side to side, and sometimes she groaned or cried (p. 82).

She was diagnosed as being in a persistent vegetative state. Although patients in a persistent vegetative state are thought to be unaware of their surroundings and unable to experience pain, the family was distressed by her thrashing and groaning, and they felt much better on days when she seemed peaceful (p. 148). The Quinlans couldn't help getting the subjective impression that their daughter hated the medical devices that were being used and was trying to fight them (pp. 88, 251).

Ms. Quinlan's doctors tried once to wean her off the respirator. In response to a request from Mr. Quinlan, Dr. Arshad Javed let her breathe on her own for half-hour periods throughout a single day, with staff standing by to reinstitute supported respiration if necessary. Karen did well during her waking periods but not during sleep. The next day, she seemed exhausted and slept for a 24-hour period, so Javed gave up on the weaning effort (pp. 103–107).

Karen Ann could definitely breathe to some extent on her own. The medical staff feared that her breathing was too shallow and that if she breathed on her own for a long time, she might develop pneumonia. The respirator had something called a "sigh volume." Periodically, it gave her a larger volume of air than usual to use her full lung capacity and thereby prevent infection (p. 189). In her case, the respirator was not critical for her very next breath; it was being used to prevent complications.

Given her doctor's hesitation to remove the respirator, Julia Quinlan, Karen's mother, felt herself to be in a dilemma. She didn't know if it would be morally correct for the family to request that the respirator be turned off. She remembered that on several occasions, when friends or relatives had been suffering in great pain from terminal cancer, her daughter had commented to her that she would not want to be kept alive under those circumstances (pp. 89, 166–167).

Mrs. Quinlan was quite active in her church, and she worked as the secretary of the priest, Father Thomas Trapasso. She consulted Father Trapasso, and he told her that turning off their daughter's respirator would not be morally wrong. He explained that the Catholic church does not require the use of "extraordinary means" to sustain life—this doctrine dated back to the 16th century. Father Trapasso gave Mrs. Quinlan the historical example of amputations before the invention of anaesthesia. The church had ruled that an individual, faced with the dilemma of having to choose either death or the ordeal of amputation, was not required to undergo the amputation in order to sustain his life. "Extraordinary" referred to the burden upon the individual (pp. 90–91).

Having been reassured by their priest that their wishes were not immoral, the Quinlans requested that their daughter's respirator be turned off. At first it seemed as if the hospital would cooperate. They asked the Quinlans to sign a release (p. 117). But then, the doctor, after consulting a colleague decided that he would not do it (p. 118).

The hospital's lawyer, Theodore Einhorn, told Mr. Quinlan that they could not honor his request because he was not even his daughter's official guardian. Mr. Quinlan asked whether if he did become the guardian, they would honor the request. Einhorn replied that he didn't know. It was this impasse that inspired Mr. Quinlan to seek legal help (p. 121).

The Quinlans' opposition to the hospital's treatment of their daughter was focused upon the respirator. Their position was very far from the position of current advocates of physician-assisted suicide and euthanasia. They did not want Karen Ann Quinlan to die. The Quinlans never asked for her artifically supplied nutrition or her catheter to be disconnected. It was only the respirator that they felt was keeping her from being in a "natural state."

Mr. Quinlan said to Karen Ann's doctor, Dr. Robert J. Morse,

we understand that conceivably *all* treatment of Karen is extraordinary. That means the antibiotics and the food and the respirator. However, we personally have moral problems with our conscience, with regard to the food and the antibiotics. We have problems with it now, and we realize we would have more problems with it ten years from now. Because we know what would happen if they were taken away—we know that Karen would die. So we are not asking for the elimination of these other two things. What we are asking for is simply the same thing that we asked for all along. And that is the removal of the respirator. (p. 282)

Father Trapasso shared their willingness to go only so far in restoring Karen Ann to her "natural state." He stated on several occasions that he wanted to make sure that no one interpreted their actions as approval of euthanasia (pp. 230, 278).

It is not even clear whether the Quinlans wished the respirator to be removed abruptly. They wrote about their reactions to newspaper and magazine accounts about their case:

Whenever one of the stories would use the phrase "pull the plug," we would wince. It was such a crude, terrible way of putting it. It makes it sound like an execution. And of course, it's not realistic at all. No one would ever "pull the plug," because if they ever pulled the plug of the respirator and left all the stale air in the machine, Karen would be breathing that stale air—she would choke on it. We would never allow that to happen. (p. 221)

Later, when Karen Ann Quinlan had been weaned from the respirator and was being transferred to another facility, the Quinlans' terrible fear that something would happen to her along the way showed that her death was not really their goal (pp. 317–318, 321, 323).

In a fascinating exchange during the proceedings at the Supreme Court of New Jersey on January 26, 1976, the Quinlans' attorney, Paul Armstrong, was asked if the Quinlans had tried to dismiss the doctor who wouldn't carry out their request, and he replied that they had not. The justice's response was "why are you here at all?" (*In the Matter*, Vol. II, 1976, p. 215). If the Quinlans had simply encouraged their doctor to try again with the weaning effort, emphasizing Karen Ann's apparent discomfort and her capability for independent respiration rather than her desire to proceed with her afterlife, the court battle could have been averted.

Why then, did the Quinlans' lawyer not advise them on how to avoid litigation by selecting the least controversial basis for the removal of the respirator; that is, the possibility that she could do without it? Why, instead, did he encourage them to select the most controversial basis for removing the respirator; that is, their right to choose for her to die? Why did he encourage them to jump into a gigantic constitutional confrontation? Why did he feel so strongly about pursuing this case that he quit his job as a Legal Aid lawyer and interrupted his graduate studies in Constitutional Law so that he could work on the case full-time, asking for no payment whatsoever (Quinlan & Quinlan, 1977, pp. 135, 137)? It was not exactly sympathy for Karen Ann Quinlan herself, because Armstrong believed that she would die very soon even with the respirator. For some reason, he and many other people believed that a time in history had come when our technology was so threatening that our ordinary ethical framework needed to be explicitly and drastically revised because of an impending emergency.

Let us briefly review some of the cultural background of the mid-1970s as well as the development of medical technology at that time and see if we can understand the eagerness with which Armstrong and many other people embraced this case.

Karen Ann Quinlan's generation grew up during the Cold War. They grew up with the idea that the highly developed character of our group life and our technology could be dangerous rather than beneficial. Devotion to large social collectivities was seen not as an inspiring part of life that fostered social harmony and cooperation but, instead, as a dangerous delusion that could result in nuclear destruction. They were a generation that contemplated the possibility that at any time, their lives could be threatened by a crazy competition between two superpowers with overdeveloped military technology. Authority figures were feared as promotors of this delusion.

The philosophy of personal autonomy was a protection from these dangers. If each person did only what made sense to him, these larger collectivities would lose their dangerous power. The return of American troops from Vietnam in

1973, just two years before Karen Ann Quinlan's collapse, signified to many that those who had fought in the war had done so in vain.

The Quinlans subscribed to the view of the importance of personal autonomy that was popular at the time. Like many parents in the 1970s, they believed that their child should be free to develop her own set of values and follow it. They made some sacrifices to follow their belief in personal autonomy. Mr. Quinlan didn't really approve of Karen Ann's job (Quinlan & Quinlan, 1977, p. 70) or her choice of roommates, but he withheld his comments. Mrs. Quinlan believed that you couldn't force religion upon your children (p. 54). Therefore they felt obligated to pursue what they thought Karen Ann would have wanted, even though the doctors reassured them that she wasn't feeling pain and that her moans and groans and grimaces were reflexes.

The combination of their religious beliefs and their belief in the more modern concept of personal autonomy was what made their dilemma so compelling. They believed that there was an afterlife and that Karen wanted to go to it. They didn't have the traditional confidence that God could do whatever he wanted to. They feared that God couldn't take her unless the doctors turned off the respirator. Instead of feeling that their daughter's situation was God's will, they felt compelled to carry out what they believed was Karen Ann's will. Their plea was "Karen wouldn't have wanted this."

Like many people in the Vietnam era, the Quinlans and their lawyer saw the great social issue of their time as being the individual's right to autonomy versus the right of the state to interfere. Karen Ann Quinlan was, to them, a conscientious objector in the war against death. They felt that she did not wish to fight in the war, and they had argued that she was part of a religious group that did not feel compelled to fight in the war.

A rapid growth in medical technology was occurring at the time. In 1974, one year before Karen Ann Quinlan's collapse, a special supplement to the *Journal of the American Medical Association* was published (Standards for Cardiopulmonary, 1974), which was entirely devoted to cardiopulmonary resuscitation. The cover of the issue contrasts the new techniques of cardiopulmonary resuscitation with obsolete techniques such as flagellation, applying heat, and other varied practices. The new techniques were explained in great detail and plans were made for these techniques to be applied in every hospital and taught to not only hospital staff but also police, firemen, rescue personnel, and finally, as many laypersons as possible, beginning with eighth graders (p. 850). The Red Cross and the YMCA and school systems were all to cooperate in training efforts, and life support units were to be found at all places where large numbers of people congregated (p. 861). Respirators were also relatively new. During the polio epidemic in the 1950s, many of the 300,000 victims had been treated with the famous "iron lung" (life-sustaining, 1987, p. 230).

The fear of overpopulation may have reached a peak in the 1970s, contributing to the fear that mankind in general, by reproducing and by developing their destructive technology had reached some sort of a disastrous brick wall and that they had to retreat rather than advance. In 1968, Paul Ehrlich published the book *The Population Bomb* (Ehrlich, 1971). Predicting mass starvation, wars, uncontrollable plagues, and ecological disasters, this best-seller definitely communicated the idea that mankind could not continue on the same course as it had been.

The disillusionment with government and science resulting from the Cold War, and the fears of overpopulation may have given a sinister twist to the fear of medical technology. People were not worried about the unintended discomforts and side effects of medical progress, but instead they worried about the very progress itself. Just as it had seemed plausible that advanced weapons would blow up the whole world, or that government leaders would needlessly send a generation of young people into a pointless war, it seemed plausible that doctors were frightening authority figures with the power to draft helpless sick people into a painful and futile war against death.

These fears, in fact, constituted a different slippery slope argument, but it was not openly identified as such. The essence of this slippery slope argument is that life-support technologies are so good that there will be a dangerous accumulation of the virtually dead or permanently suffering. This frightening scenario was conceived at times as a subjective disaster. Continuing to practice medicine to our full capability would trap people in an agonizing mesh of machines and wires. Sometimes it was conceived as a financial disaster. Continuing to practice medicine with its newest developments would cause patients in a chronic or in a terminal state to accumulate indefinitely and drain the vital resources that were needed to sustain the healthy.

This fear was not based upon any historical evidence. There never was a society that faltered because it gave good care to all of its disabled people. Nor was it based upon any explicit calculations or trends. It was based, rather, upon unarticulated speculation and extrapolation. It was against the background of these fears that the Karen Ann Quinlan case took place.

On September 10, 1975, Joseph Quinlan, Karen Ann's father, became the plaintiff in a civil action complaint in the Superior Court of New Jersey. He asked to be appointed Karen's Ann guardian "with the express power of authorizing the discontinuance of all extraordinary means of sustaining the vital processes of his daughter. . . ." (*In the Matter*, 1975, p. 3). On September 15, 1975, the court appointed Daniel Coburn as guardian to represent Karen Quinlan (p. 11). On September 16, 1975, Joseph Quinlan filed another complaint, asking that the prosecutor be enjoined from "interference with or criminal prosecution" and that the doctors and hospital be enjoined from "interference" in case the court granted "relief" in this case (pp. 13–14).

The *New York Times* reported on September 17, 1975, that past cases dealing with abortion or euthanasia occurred "after the fact" but that in this case, the court was being asked to "condone in advance the cessation of life-sustaining medical procedures" and to "become a party to the act" (Sullivan, 1975).

The guardian, Daniel Coburn, filed an affidavit on September 19, 1975, that touched upon many important issues. Having visited Ms. Quinlan, he noticed that her eyes were open and moving, that she blinked and moved her tongue, and that she seemed to gasp as oxygen entered her windpipe. He went over the criteria he had learned from his survey of the medical literature on the question of "brain death" and concluded that she did not appear to meet the criteria (*In the Matter*, 1975, p. 22).

In 1968, only a few years before Karen Ann Quinlan's illness, the Harvard Medical School ad hoc committee to examine the definition of brain death had published a description of irreversible coma (A definition of irreversible, 1968). Because of modern resuscitative technology, it appeared that the prior definition of death was becoming harder to use. Because of the technology of resuscitation, the heart no longer stopped after irreversible brain damage. With the help of a respirator, the heart, because it was being continuously supplied with oxygen, could keep on beating even in an individual whose brain had been entirely destroyed.

The committee described the characteristics of irreversible coma or brain death as including complete unreceptivity and unresponsiveness, no movements or breathing, and no reflexes. In other words, no response to painful stimuli, no movements, groans, or vocal responses, no spontaneous breathing or efforts to breath, no head turning, blinking, swallowing, yawning, or pupillary responses. They cited a flat encephalogram as a confirming sign. They stated that these observations must be made again after 24 hours and that death must be declared first before the respirator is turned off.

Coburn's conclusion that Karen Ann Quinlan did not meet the new criteria for irreversible coma or brain death completely anticipated all the expert testimony in the subsequent legal proceedings. In spite of the fact that the issue of brain death is brought up over and over again in the briefs and in the proceedings, not one of the experts testifying believed that Karen Ann Quinlan met the criteria.

Coburn's legal research indicated that "no court has authorized the cessation of supportive mechanical devices necessary to sustain life" (*In the Matter*, 1975, p. 23). The only kind of precedent he could find was an analogy to "heart transplant cases where removal of the heart from the body has apparently been authorized" (p. 23).

From the very beginning, the Quinlan case attracted international attention. On September 19th, 1975, Judge Robert Muir barred television and radio equipment from the courtroom and set aside certain seats for the media (p. 25)

Some of the legal arguments advanced in the Quinlans' case were that to be kept alive by "extraordinary" means would be a violation of Ms. Quinlan's religious freedom, that to be sustained in such a manner was cruel and unusual punishment, that she had a right of privacy to make this life-and-death decision for herself, and that, since she was incompetent, her parents could exercise this right on her behalf (pp. 34–51). These arguments did not persuade Judge Muir, who ruled against the Quinlans.

Judge Muir limited his role to the "facts of this case and the issues presented by them. . . . In this age of advanced medical science the prolongation of life and organ transplants, it is not my intent nor can it be, to resolve the extensive civil and criminal legal dilemmas engendered" (p. 554). He notes that previous cases in which parents were able to authorize medical procedures were in order to preserve the life of the patient, not to cause their death. He states that "A patient is placed, or places himself, in the care of a physician with the expectation that he (the physician) will do everything in his power . . . to protect the patient's life" (p. 559). He concludes on this point that physicians must follow medical tradition, that

None of the doctors testified that there was *no* hope. . . . There *is* a duty to continue the life assisting apparatus, if within the treating physician's opinion, it should be done. Here Dr. Morse has refused to concur in the removal of Karen from the respirator. It is his considered position that medical tradition does not justify that act. There is no mention in the doctor's refusal of concern over criminal liability and the Court concludes that such is not the basis for his determination. (p. 560)

He concludes that Karen Ann's earlier statements about not wishing to have her life sustained artificially were theoretical (p. 560). He concludes that the decision is medical rather than judicial (p. 561). He declined to make it part of his decision whether Karen Ann Quinlan could be removed from the respirator in the future, should she meet the criteria for brain death. He said this is "a decision that will have to be based upon the extant ordinary medical criteria at the time" (p. 563).

He found with regard to privacy that the cases in which medical treatment had been declined were cases in which it was declined by competent adults. The only privacy rights successfully asserted by parents on behalf of their children had to do with life styles. Similarly, he found that it was not Karen who was asserting her religious beliefs but her parents. This had been done by parents on behalf of children for life conduct but not for the ending of life. He also found that the issue of cruel and unusual punishment was not applicable to Karen Ann's situation.

Judge Muir's decision did not rule out discontinuance of medical devices if the physician thought it was appropriate, but only if the physician thought it was not.

Although Judge Muir was careful to confine his decision to the case at hand, the argument about the fear of medical technology came up several times. In the brief prepared for the Quinlans, it was argued, "For the court to mandate continued treatment in such circumstances would . . . create a precedent requiring that the vital functions of all persons in similar circumstances be indefinitely sustained—a grotesque distortion of Hippocratic ideals" (pp. 41–42).

Conceding that the state has an interest in protecting bodily integrity, the argument on behalf of the Quinlans continued as follows:

In the absence of . . . bodily integrity the state can derive no constitutionally sufficient secular benefit from the artificial maintenance of the bodily functions of an individual. Indeed, continued maintenance would place an almost intolerable burden on society's resources by creating in every individual a right to receive like treatment in similar circumstances. (p. 48)

When the case was appealed to the New Jersey Supreme Court, the arguments about religious freedom, privacy, and cruel and unusual punishment were presented again. The frightening scenario of the fear of medical technology also came up again.

Justice Morris Pashman asked William F. Hyland, the Attorney General of New Jersey: "really doesn't the horror of continued pseudo life cry out for some type of handling, some type of treatment by a court, to perhaps eliminate that situation, or to diminish the impact of that situation?" Hyland replied, "I'm not really persuaded, Justice Pashman, by that kind of emotional concern. I recognize that life has a great many burdens, a great many pains and anguish." Pashman replied, "I didn't say 'emotion.' When I'm talking about truly a horrible existence, that's not emotion; that's a fact, in given cases" (*In the Matter*, Vol. II, 1976 p. 260).

The fact that the Quinlan case attracted "wide attention" (Sullivan, 1975) indicated that the general public was concerned about the problems raised by the issues involved. Information about the case was juxtaposed in the news with information about how "courts around the nation" were establishing "legal definitions of death," and it was reported that even some attorneys said that the case might "turn on whether the court finds the is [sic] girl is legally dead" (Sullivan, 1975).

It took a while before people realized that declaring Karen Ann Quinlan to be brain dead was an unworkable strategy. The criteria for brain death were new and the case was new. People weren't familiar enough with the criteria or with the case to realize that the criteria did not apply to the case. Judge Muir, in his opinion, stated that the plaintiff initially claimed that Karen Ann Quinlan was legally and medically dead, but he had to change his position before the trial and admit that she was alive (*In the Matter*, 1975, p. 541.

It finally became apparent to those involved in the case that there was no possible way that Karen Ann Quinlan could be declared legally dead, even with the new criteria. In the court transcript of the proceedings at the New Jersey Supreme Court, we can see how the justices and Armstrong worked together on this problem. One of the justices made it clear that he was not content, to focus, like Judge Muir, on the case at hand. He wanted to make a contribution to the general problem as he perceived it (*In the Matter*, Vol. II, 1976, p. 264).

The court asks Armstrong, the Quinlan's attorney, whether they could "reconsider what has become the traditional definition of death" (p. 232). They even suggest moving to a definition of death that considers the death of only part of the brain, the cerebrum (p. 233). But Armstrong had to admit that she failed to pass even this test.

At several points in the transcript, the court asks Armstrong, for guidance as to what they could do to help him with the case. He is asked whether they must say that the Quinlans have a constitutional right to make the decision (p. 217). Armstrong states that there is another way: they can indicate that it was in her "common law best interests" to have her life support terminated (p. 217).

The court pursues the issue of a possible constitutional right, but Armstrong cannot satisfy them about the conditions. He says that the individual should be "terminally ill" and "comatose" and that "the family who knows this individual best can exercise on her behalf that judgment to terminate futile medical measure which do no more than ford the death process" (p. 222). The court did not think this route was a good route for the case to take. They challenged Armstrong's assumption that the medical measures were futile because they were in fact keeping her alive and maintaining her on a plateau (p. 225). Armstrong believed that Karen was deteriorating and that the doctors considered that she would die very soon, but the medical testimony was not clear on this point (p. 226). In fact, as subsequent events revealed, Karen Ann Quinlan was not in fact going to die soon, and her condition was very stable.

The court offers Armstrong another line of argument. They say: "Mr. Armstrong, I suspect that philosophically behind your position is something that has not been proven . . . the assumption that many physicians . . . every day make decisions to stop giving life-sustaining help to people who are hopelessly ill . . . to me that might be influential if it were proven" (p. 228).

Armstrong and the justices mutually develop this argument that there was already an underground tradition of ongoing medical practice that supported the Quinlans. They all talked about how they had heard that doctors were using a policy of judicious neglect for certain patients, but none of the participants in the proceeding provided any definite evidence. They all agreed that definite evidence would not be forthcoming because of the threat of criminal penalties (p. 229).

One of the justices asks, "Isn't it naive on our part to expect that anyone will ever prove that this is a common practice despite the fact that down deep we all know it is?" (p. 229).

This is a very curious argument. The Harvard criteria carefully state that the respirator should not be disconnected until the patient has been declared brain dead. Moreover, the lawyers representing the doctors involved and the hospital were making eloquent arguments against disconnecting the respirator. Nevertheless, Armstrong and the justices assumed, in spite of the Harvard criteria and in spite of arguments advanced by Dr. Morse, Dr. Javed, and St. Clare's hospital, that the medical profession wanted to move toward disconnecting life supports for patients who were not dead, but that they didn't dare to go any further than the Harvard criteria simply because they feared criminal sanctions.

The court concludes that the true medical consensus is the exact opposite of the published guidelines and opposite to the wishes of the medical parties who had standing in the case. Instead of seeing the Harvard criteria as the limit on how far the medical profession would go, the court saw them as only the beginning of a change in the direction of reducing the responsibility to prolong life. They saw the gap between the criteria and the case at hand and concluded that the medical profession wanted and needed their help in bridging this gap.

A perusal of medical journals at the time of the Karen Ann Quinlan case does, in fact, reveal some open, explicit discussion about the idea that certain life-sustaining actions were not appropriate for all patients. However, this discussion was in reference to a completely different sort of medical intervention, that is, cardiopulmonary resuscitation.

On August 12, 1976, just a few months after the March 31, 1976, New Jersey Supreme Court opinion regarding Karen Ann Quinlan, the *New England Journal of Medicine* published a few articles discussing sample hospital policies that allowed for "do not resuscitate" orders for certain patients (Optimum care for hopelessly, 1976; Rabkin, Gillerman, & Rice, 1976). In these articles, reference is made to the earlier *Journal of the American Medical Association* supplement devoted to cardiopulmonary resusciation (Standards for Cardiopulmonary, 1974). In this supplement, it was acknowledged that there were certain cases where death was imminently expected in which cardiopulmonary resuscitation would be considered futile.

An examination of the *Journal of the American Medical Association* issue to which these articles referred is very revealing. The discussion of "do not resuscitate" orders is one tiny paragraph of acknowledgement that cardiopulmonary resuscitation will not solve every problem (p. 864). Far from being a document about accepting the inevitability of death, this issue of the *Journal of the American Medical Association* is one of the best examples of the enthusiastic promotion of life prolongation techniques that I have ever seen.

The justices, in their very imprecise discussion of this topic, failed to distinguish between cardipulmonary resuscitation (CPR) and other kinds of life supports such as respirators. CPR requires continuous effort by medical staff. Other life supports—for example, a respirator—are completely different: They are mechanical and can be continuously applied over a long period of time. They require only intermittent support by medical personnel. Despite the fact that ethicists are fascinated by the dilemmas that would be involved if there weren't enough respirators to go around, the fact of the matter is that in the United States, lack of respirators is rarely a problem.

The fact that the medical profession accepted the concept of "do not resuscitate" orders for CPR does not mean that they accepted the concept of withdrawing respiratory supports. Acknowledging the limitations of CPR—that some patients would not wish to undergo a painful attempt to get their heart started again if they were already almost dead from other causes or that we cannot require medical personnel to try over and over again to start a heart that simply won't beat—is not the same as saying that it is futile to provide continuing mechanical respiratory support to a patient who, with this support, can remain alive.

Nevertheless, the unsubstantiated conclusion that the medical profession had a secret consensus to remove life supports was an important focus in the final opinion written by Justice Hughes. Beresford wrote that the court "discounted the assertion of Ms. Quinlan's attending neurologist that his reluctance to remove the respirator stemmed from uncertainty over whether this was a medically appropriate action. The court—without supporting evidence—simply assumed that his reluctance reflected fear of adverse legal consequences" (Beresford, 1997, p. 387).

Justice Hughes wrote that the "unnerving possibility of criminal sanctions would seem, for it is beyond human nature to suppose otherwise, to have bearing on the practice and standards as they exist . . . we cannot believe that the stated factor has not had a strong influence on the standards" (*In the Matter*, Vol. II, 1976, p. 309).

The judge finally stated:

We would hesitate, in this imperfect world, to propose as to physicians that type of immunity which from the early common law has surrounded judges and grand jurors . . . so that they might without fear of personal retaliation perform their judicial duties with independent objectivity. . . . Nevertheless, there must be a way to free physicians, in the pursuit of their healing vocation, from possible contamination by self-interest or self-protection concerns which would inhibit their independent medical judgments for the well-being of their dying patients. We would hope that this opinion might be serviceable to some degree in ameliorating the professional problems under discussion. (p. 311)

When the justices asked Armstrong what distinguished the Quinlans' exercise of their privacy right from euthanasia, Armstrong referred to a statement by Bishop Lawrence B. Casey, the Bishop of Paterson New Jersey (p. 205). Armstrong replied: "Well, essentially we follow the definitions set forth in Bishop Casey's statement that has been filed by the New Jersey Catholic Conference and adopted by all the Bishops in the State of New Jersey. . . . Merely removing these futile medical measures and allowing the body to follow its natural process is not the act of taking a human life in the sense of injecting with an air bubble or injecting with an overdose of morphine" (p. 225).

The justices do not sound convinced by these nuances and question whether a treatment that prolongs life can truly be considered futile (p. 225).

In the court opinion, however, the justices, like Armstrong, also rely on Bishop Casey's statement as an assurance that their decision is not license for euthanasia. Interestingly enough, Bishop Casey's argument also consists of the idea that doctors are already withdrawing treatment: "people involved in medical care . . . have exercised the freedom to terminate or withhold certain treatments . . . it has been without sanction in civil law . . . such actions have not in themselves undermined society's reverence for the lives of sick and dying people" (pp. 299–300).

Bishop Casey's statement continues to the effect that it is important to be able to terminate treatment without "leaving an opening for euthanasia" (p. 300). He assumes, because this is already being done, "to accomplish this, it may simply be required that courts and legislative bodies recognize the present standards and practices of many people engaged in medical care who have been doing what the parents of Karen Ann Quinlan are requesting authorization to have done" (p. 300).

It is first of all remarkable that the justices, in support of their decision that the termination of Karen Ann's life is not euthanasia, do not cite legal sources but instead turn to the Catholic Church for support. What is even more remarkable is that Bishop Casey's main argument does not really have a solid source. His source of support is simply the belief that these practices are already going on and that he is so far unaware of any resulting harm. The law and the church, instead of backing up the official medical standards, are to take as their model the underground standards. No one knows what these standards are. No one knows who to ask, because the parties involved are only identified by hearsay.

No one profession took responsibility for these actions. The judges assumed, because of the nonspecific testimony to this effect, that they were simply rubber-stamping an assumed but anonymous consensus among doctors. The court cited at length the opinion of Bishop Casey, but Bishop Casey's argument also depended upon an assumed consensus among doctors. Pope Pius XII's 1957 statement, upon which Bishop Casey relied to some extent, also stated that it was "not obligatory" to use "artificial respiration in seemingly hopeless cases" because these techniques "go beyond generally accepted medical standards" (Hofmann, 1957, p. 20).

Justice Hughes was not impressed by the arguments about religious freedom or cruel and unusual punishment. He justified his decision in favor of the Quinlans by her right to privacy. Although earlier in the proceedings, the justices had expressed some skepticism about the solidity of the privacy argument (*In the Matter*, Vol. II, pp. 223–224), Hughes used it as justification in his opinion, finding that the state's interest in preserving life decreased as the "prognosis dims" and "the degree of bodily invasion increases" (p. 305).

In this decision, he was following the advice of Paul Armstrong. Armstrong had said that one vehicle for deciding in favor of the Quinlans would be to argue that the common man believed that to die was in Karen Ann Quinlan's best interest, so that this could be seen as a permissible decision for the guardian to make in the normal course of a guardian's duties of making decisions in the best interest of the client. Hughes didn't think that Karen Ann's statements had any weight (p. 305)—he allowed her parents to request the termination of the respirator on her behalf, not because they had proved that she wanted it, but because it made sense as being in her best interest (p. 306). Hughes said that these "determinations" should be "responsive not only to the concepts of medicine but also to the common moral judgment of the community at large" (p. 308).

Justice Hughes suggests in his opinion that hospitals form ethics committees (pp. 311–313). This mechanism allows the same kind of diffusion of responsibility as took place in the Quinlan case. The doctor thinks he is being given his instructions by the family. The family assumes that, because they are being given this choice, that it conforms to medical practice. Often the members of ethics committees perform their functions anonymously. The decisions made about these patients aren't reflected in medical records. The cause of death is given as the disease that the patient was suffering from.

In their decision, the justices seemed to share the fears and strategies of those in the general culture at the time. First, they feared the direction medical technology would take if it were left unrestrained. Second, they shared the popular idea that this danger could be avoided by a sort of revolution against authority figures.

Just as many conscientious objectors had needed to establish that they were part of an organized religion, and just as Paul Armstrong had pleaded that Karen Ann's religion exempted her from extraordinary medical treatment, so, too, the justices turned to the church to justify their rebellion against the medical authorities.

The statements of the leaders of the medical field and the statements of the doctors in the case were ignored in favor of a hypothetical set of unidentified doctors who were thought to be acting in accordance with the views of the "common man." No limits were set to ensure that these views did not lead to euthanasia.

After all the court proceedings were over, Mrs. Quinlan went through a crisis very much like Louise, the patient we discussed in Chapter 2, who had planned her suicide but, when faced with the prospect of doing it soon, wanted more time to live. Mrs. Quinlan experienced great sadness about the idea of losing her daughter. She appreciated that however limited her daughter's life was, at least she was alive. She wrote that she would no longer have her daughter to kiss any more (Quinlan & Quinlan, 1977, p. 278). She hesitated. However, just as in the case of Louise, her "helper," Armstrong, encouraged her to carry through on the court decision (p. 278). Father Trapasso also experienced hesitation. He expressed the wish that Karen Ann would die before her respirator was disconnected (p. 277). He also hoped that when it was disconnected, she wouldn't die right away (p. 300).

What happened next was a great surprise to the Quinlans. After the New Jersey Supreme Court case had been decided in their favor, Mr. Quinlan felt sorry for the doctor, because he assumed that the doctor had to decide whether to remove Karen Ann's respirator or resign. To the Quinlans' surprise, however,

Dr. Morse did not even read the decision (pp. 281–282). To the doctors, the pronouncements of the state were not particularly pertinent. Their everyday decision making was guided by medical standards and by their personal morality. The Quinlans had thought of their problem as a struggle between the individual and the state. What they didn't realize was that although the court had taken their side, the law was only one part of our society's ethical infrastructure.

Professional ethics and personal ethics were also a force with which they had to contend. The court did not compel the doctors to go along with the Quinlans' wishes. The court only said that if the doctors did go along with the Quinlans' wishes, it would not be considered homicide.

In this sense, the Karen Ann Quinlan case was hypothetical. The court decided whether it would be homicide to discontinue a respirator if her doctor deemed it appropriate, but in fact her doctor did not.

Karen Ann's doctors still refused to disconnect her respirator (pp. 282, 287, 291). Instead, they succeeded in weaning her off it gradually. The process only took about two weeks (p. 297–298). After this, she was safely transferred to another facility, where she continued to survive without the respirator for another nine years (Stryker, 1996, p. 5). In this facility, she was treated with an anti-convulsant, Dilantin, which seemed to help her remain in a more peaceful state, and the family was greatly relieved by this (Quinlan & Quinlan, 1977, p. 342).

The justices interpreted the Harvard criteria as an attempt by the medical profession to deal with the accumulation of the virtually dead. Did the medical profession share the common man's fears? Were the Harvard criteria, in fact, their attempt to move in the direction of limiting their responsibility to prolong life?

Peter Singer, a philosopher with controversial views on bioethical issues, believes that they had no such intentions. Singer argues that the criteria were changed at that time because of the possibility of heart transplants (Singer, 1994, pp. 25–26). Singer explains that for a successful transplant, the heart must be removed as soon as possible (pp. 23–24).

Singer points out that the Ad Hoc Committee of the Harvard Medical School to Examine the Definition of Brain Death was set up within a month of the news of the first heart transplant (p. 24). The committee's statement about the purpose of the new definition declares that "Obsolete criteria for the definition of death can lead to controversy in obtaining organs for transplantation" (p. 25). According to Singer, an earlier draft of the statement contained an even more explicit mention of transplants: "there is a great need for tissues and organs of, among others, the patient whose cerebrum has been hopelessly destroyed" (p. 25). Singer also quotes the chairman of the committee, Henry Beecher, in his address to the American Association for the Advancement of Science: "There is indeed a life-saving potential in the new definition, for, when accepted, it will lead to greater availability than formerly of essential organs in viable condition, for transplantation, and thus countless lives now inevitably lost will be saved" (p. 26).

If Singer is correct about the motivation for the Harvard criteria, this statement was not an acceptance of the inevitability of death but, instead, just the opposite. It is a preparation for an anticipated leap into an era of greater life prolongation through organ transplantation.

The Quinlan case was indeed a public-relations triumph for the advocates of managed dying. By taking this hypothetical case, in which the medical authorities were refusing to discontinue a respirator, somehow Paul Armstrong managed to persuade the court that to discontinue the respirator was consistent with standard medical practice, simply by asserting that this was the case. By getting the court to agree to this, and by getting all the publicity that the case engendered, he in fact promoted this approach to medical care.

The fact that Justice Hughes justified his decision on the basis that dying was considered by the common man as being in Karen Ann's best interest left the door wide open for future cases. The fact that Karen Ann Quinlan was not suffering from pain or from a rapidly deteriorating fatal illness but, rather, from something that impaired her consciousness, also set a precedent allowing quality of life considerations.

The fact that the case was hypothetical, that the justices' discussions lacked precision, and that the doctors in Karen Ann Quinlan's case ignored the decision are obscure facts unknown to most. The confusing and rapid cultural and technological changes going on at that time—the end of the Vietnam war, the beginnings of CPR and heart transplants—are not invoked to excuse the conceptual confusion of this case. The possibility that the public's fears about the torturous accumulation of the virtually dead might be based more upon hysteria than upon medical reality is not considered.

What remained clearly etched in the public consciousness was that life supports could be legally disconnected upon the request of the family. No restrictions were set down about the kinds of circumstances under which these family requests would be allowed. Just as Schoevers, Asmus, and Van Tilburg (1998) had hope that the next set of detailed guidelines developed by the Dutch Board of Psychiatrists might overcome some of the serious problems that they found with the guidelines being used in 1998, the justices and the public were satisfied that somewhere out there the ordinary doctor, inspired by the common man, had already developed a set of such guidelines. In reality, however, the only guidance given was to form a committee and to assess the views of the "common man." The future limits of family requests were very much open. It would all depend upon how far the "common man," whoever that is, was willing to go.

REFERENCES

A definition of irreversible coma: Report of the Ad Hoc Committee of the Harvard Medical School to examine the definition of brain death. (1968). *Journal of the American Medical Association, 205,* 337–340.

Beresford, H.R. (1997). The persistent vegetative state: A view across the legal divide. *Annals of the New York Academy of Sciences, 835,* 386–394.

Ehrlich, P.R. (1971). *The Population Bomb.* New York: Sierra Club/Ballantine Books.

Hofmann, P. (1957, Nov. 25). Pius gives view on saving dying; Tells when doctors may give up. *The New York Times,* 1, 20.

In the matter of Karen Quinlan: The complete legal briefs, court proceedings, and decision in the Superior Court of New Jersey. (1975). Arlington, VA: University Publications of America.

In the matter of Karen Quinlan, Vol. II: The complete briefs, oral arguments, and opinion in the New Jersey Supreme Court. (1976). Arlington, VA: University Publications of America.

Life-sustaining technologies and the elderly. (1987, July). U.S. Congress, Office of Technology Assessment. Washington, D.C.: U.S. Government Printing Office.

Optimum care for hopelessly ill patients: A report of the Clinical Care Committee of the Massachusetts General Hospital. (1976). *New England and Journal of Medicine, 295,* 362–364.

Quinlan, Joseph, & Quinlan, Julia, with Battell, P. (1977). *Karen Ann: The Quinlans tell their story.* New York: Doubleday.

Rabkin, M.T., Gillerman, G., & Rice, N.R. (1976). Orders not to resuscitate. *New England Journal of Medicine, 295,* 364–366.

Schoevers, R.A., Asmus, F.P., & Van Tilburg, W. (1998). Physician-assisted suicide in psychiatry: Developments in the Netherlands. *Psychiatric Services, 49,* 1475–1480.

Singer, P. (1994). *Rethinking life and death: The collapse of our traditional ethics.* New York: St. Martin's Press.

Smith, W.J. (1997). *Forced exit: The slippery slope from assisted suicide to legalized murder.* New York: Times Books.

Standards for Cardiopulmonary Resuscitation (CPR) and Emergency Cardiac Care (ECC). (1974, Feb. 18). *Journal of the American Medical Association, 227* (7), supplement, 833–868.

Stryker, J. (1996, Mar. 31). Life after Quinlan. *The New York Times,* Sect. 4, p. 5.

Sullivan, J. (1975, Sept. 17). Hearing set on removal of devices keeping girl in a coma alive. *The New York Times.* p. 49, Late Jersey Edition, New Jersey Pages 000095.

CHAPTER 4

The Movement to Legalize and Otherwise Promote Physician-Assisted Suicide and Euthanasia in America

In this chapter we will discuss some of the highlights of and some of the people involved in the campaign to legalize physician-assisted suicide and euthanasia in the United States. The movement for physician-assisted suicide has been very visible and its advocates have been very visible. In contrast, the movement for euthanasia has been behind the scenes, and its advocates have been behind the scenes.

The campaign to legalize physician-assisted suicide has achieved spectacular publicity. Although physician-assisted suicide has not been legalized anywhere in the United States except Oregon, almost everyone has been exposed to the idea. Many members of the public who have not yet thoroughly investigated the idea are favorably inclined toward it.

The status of the struggle to legalize physician-assisted suicide is as follows. In the United States, physician-assisted suicide is allowed only in Oregon, where it was legalized in 1994. Implementation was delayed by court battles until 1997. On November 6, 2001, the practice of physician-assisted suicide in Oregon was challenged when Attorney General Ashcroft sent a "memo to the head of the Drug Enforcement Administration" indicating that "prescribing, dispensing, or administering' federally controlled substances" to assist suicide was a violation of the Controlled Substances Act (Meyer & Murphy, 2001, p. A10). On April 17, 2002, however, Judge Robert Jones ruled that Ashcroft lacked the authority to make this determination. Therefore, physician-assisted suicide is still legal in Oregon (Liptak, 2002, p. A16). This decision will likely be appealed. Readers can find out more about these events as they unfold from the web sites of organizations that oppose (www.internationaltaskforce.org, www.pccef.org) and advocate (www.compassionindying.org) physician-assisted suicide.

In the Netherlands, physician-assisted suicide and euthanasia have been tolerated for several decades. Until recently, these practices, although criminal, were not prosecuted if the physicians followed certain guidelines. However, on April 10, 2001, these practices were completely legalized in the Netherlands (Dutch upper house, 2001). Belgium is currently in the process of legalizing euthanasia.

In the United States, two important cases were decided by the U.S. Supreme Court on June 26, 1997. In these cases, advocates of physician-assisted suicide used a very aggressive strategy. Instead of trying to legalize physician-assisted suicide in a particular state, they tried to make it unconstitutional to ban it in any state. Four Washington physicians, three terminally ill plaintiffs, and an organization providing counseling to people considering physician-assisted suicide sued the state of Washington in *Washington v. Glucksberg*. Similarly, in *Vacco. v. Quill*, physicians and three patients sued the Attorney General in New York state. In each case it was claimed that the state's ban on assisted suicide violated constitutional rights.

In the New York case, it was claimed that the ban violated the Fourteenth Amendment's equal protection clause because, among terminally ill persons who wished to hasten their deaths, New York treated those who wished to do it by self-administering prescribed drugs differently than those who wished to do so by removing life support systems. The U.S. Supreme Court ruled that the assisted-suicide ban did not violate the equal protection clause. They disagreed

with the Second Circuit's submission that ending or refusing lifesaving medical treatment 'is nothing more nor less than assisted suicide.' The distinction between letting a patient die and making that patient die is important, logical, rational, and well established . . . and has been widely recognized and endorsed in the medical profession, the state courts, and the overwhelming majority of state legislatures, which, like New York's, have permitted the former while prohibiting the latter. The Court therefore disagrees with respondents' claim that the distinction is 'arbitrary' and 'irrational' . . . New York's reasons for recognizing and acting on the distinction between refusing treatment and assisting a suicide—including prohibiting intentional killing and preserving life; preventing suicide; maintaining physicians' role as their patients' healers; protecting vulnerable people from indifference, prejudice, and psychological and financial pressure to end their lives; and avoiding a possible slide towards euthanasia—are valid and important public interests that easily satisfy the constitutional requirement that a legislative classification bear a rational relation to some legitimate end. (*Vacco v. Quill*, pp. 793–794)

In *Washington v. Glucksberg*, where it had been claimed that assisted suicide was a liberty interest protected by the Fourteenth Amendment's due process clause, the court ruled that it did not violate the due process clause. They noted that the clause protects fundamental rights which are "deeply rooted in this Nation's history and tradition. . . . This asserted right has no place in our Nation's traditions, given the country's consistent, almost universal, and continuing rejection of the right, even for terminally ill, mentally competent adults. To hold for respondents, the Court would have to reverse centuries of legal doctrine and practice, and strike down the considered policy choice of almost every State" (*Washington v. Glucksberg*, p. 703).

Proposals allowing physician-assisted suicide have been brought to a vote by referendum and were defeated in California (1992), Washington (1991), Michigan (1998), and most recently, Maine. Maine's proposal was defeated on November 7, 2000.

According to Wesley J. Smith (2000a), in all of these states, there was a pattern of substantial early support for the measures, but that the support dwindled as the voters learned more about the possible abuses (pp. 21–22). In Maine, for example, at first, according to the *Bangor Daily News*, 70% of the voters supported the proposal, which received financial support from euthanasia organizations all over the country. But when the voters considered it in the context of HMO cost cutting, support declined to 48.5%, and the measure lost by 20,000 votes (p. 21). Even in Oregon, where the voters passed legislation legalizing physician-assisted suicide in 1994, initial voter support of 70% dwindled to 51% (p. 22).

In Wisconsin, Hawaii, New Hampshire, California, Rhode Island, Illinois, Texas, and other states, assisted suicide bills were introduced in legislatures but did not pass.

It is clear that although the movement has not succeeded in legalizing physician-assisted suicide anywhere in the United States except Oregon, popular support runs high and it takes continuous effort to keep the public well informed enough to defeat these initiatives.

These attempts to legalize physician-assisted suicide have been opposed by coalitions of "hospice professionals, religious organizations, pro-lifers, and medical associations." These groups have "set aside their differences on other controversial issues" to join together to defeat these measures (p. 22).

Because advocates of these measures claim to be working on behalf of dying patients, one might expect that the people who work the most closely with dying patients would favor physician-assisted suicide and euthanasia. This is not at all the case. In fact, hospice organizations are most often active opponents of these practices. Eric Chevlen wrote the following:

"As a hospice medical director and board-certified specialist in pain medicine, I know the reality behind the distortions of the euthanasia lobby. My experience is consonant with that of numerous government-appointed blue ribbon panels. They, like I, have found that 90% of cancer patients in pain can have dramatic relief with relatively simple oral therapies. Virtually all the rest of them can achieve relief with more sophisticated therapies. . . . Innumerable published medical studies have confirmed what I have witnessed in my own practice, that a request for assisted suicide is almost always an expression of clinical depression. Depression in the face of advanced illness is as treatable as it is in those who are otherwise healthy. The treatment might include medicine, counseling, or prayer, but it surely does not include a lethal injection." (Chevlen, 1998)

Oncologists, who spend their medical careers treating the very kinds of terminally ill patients that advocates of physician-assisted suicide are worried about, have a low rate of support for physician-assisted suicide and euthanasia, and it is declining. Emanuel et al. (2000) reported that oncologists' support for physician-assisted suicide for patients in unremitting pain declined from 45.5% in 1994 to 22.5% in 1998.

Given that the support for physician-assisted suicide and euthanasia has not come from the medical profession, particularly not from those concerned with the dying, and not from cancer patients in pain, from where has the support come? Much of the support for the movement has come from people who decided to help a dying person die and then published accounts of what had happened.

The story of Derek Humphry is told by Rita Marker in her book *Deadly Compassion: The Death of Ann Humphry and the Truth about Euthanasia* (1993). Humphry's first wife, Jean, was dying of breast cancer, and they "made a pact" that he would help her commit suicide. If "she . . . asked him if it was time" to commit suicide, "he would give her an 'honest' answer" and "he would provide her with the means" to do it (p. 32). After her death, and after Humphry married Ann Wickett, he, with the support of Ann Wickett, wrote a book about Jean's death called *Jean's Way* (1978).

The book received a lot of publicity, and Derek Humphry, an unemployed journalist with a charismatic speaking style, began a speaking career. In 1980, he and Ann Wickett started the Hemlock Society, and the *Hemlock Quarterly*. They were interested in training counselors to help with "self-deliverance" (Marker, 1993, pp. 44–45). From the beginning, Humphry's goal was not just physician-assisted suicide but the legalization of euthanasia (p. 67). Humphry, along with a new organization, Americans Against Human Suffering, tried to legalize euthanasia by putting an initiative on the California ballot in 1988 to amend the existing living will legislation (p. 77). This effort failed in California and in Washington (p. 86).

Earlier drafts of the bill that eventually passed in Oregon allowed lethal injection, but because of the Washington and California defeats, the version that appeared on Oregon's ballot prohibited instead of allowing lethal injection (p. 4). The phrase "assisted suicide" was also not used in the Oregon version. Terms such as "death with dignity" were used instead (Marker, 2000, p. 4). Within a short time after the measure passed, physician-assisted suicide was described as "comfort care" in Oregon's reimbursement categories (p. 6).

To euthanasia supporters, the legislation to allow physician-assisted suicide and public acceptance of such measures as removing food and fluids from incapacitated patients are stepping stones toward the acceptance of euthanasia. Helga Kuhse said that if people come to accept the removal of care and removal of food and fluids, and then see how uncomfortable this method of dying is, they will then, in the patient's best interest, accept lethal injection (Marker, 1993, p. 94).

Marker describes an important conference of the World Federation of Right to Die Societies, a world-wide umbrella organization for euthanasia societies, held in Nice in 1984. At this time the organizations supporting the international movement for euthanasia claimed a membership totalling 415,000 (p. 49). Six hundred people applauded thunderously as a French physician, Dr. Leon Schwartzenberg, described giving a lethal injection to a woman in her mid-1950s in the presence of her daughter and infant grandchild (pp. 59–62). Schwartzenberg's background, shows the same pattern as Humphry's. He first helped a close personal friend die, then, later, patients he'd known for a long time. Finally he began to help people die that he hardly knew (p. 63).

Humphry's success with *Jean's Way* (1978) was followed with other books, for example, *Right to Die: Understanding Euthanasia* (1986), and ultimately, *Final Exit: The Practicalities of Self-Deliverance and Assisted Suicide for the Dying* (1991), the best-seller that gives instructions about how to commit suicide. Humphry and Ann Wickett also helped Ann's parents commit suicide. Ann wrote a fictionalized book about their suicides (Marker, 1993, p. 72) called *Double Exit* (Wickett, 1989).

Recently, when it appeared that the Pain Relief Promotion Act, which proposed to prohibit using controlled substances for the purpose of physician-assisted suicide, might become law, Humphry helped organize a conference to provide information about other methods of suicide. At a conference of the Self-Deliverance New Technology Group on November 13, 1999, in Seattle, Washington, masks, plastic bags, a DeBreather, and other suicide gadgets were displayed and discussed (Euthanasia gurus meet, 2000). Humphry put the information from his book *Final Exit* on a video, which was aired on Oregon television. In discussing this video on a televised discussion program, he articulated his justification. He stated that he was first and foremost a journalist with a commitment to dispensing information rather than a doctor or a nurse practicing medicine.

Groups like the Hemlock Society facilitated the work of all the other supporters of physician-assisted suicide and other forms of deliberate discontinuation of life. Timothy Quill, a physician who became a famous advocate of physician-assisted suicide when he wrote an article in 1991 for the *New England Journal of Medicine* about his patient "Diane," and then wrote her a lethal prescription (Marker, 1993, p. 187). Nancy Cruzan's parents consulted "with the Society for the Right to Die" (Smith, 1997, p. 46). Even Kevorkian's first patient, Janet Adkins, was a member "of the Hemlock Society" (Smith, 1997, p. 24).

By far the most famous promoter of physician-assisted suicide is Jack Kevorkian. Jack Kevorkian's background before he helped Janet Adkins, his first physician-assisted suicide case, inject herself with lethal medication in the back of a van, was not as an advocate for patients dying of disease. The group to whom he devoted his energies was convicted criminals sentenced to death. He felt that it was an outrage to these individuals not to allow them to donate their organs for transplantation. Donating organs would allow them to feel that their execution wasn't a complete waste and that they could contribute to society.

In his book, *Prescription—Medicide: The Goodness of Planned Death* (1991), he gives a detailed description of his quest beginning in 1958, when he was inspired by an obscure German article that described how condemned criminals in ancient Alexandria were used in anatomical experiments (p. 28). For many years he corresponded with death-row inmates. He met many of them and arranged for surveys to demonstrate their support for his ideas. His plan was to begin sedating convicts at the moment of the official execution and then to use their bodies for medical experiments and organ donations, never allowing them to recover consciousness. An important obstacle that he encountered in his plan was that the medical profession had traditionally refused to participate in executions, a refusal that he severely criticized (pp. 122–124). He actually blames doctors for allowing the cruel executions throughout history. He questions why the medical profession "stood by idly while thousands were being brutally crucified, crushed, and burned to death" (p. 187). He questioned why they didn't "rise up as a whole and scream, 'No! Let *us* do it humanely. Let us kill him with an opiate' " (p. 187).

After a visit to the Netherlands in 1987, during which he could not gain any support for his idea of combining euthanasia with medical experimentation (pp. 189–190), Kervorkian decided to start helping suffering people to die (p. 192). He explained to a man with terminal lung cancer who was interested in his services that his aim was "not simply to help suffering or doomed persons kill themselves—that is merely the first step, an early distasteful professional obligation . . . that nobody in his or her right mind could savor. I explained that what I find most satisfying is the prospect of making possible the performance of invaluable experiments or other beneficial medical acts under conditions that this first unpleasant step can help establish" (p. 214).

Kervorkian sees the terminally ill and the condemned as similar in that they both are facing an inevitable death. He was hopeful that his suicide machine, the Mercitron, could also be used in executions, allowing the condemned some autonomy in activating the machine themselves (pp. 234–237).

We have already discussed, in Chapter 2, how technical problems frequently arise as people try to kill themselves and how they often need help. These problems, although euthanasia activists are fully aware of them, were concealed for many years. Euthanasia activists know that the public would have to first be highly attached to the idea that people should be allowed to die before they could even consider, without revulsion, the idea that they should be allowed to be killed.

Now that these facts about how symptoms of nausea, vomiting, convulsions, and other problems occur fairly frequently when the physician's role is limited to prescribing lethal doses of medication have been published even in the *New England Journal of Medicine* (Groenewoud, van der Heide, Onwuteaka-Philipsen, Willems, van der Maas, & van der Wal, 2000), they can no longer be concealed.

The public may have had the impression, from both Humphry and Kevorkian, that physician-assisted suicide was a trouble-free way of ending life, but the inevitable problems of this procedure eventually haunted them. Humphry claimed in *Jean's Way* that his wife died quietly from taking the medication. His second wife, Ann Wickett, claimed in a note to Rita Marker that he had smothered Jean with pillows (Marker, 1993, p. 230). Similarly, Kevorkian claimed at first that the suicide of his patients was entirely in their own hands. Eventually, he lethally injected Thomas Youk on national television (Johnson, 1998), after which he was successfully prosecuted.

Timothy Quill as mentioned earlier in this chapter, entered the limelight when he published an article in the *New England Journal of Medicine* in 1991 about "Diane," a woman with leukemia whom he referred to the Hemlock Society (Marker, 1993, p. 187) and for whom he provided a prescription of barbiturates. His patient's "identity . . . was discovered" and her case was "presented to a grand jury" for consideration of criminal prosecution. They did not prosecute, however (Quill, 1993, p. 21).

Having begun with this case, he continued to write books in this area, publishing *Death and dignity: Making Choices and Taking Charge* (1993) and *A Midwife through the Dying Process: Stories of Healing and Hard Choices at the End of Life* (1996). He was one of the plaintiffs in the *Vacco v. Quill* lawsuit against the state of New York, which was an unsuccessful attempt to end New York's ban on assisted suicide.

Although the writings and other activities of these advocates of physician-assisted suicide and euthanasia have so far not resulted in the legalization of physician-assisted suicide for competent adults anywhere in the United States except Oregon, they have nevertheless, I believe, had a profound effect upon the treatment of critically ill incompetent patients.

The traditional beliefs of families about the treatment of their incompetent loved ones have been shaken. Because of the current rhetoric, family members are acutely aware that by requesting treatment for their critically ill loved ones who may be close to death, they may be simply causing them unnecessary pain. Consequently, when doctors approach the families of critically ill patients and suggest disconnecting life supports, families often agree to this without taking any precautionary steps. They may not be considering the possibility of a medical mistake or that the medical facility might be under pressure to reduce costs. They may not be considering that the doctor's ethical beliefs might be different from the family's. They may not be seeking additional medical consultations. They may not realize the value of consulting clergy.

It has become so common for families to go along with pressures to disconnect their loved ones, that this is almost expected, and the family that wants treatment sometimes has to struggle to get it.

Shaywitz, a medical intern (Shaywitz, 2000), wrote an Op-Ed piece in the *New York Times* about his terminally ill uncle, who was suffering from metastatic cancer and developed a lung infection. Instead of treating this infection, his uncle's doctor hesitated. Since his uncle was dying anyway, his uncle's doctor felt that treating the infection would be pointless. His aunt had to plead with the oncologist on the telephone in the middle of the night. Fortunately, she was successful. His uncle recovered from the lung infection and enjoyed the next few months tremendously. Shaywitz was impelled to write an Op-Ed editorial to point out "how much living some patients can compress into an additional day, an extra week, an unanticipated month." He concluded, "I have the pictures to prove it" (p. A25).

In an era of reverence for life, Shaywitz would not have had to write his editorial; the advantage of life over death was something that most people understood and took for granted. However, in this era, the editorial was necessary and was a great contribution. How did Shaywitz know how important it was to express these points? Shaywitz was in medical school, and he knew the current concepts that are being conveyed to future doctors. He had been taught that "aggressive medical intervention in terminal cases is increasingly considered an avoidable cruelty, inflicted on a suffering patient by . . . a family member unable to acknowledge the inevitable" (p. A25). Against the background of this approach, Shaywitz realized that his own personal experience with his uncle was critical for new doctors to hear. He felt that the preciousness of extra time to live is not being conveyed by medical professors or by our general culture.

A remarkable example of relatives struggling with a medical facility took place in Great Britain. A 12-year-old boy, David Glass, born with hydrocephalus, blind, and with severe learning disabilities and spastic quadriplegia, was hospitalized with a chest infection. Doctors refused to treat the infection but instead treated him palliatively with diamorphine and told the family he should be allowed to die with dignity. Aware that in the absence of other treatment, this medication would simply tranquilize him and possibly make it even harder for him to breathe, bringing on his death, members of his family showed up at the hospital to revive him by rubbing him, banging on him, and pulling him out of bed. The doctors tried to stop them. When the boy was visited at home by the official solicitor some time later, he was sitting in bed laughing and smiling, surrounded by his sisters. He was being taken out to shops and parks. Two years later, this boy is still alive. Even though it was acknowledged that they had saved their nephew's life, his aunts and uncle were convicted of assaulting two doctors and jailed. According to an editorial in the London *Daily Telegraph*: "It is difficult not to conclude that the intervention by his aunts and uncle saved his life. It is a warped idea of 'intensive care' that tries to induce avoidable death" (Disabled boy's relatives, 2000, p. 6).

Not every patient has someone like Shaywitz's aunt to plead for him. She had her oncologist's home phone number and was aware enough not to take his initial refusal as final. She was also articulate enough to persuade him. Not every patient has a family like David Glass's—who would come to the hospital to retrieve him. Most families whose doctor says he can do no more for their family member simply accept the doctor's word and sign what he asks them to sign. This means that patients like Shaywitz's uncle and David Glass are dying unnecessarily.

Examples like these are not hard to find. Shoff (2000) wrote that when she flew to the East Coast to visit her father who had had a stroke, she found that he was not receiving any food. She was told that he had seven to ten days to live. After consulting with clergy, the family insisted that he be fed and insisted upon a neurological consultation. The neurologist began by asking the patient, "Sir, if you can hear me, put up one finger." His finger went up immediately. He was able to leave the hospital and survived for eleven months, during which time he was able to speak and make intelligent conversation. This time was regarded by the family as high quality time for all of them. Why did the family of this man, who had the potential to live longer, have to save his life by insisting upon food and fluids and neurological consultation? Why wasn't nourishment and neurological consultation provided as part of his treatment?

These kinds of cases are not even restricted to people who are elderly or terminally ill or previously handicapped. Smith (2000b) gives an example of a teenager, "unconscious for three weeks" after an auto accident, who "developed a 105-degree fever." His father "asked the nurses" to treat the fever. The nurses refused because they had no medical order. The doctor on call refused to write the order, and the boy's regular "physician was out of town" (p. 1). The boy's temperature kept rising, until it was 107.6. The on-call doctor, who had "refused to take" the desperate father's calls, was finally pressured by the nurses into speaking to the father. He explicitly refused the father's request. The "doctor actually laughed. The boy was unconscious. His life was effectively over. What was the point?" (p. 2). The father had to angrily insist that that doctor do something about the fever, which had been allowed to rage for "twenty hours."

With treatment, the boy's "temperature subsided." He is still alive, lives at home with his parents, is in rehabilitation, and is "learning to walk." He "works at a local youth center," counseling "at-risk teenagers," and is "glad to be alive" (p. 2).

What if his father hadn't been there that day? Why was his medical treatment dependent upon his father's expression of outrage?

The Shatter family was not so lucky. When their "healthy seventy-six-year-old" father suffered a head injury and was intermittently unconscious after surgery, his "medical caregivers," who had previously treated him optimally, changed their strategy and tried to pressure "the family into authorizing the withholding of his tube-supplied food and fluids." (p. 3). The family was "appalled" and the hospital staff had to accept the family's decision. He was "transferred to a rehabilitation hospital." On the "day of the transfer," he "spoke briefly with his family," and they were becoming hopeful. One day, he "developed a high fever," and the medical staff did nothing. The family "spoke with an administrator" and he "hemmed and hawed and reminded us that Dad wasn't making progress" (Smith, 2000b, p. 4). The medical staff didn't begin treatment until someone in the family shouted "I am calling the police and telling them you are murdering my father by refusing to help him! Get a doctor to my dad's bedside!" (p. 4). By that time, it was really too late, and their father died.

Many people are polarized on the issues of physician-assisted suicide and euthanasia, but they believe, when their loved one is sick, that when they get to the hospital, they will be able to specify, according to the patient's deeply held conviction, which manner of medical treatment is to be used. Is their loved one's life to be extended as long as possible? Or is their loved one going to be subject to a calculation of their potential pains and pleasures and allowed to die if there seems to be little chance of any future pleasure?

When they first get to the hospital, it seems as if the staff is doing everything that can be done for the patient. Only later, if the patient's organ systems begin to fail, does it become clear to the family, that members of the medical staff are just as polarized as other people on these issues.

When your loved one is hanging by a thread and has a chance of dying or recovering, there may be some members of the medical staff who believe it is still worth treating her and others who believe it is cruel to keep trying. And it is difficult for the family to maintain the round-the-clock surveillance necessary to ensure that those who want the patient treated can prevail. Our medical facilities are not characterized right now by a harmonious devotion to patient autonomy. There is instead, a chaotic and unpredictable blend of different ideologies, creating bitter disputes.

These conflicts between families seeking medical care and facilities refusing it are not isolated situations. If we look at individual doctors and nurses, we see that each of them has his or her own personal philosophy about the right or wrong of terminating a patient's life. Some are tortured by the idea of taking a life and will not do it even if they are reprimanded for not doing it. Even advocates of euthanasia who believe in it thoroughly find it difficult to take a human life. Herbert Cohen, one of the leading practitioners of euthanasia in Holland, says he cannot sleep for a week after performing euthanasia (Hendin, 1997, p. 52).

On the other hand, some doctors and nurses believe, like the advocates of euthanasia, that continued medical treatment is cruel. Mitchell (2000) spoke with some doctors and nurses who felt terrible because they had tried to resuscitate a little girl on the request of her parents and believed they had done too much. "It was horrible. . . . We tried to resuscitate her for over an hour. It's the worst thing I've ever done. I actually felt sick" (p. 12).

This fact of life—the attachment of individual doctors and nurses to different principles—has unfortunately not been taken into account by those who believe that we can ask doctors and nurses, regardless of their deepest personal goals, to reverse their strategies 180 degrees upon request in each individual case.

Unfortunately, people cannot change their deepest values so easily, and, instead of a situation in which everyone has his choice, we instead have a struggle going on for control of our medical institutions.

The chaotic blend of individual values that we are currently experiencing may give way to more organized procedural methods of deciding who is eligible for care. In the construction of these new policies, medical facilities have leaned heavily on a new field called "bioethics." In the past, many hospitals were founded and supported by religious groups, and for difficult questions they turned to the clergy for answers. Currently, hospitals are run for profit, and for difficult questions they turn to a new kind of advisor: bioethicists. Wesley Smith's book, *Culture of Death: The Assault on Medical Ethics in America* (2000b) is an exploration into the ideas and conclusions of these bioethicists who are being given so much power in the world of public health policy today. Bioethics has become a new academic specialty, and many short courses in bioethics have been offered to medical personnel.

One of the most well-known bioethicists is Peter Singer, and many bioethicists follow his way of thinking. Singer is a philosopher who occupies a prestigious professorship at Princeton University. He has written many popular books that are easily available in public libraries. Singer (1994) has called traditional ethics into question and has tried to put in its place a system based upon the principle of utilitarianism. Actions are right or wrong, according to Singer, not according to the nature of the action but according to the consequences of the action.

Singer has outraged many by taking the position that our society could consider it acceptable for the parents of a disabled infant to decide to kill it (pp. 210–215). Protesters in Germany caused a symposium including Singer to be cancelled because of his views (pp. 201–202). His appointment as a professor at Princeton University was protested actively by student groups and by groups advocating the rights of the disabled.

Singer describes what he considers a moral dilemma powerful enough to topple traditional ethics. He attended a conference in Melbourne in 1991 (p. 38) where the following dilemma was presented by Dr. Frank Shann (pp. 41–42). He described two infants lying side by side. One had sustained massive damage to its cerebral cortex. The other had a hopeless heart condition. According to Singer, traditional ethics forbids the doctor to remove the heart from the child without a functioning cerebral cortex and transplant it into the other child.

It bothers Singer that the reason traditional ethics doesn't allow a living person to become an organ donor is that traditional ethics considers human life to be something precious that we should not tamper with. Singer questions this specialness of the human being. He maintains that many animals gain much more benefit from their continued life than the infant without a cortex and that therefore, we should rig our categories differently and forbid the killing of such animals and allow the killing of certain humans (p. 204). He would like to have us declare that it is perfectly acceptable to take hearts from impaired human patients who are still alive (p. 52).

Those who follow his logic may find some unpleasant surprises. Having shed the obligation to maintain certain humans, followers may find that they have acquired other equally onerous burdens, such as maintaining certain animals that Singer feels qualify as persons (pp. 205–206).

The interaction between a philosopher trying to draw out the implications of a philosophic system and those who try to use his conclusions for practical affairs can go awry. Unfortunately, most ordinary people who support the idea of allowing terminal patients in pain to die if they wish are counting upon the distinction between allowing somebody to die of his or her underlying disease process and killing him or her with a lethal injection. They base their sense of where we can draw an ethical line on practical issues on which they feel there is a strong consensus in our culture.

Singer, however, comes up with examples cleverly rigged to show the difficulties in maintaining these distinctions. His solution is to substitute an entirely different ethical system.

Bioethicists are indeed creating categories that decide whose life is to be considered precious enough to protect. Wesley J. Smith (2000b) gives a fascinating example of a hospital, Loma Linda University Medical Center, that decided to allow anencephalic infants, that is, infants born with critical brain areas missing, to become organ donors. The program had to be terminated because doctors referred many infants to the program who had abnormalities that were much less severe. The drafters of the program found themselves educated about the reality of the slippery slope (pp. 177–178).

The philosophies of the bioethicists have made it possible for hospitals to draft protocols that systematically refuse medical treatment to certain patients. In spite of the fact that the public thinks patient autonomy is the basis for such decisions, these hospitals nevertheless have policies that override patient autonomy. Some have bureaucratic procedures whereby when the patients and doctors disagree, the ethics committee can make a decisions to terminate care unilaterally (pp. 131–132). These committees have anonymous membership, no particular qualifications for membership, confidential deliberations, often no written records, no oversight, and no appeals (p. 133).

Others have policies that stipulate "in advance the specific medical conditions for which treatment is deemed futile." The "Alexian Brothers Hospital of San Jose, California," instituted "such a . . . policy in . . . 1997" (p. 132). The policy "presumes that requests for medical treatment or testing are 'inappropriate' for" people who have "permanent dependence on intensive care" or who have "neurological, renal, oncological, or other devastating disease" or "untreatable lethal congenital abnormality" or "severe irreversible dementia." Smith (2001) reports that "in hospitals nationwide they are quietly promulgating formal, written futile care protocols that establish procedures under which wanted treatment can be refused" (pp. 27–28).

The bioethical ideologies discussed by Wesley Smith are not limited in their influence to hospitals such as Alexian Brothers that have included them in their medical protocols. The idea that the pros and cons of continuing an individual human life can be weighed without giving priority to life enables guardians and judges to make decisions ending the lives of patients in other facilities as well.

What are the actual considerations that judges and guardians are using in making these decisions? Wesley Smith's discussion of the Robert Wendland case offers illumination on this point. Robert Wendland was injured in an accident and woke up from a coma with considerable brain damage (Smith, 1997, p. 40). He could operate a "motorized wheelchair" and even write some "letters of his name" (Smith, 2000b, p. 75), but his wife believed that he wouldn't want to live this way, and she tried to have his feeding tube disconnected. Until he died of pneumonia (Saunders, 2001), his mother fought his wife in court to try to save him. The legal proceedings went on for several years. The case reached the California Supreme Court and received national attention. Dr. Vincent Fortanasce, a Los Angeles neurologist who examined Wendland, said that the ruling could affect "hundreds of thousands of brain-injured people who need feeding tubes to survive" (Ressner, 2001).

During the legal proceedings, Janie Hickock Siess, the attorney for Robert Wendland's mother was questioning Dr. Ronald Cranford, an expert witness. Dr. Ronald Cranford is a good example of one of the behind-the-scenes personalities promoting euthanasia in the United States. Although he has not come to the notice of the general public, he served as an expert witness in the famous case of Nancy Beth Cruzan, where he testified in favor of removing her feeding tube (Smith, 2000b, p. 73). After the Cruzan case, he testified in favor of disconnecting feeding tubes in other cases, such as the Michael Martin case (Smith, 2000b, p. 73) where a wife sought to disconnect her husband's feeding tube even though he was capable of communicating with a "communication augmentation system" in which he pointed to letters to express himself and "enjoyed watching television and listening to country-and-western music" (pp. 72–73). Cranford also testified in the case of Christine Busalacchi (Smith, 1997, p. 47).

A clear articulation of Cranford's philosophy can be found in an editorial he wrote for the *British Medical Journal*. Andrews, Murphy, Munday, and Littlewood (1996) had published an article reporting that of 40 patients diagnosed as being in a persistent vegetative state, 17 were misdiagnosed. Of those that were misdiagnosed, many were blind or visually impaired. This had complicated the assessment given by their caretakers, and their state of awareness had not been noticed. Of those in a persistent vegetative state, 13 slowly emerged from this state. Of the original 40 patients, only 25% remained vegetative. Cranford, in the same issue, wrote an editorial in which he acknowledged that although "patients who retain some degree of awareness must be recognised if their quality of life is to be maximised and inappropriate withdrawal of tube feeding prevented," he nevertheless concluded, "I would speculate that most people would find this condition far more horrifying than the vegetative state itself, and some might think it an even stronger reason for stopping treatment than complete unconsciousness" (Cranford, 1996).

Dr. Cranford was asked by Jane Siess, the attorney for Robert Wendland's mother, "Why in your opinion as a clinical ethicist should . . . the error not be on the side of caution . . . and just let Robert [Wendland] live?" Cranford replied that there wouldn't be harm to Wendland himself but that his family "should be able to go through the grieving process . . . the family should be allowed to live their lives . . . Robert should be allowed to die so the family can grieve" (Smith, 2000b, p. 77).

We find then, that this witness, called in because of his expertise in neurology, is not basing his conclusions upon facts of neurology at all, but upon his limited understanding of psychological concepts!

The vast and highly popular literature describing stages of grief is probably useful to counselors to enhance their understanding of the various possible thoughts and emotions that might be troubling their bereaved clients. However, these stages describe possibilities, not necessities. The process of grief is not mechanical; it is a highly individual matter. Not all bereaved people necessarily go through all the stages described by any particular author before they can experience consolation and readjustment.

Wortman and Silver (1989), in an important review of the empirical research relating to bereavement, concluded that the assumptions that are prevalent in our culture and in our clinical lore—that a loss is followed by intense grief, that the absence of this grief is pathological, that the grief has to be experienced and worked on—are not supported by the data and are, in fact, contradicted.

The public often misinterprets these kinds of descriptions of psychological stages and have a sort of naive psychological theory according to which certain external events have to happen before a person's emotions can be soothed. This theory vastly underestimates the power of the human mind to respond to situational difficulties with creative, constructive ideas. It also underestimates the power of psychotherapy to encourage individuals to grow stronger and adapt in healthy ways even to undesirable situations.

This popular naive psychology, in combination with the best-interests analyses of the bioethicists, makes for a dangerous philosophical combination that enables the weird conclusion that the patient must die to comfort the family.

In Cranford's reasoning, not only is the concept of stages of grief taken too literally, but it is also applied to a totally different situation. It is quite a leap of logic to assume that if you only—no matter how—get the person whose loved one is lingering between life and death into a normalized situation where the loved one is now dead, that they can proceed through the stages of grief as if the death occurred normally.

Can an individual who takes the step of ending a friend's or a family member's life to facilitate his own bereavement truly proceed to a normal, uncomplicated bereavement? I believe that it would be naive to automatically assume that this is the case. Many kinds of situations such as suicide or homicide necessarily complicate the bereavement process.

I am not aware of any statistical studies on this issue, but there is much anecdotal evidence to indicate that deliberately ending the lives of loved ones is sometimes at least associated with lasting emotional complications. Many families have at least found that participating in helping their loved one die didn't give them the peaceful feelings that they had hoped for.

Stephen Jamison, in *Final Acts of Love: Families, Friends, and Assisted Dying* (1995) reports "conversations with hundreds of individuals, and in-depth interviews with 160 participants in some 140 assisted deaths" (p. xvi). Jamison tells the story of Michael, who had a "secret pact" with his father to help the father die. He had to keep their plans a secret from his brother and from his father's girlfriend. As his father's condition worsened, Michael began "excluding others" for fear that they would interfere. The "pressure built" until Michael himself had to go to "a hospital emergency room" with "chest pains." When his father finally took the lethal medication Michael had obtained for him, he didn't die. Finally Michael used "two dry-cleaning bags" to asphyxiate his father.

Michael then went into a "state of shock . . . his father's girlfriend blamed him." He felt he had "no support" for everything he had done. "A month after" the death, he went into "a treatment facility for his insomnia and depression." He kept "replaying the event over and over again." He would "think about the plastic bag, of asking him questions, of waiting for his breathing to stop, or watching him die, of pushing people away in the last days" (pp. 141–144).

Jamison makes it clear that Michael's case was not unusual. He wrote, it "exemplifies several, though not all, of the features of what can go wrong in an assisted death . . . the serious lasting effects for those involved—the most obvious of which were exemplified in his depression and sleeping disorders" (p. 144).

Jamison gives multiple examples of the suffering of those involved in helping a patient die. "One support-group member with AIDS" said he "bore the emotional scars" from helping "his partner die some years before." He was angry at his partner "for not taking repsonsibility for his own death." The man had "pleaded with him to 'do something.' " After "providing his partner with . . . pills, he had "smothered him with a pillow" (p. xiv). A father called Jamison to say that helping his son die had "taken its toll" (p. xvi).

Many other published examples exist of serious consequences to family members and friends involved in assisted dying. Several people who became famous by pioneering managed death for their family members ended up committing suicide. On August 17th, 1996, Nancy Beth Cruzan's father, Lester Cruzan committed suicide by hanging himself. He was said to have "expressed uncertainty" about the rightness of the Cruzans' actions. He had said: "I've wondered sometimes if we have finally accomplished for God what he set out to do. . . .

People say that's blasphemy, but I don't mean it that way. I mean it as, 'Where does God fit into the equation?' " (Pace, 1996, p. B12).

The case of Ann Wickett is another example. Ann Wickett, as discussed earlier in this chapter, was the second wife of Derek Humphry, and had worked with him to form the Hemlock Society. She and Humphry participated together in the suicide pact of her parents. Her 92-year-old father wanted to die, but Ann believed that her 78-year-old mother was not ready (Marker, 1993, pp. 68–69). Marker describes Ann's reaction after she and Derek helped her parents die, an event that Ann fictionalized in a book called *Double Exit*. Ann's mother's breathing got "agitated" after taking the lethal medication that Ann fed to her, and Ann got "scared." Derek had told her to "use a plastic bag" to smother her mother, and she did. She later said, "I have never gotten over that. . . . I walked away from that house thinking we're both murderers and I can't live like this anymore" (Marker, 1993 p. 72). Ann had "written about 'helping people die' for years," but "in real life, however, it wasn't turning out the way it had on paper. Ann couldn't stop thinking about her parents. She cried. She looked at old family pictures. All she wanted to do was talk about her mother and father" (p. 72). Ann ultimately committed suicide herself.

Another famous case of a family member who had trouble coping with managed death (also discussed in Chapter 7) was the 50-year-old woman in the Netherlands whose psychiatrist, Chabot, gave her lethal medication. One of her sons had died of suicide (Hendin, 1997, p. 62). The surviving son was on chemotherapy for an inoperable cancer and his white cells were destroyed. She agreed to disconnect his respirator (p. 64). The woman attempted suicide the same day he died, so that she could be buried with her son (p. 62). It is incredibly ironic that this particular case, which some have taken as an illustration that managed dying could be a solution for emotional pain, could very plausibly be used to illustrate just the opposite—that suicide and managed dying can cause overwhelming distress.

What I have used as examples here are not isolated reports. Even in more conventional medical cases, families often feel guilty later about decisions that were made. Advocates of managed dying would like to imply that this guilt can be dissipated if we accept these practices, but this may not be the case. Lo and Jonsen (1980) describe the case of a man who had discontinued his chemotherapy a year after cancer surgery and then was hospitalized about a year later with a pelvic mass. At this point, he refused further testing and treatment. A few months after he had died, his wife came back to the ward and "asked whether she should have encouraged her husband to continue the post operative chemotherapy" and if she should have "brought him to the hospital" earlier (p. 110).

Meier (1986) also makes a similar point. He reports that at the time of illness, the family is distraught and can only focus on pain and suffering, but later, in his clinical experience, they think about how they should have perhaps have consulted someone else, changed to "a different hospital" with better nurses or more aggressive medical actions. He recommends that the doctor not be swayed by the family's urgency. If the family has pressing needs, they should receive "mental health assistance" (p. 40).

Bill Moyers' television special about managed dying, aired on public television on Sept. 10 to Sept. 13, 2000, in spite of his bias towards managed dying, it also showed an example of a family member whose suffering was increased because her husband wanted his death managed. A veterinarian with amyotrophic lateral sclerosis (ALS) had wanted help in committing suicide, but he didn't want to die right away. He wanted to wait until he found his suffering unbearable, but he was afraid that by that time, he wouldn't be able to take lethal medication without someone's assistance. His wife didn't want to help him. He cried bitterly that because of the law against physician-assisted suicide, he would have to commit suicide earlier than he really wanted to (while he could still swallow the lethal medication without assistance). As she went about her nonstop round of chores taking care of him, she had to constantly turn over in her mind what she would do at the end, when he was in need of emergency medical assistance. Would she call an ambulance or not? She tearfully said that it would be hard for her not to call the ambulance.

It was very clear that the idea of managed dying put considerable pressure on his wife. She was doing so much for him, and yet, she felt guilty about wanting to keep him alive.

The children of Joan Lucas, a 65-year-old Oregon woman who committed suicide with the assistance of the organization Compassion in Dying (Kettler, 2000b, p. 3A), also felt much distress about the suicide. Her daughter Lisa said, "We went through this hell that she was going to take her life to protect us . . . Then we didn't talk about it again" (p. 8A).

Andrew Solomon (2001), author of the popular book *The Noonday Demon: An Atlas of Depression*, says that his mother's death by assisted suicide—the family was with her when she died—precipitated his first episode of depression (p. 278). Although he favors the cause of assisted suicide, he wrote of the difficulty it poses for those left behind, ". . . suicide is the saddest thing in the world. Insofar as you assist in it, it is still a kind of murder, and murder is not easy to live with . . ." (p. 279).

The acceptance of assisted suicide as a possible option puts the families and friends of a dying person in a dilemma eloquently described by Lonny Shavelson. He writes, "We live in torment if we acted; we agonize if we did not. . . . Either decision would have been—and has become—my life's worst nightmare" (p. 33).

As we learn from the many bitter lawsuits in which family members have faced each other in court, medical decisions about ending life leave many families with possibly irremediable schisms. It is not clear how many other families experience this agony privately.

Clearly Cranford's speculations about how ending the patient's life is good for the family are questionable. Nevertheless he, and others of his philosophy, have been successful in attaining legal sanction for some guardians to remove life supports from conscious patients, and they continue to try to extend this to other patients.

The public has very little understanding of how these confused philosophies, which can have powerful results when they are held by expert witnesses, guardians, judges, doctors, and hospital administrators, can now be used by institutions as part of their regular procedures. In hospitals where the philosophy of managed death prevails, hospital and HMO managers are making use of the kind of utilitarian bioethical arguments so well studied by Wesley Smith (2000b). They are making policies designating certain categories of patients as unworthy of expenditures of society's resources.

Moreover, this pattern is worsening. Advocates of physician-assisted suicide and euthanasia have been very active in rewriting medical textbooks and adding bioethics to the medical school curriculum to try to influence young doctors at formative stages in their careers before their goals have chrystallized.

For example, only a few decades after doctors were taught that their job was to sustain life, a current critical care textbook puts the goals of medical care in a different frame of reference. In spite of the fact that a nonnegligible proportion of patients in a persistent vegetative state regain consciousness eventually, and in spite of the fact that many patients diagnosed as being in a persistent vegetative state are misdiagnosed and are actually in a state of awareness, the critical care textbook states, "the indefinite maintenance of patients in a persistent vegetative state raises ethical concerns both for the dignity of the patient and for the inappropriate utilization of health care resources" (Luce, 1998, p. 250).

The changing of medical education has been successful in changing the attitudes of young doctors. Macklin (1993, pp. 148–151) discusses a conference on medical ethics with third-year medical students in which some talked of resources "wasted" on patients from the "margins" of society. Macklin points out the students' lack of understanding of the fact that, in our health care system, depriving one patient doesn't necessarily help another. They didn't realize the inevitable unfairness of treating different groups differently. These students who have absorbed concepts from the new bioethics can become dangerous bedside rationers of resources. Christakis and Asch (1995) found that younger physicians are indeed more likely to withdraw life supports.

Macklin (1993) reports that physicians who are already working in health care facilities are experiencing pressure. She reports that those who give medical approval for expensive power wheelchairs and communication augmentation devices say they are being pressured not to issue these approvals (p. 155).

Weeding out doctors who allocate resources too generously to patients or aggravating them so much that they retire early has the effect of producing a cadre of medical workers who are more inclined towards managed death. Sulmasy, Linas, Gold, and Schulman (1998) found, using a random sample of general internists from six urban areas, that those whose choices about hypothetical medical scenarios indicated more concern about saving resources were 6.4 times more likely to agree to help a hypothetical patient commit suicide.

A vicious cycle has been instituted. The more we are intimidated by claims that society cannot afford good care and the more we compromise on quality of care, the more our patients suffer. The more they suffer, the more the advocates of euthanasia claim that they have an easier solution.

A recent article in *Scientific American* contained an analogy that may capture the unidirectional push of our changing medical ethics without the difficulties of the slippery slope metaphor. Astumian (2001), in an article about moleculor motors, uses the analogy of a car pelted with hundreds of hailstones, each one of which moves it a tiny distance. If every time the car moves forward, a brick is placed behind the rear wheel to keep it from getting pushed back, the car would keep inching forward, even up a hill.

So it is with our medical ethics decision making. Ever since the Karen Ann Quinlan decision removed the barrier in the direction of deliberately producing death, we have been moving farther and farther in that direction, finding more and more ways to deliberately produce death in more and more circumstances. Despite the steepness of the uphill terrain—the outrage of the prolifers, the fear in the disabled, the distress of medical personnel who do not wish to participate, the conflict in the health care team, the fear among the public who point to the managed care company's conflict of interests, the unnecessary deaths—we inch along relentlessly. Whenever there might be the possibility of moving in the opposite direction, advocates of managed dying quickly block the motion. Anyone who suggests moving in the other direction is confronted with the terrors of being hooked up indefinitely to life supports, subject to nothing but pain and degradation, and the terrors of having so many invalids around that we will all be trapped in a nightmarish caretaker role and have no time or resources for anything except caring for these tortured bodies.

It doesn't matter if we disagree with each other about the exact time that we reach the point where we have gone too far with managed death. For some of us, that time has already passed. For some, it might occur in the next few years. In any case, it is clear that whenever the time occurs that a sufficient consensus builds up that we have gone too far, we will have to have a strategy for dealing with these fears.

It is not just a question of reminding families that more can be done for their loved one. The fears of families have an irrational component that will have to be addressed. The rhetoric of the movement for physician-assisted suicide has made it seem not just possible but very likely to families that they are causing their relatives unnecessary agony by requesting treatment.

Who, if not the mental health profession, can sort out these fears and reassure the public that they are exaggerated and will not come to pass?

Unfortunately, we ourselves, even in our own field, have been intimidated by false claims that mental health treatment is a drain on the economy. We have settled for doing much less than could really be done for our patients. The consequent suffering of patients has then been misattributed to their chronic condition instead of being correctly attributed to undertreatment.

Even with our help, it might seem as if it will take extraordinary courage for families to overcome their fears, but when we begin to truly examine the arguments that people in our culture are making—that we can't afford good medical care and that the sick and handicapped are beyond consolation—we will see that it is not that difficult to find holes in these arguments. We will see that the risk of increasing the suffering of your loved one by pursuing medical treatment is not as great as we might have thought.

Advocates of assisted suicide and euthanasia believe that they are easing the physical and emotional discomforts of seriously ill patients and their families, but instead, they are imposing new burdens. The sick person, instead of having some license to complain without embarrassment about dying and about his discomforts and fears, must instead worry that others regard his pains as something preventable that he should have avoided by killing himself. The family of any person with an uncomfortable illness of any age has to worry that their loved one will fall prey to the assisted-suicide rhetoric and kill herself or that her doctor will consider her hopeless and discontinue treatment.

A patient who gets caught up in the desire for assisted suicide has even more burdens. During his last weeks when his strength is ebbing and the basic tasks of daily living are a struggle—instead of clinging, as best he can, to the thoughts and feelings and relationships that sustained him throughout his life, he must instead give his attention to the elaborate task of orchestrating his death. Jamison (1995) gives long lists of things a person planning assisted suicide should consider. If you were worried—before the possibility of assisted–suicide that you would appear undignified in your pajamas with tubes attached to your body, just imagine how you would feel if you were expected to do all the things Jamison suggests, if your friends and family were discussing how well you succeeded in deciding "who should and should not be present" and "whether the attendance of some may negatively affect those closest to you" and whether the gathering you planned helped "both you and others obtain a sense of closure" and whether you gave those close to you "time for anticipatory grieving, letting them talk about what your death will mean to them," and whether you consulted with "those closest to you" about "what they might like to accomplish from the event and what elements they'd like to include in it" and whether "by the addition of special shared words or acts" the participants "might be better able to achieve a sense of peace" (pp. 183–184). Friends and family believing in the assisted-suicide way of dying are burdened as well. They can be left always wondering if they encouraged someone to die who didn't need to or if they caused someone extra pain by encouraging him to stay alive.

When we consider these emotional burdens that advocates of physician-assisted suicide are suggesting that we endure, the ordinary burdens of dealing with illness seem simple by comparison.

We have believed falsely that we had to make choices between good medical care and a healthy economy. We have suffered unnecessarily because of this belief. As we shall see, this dilemma is more apparent than real. When we develop a more responsive medical community, and a cooperative alliance between medicine and the mental health professions, we will be able to demonstrate that patients' pain and suffering can be soothed by palliative care and skilled emotional support, and their fears can be eased by good patient education. We can show society how to minimize stress instead of minimizing expenditures. We can lead the way to a culture that encourages healthy human interdependence that enables even sick and handicapped people to thrive psychologically.

REFERENCES

Andrews, K., Murphy L., Munday R., & Littlewood, C. (1996). Misdiagnosis of the vegetative state: Retrospective study in a rehabilitation unit. *British Medical Journal, 313*, p. 13–16.

Astumian, R.D. (2001). Making molecules into motors. *Scientific American, 285* (1), 56–64.

Chevlen, E.M. (1998, Jan. 3). Killing the dying is not palliative care. *Update, International Anti-Euthanasia Task Force*, pp. 26–27.

Christakis, N.A., & Asch, D.A. (1995). Physician characteristics associated with decisions to withdraw life support. *American Journal of Public Health, 85*, 367–372.

Cranford R. (1996). Misdiagnosing the persistent vegetative state. *British Medical Journal, 313*, pp. 5–6.

Disabled boy's relatives convicted for saving his life. (2000). *International Anti-Euthanasia Task Force Update*, No. 2, p. 6.

Dutch upper house backs aided suicide. (2001, Apr. 11). *The New York Times*, p. A3.

Emanuel, E.J., Fairclough, D., Clarridge, B.C., Blum, D., Bruera, E., Penley, W.C., Schnipper, L.E., & Mayer, R.J. (2000). Attitudes and practices of U.S. oncologists regarding euthanasia and physician-assisted suicide. *Annals of Internal Medicine, 133*, 527–532.

Euthanasia gurus meet to discuss ghoulish ways to die. (2000). *International Anti-Euthanasia Task Force Update*, Year 2000 (2), 4.

Groenewoud, J.H., van der Heide, A. Onwuteaka-Philipsen, B.D., Willems, D.L., van der Maas, P.J., & van der Wal, G. (2000). Clinical problems with the performance of euthanasia and physician-assisted suicide in the Netherlands. *New England Journal of Medicine, 342*, 551–556.

Hendin, H. (1997). *Seduced by death: Doctors, patients, and the Dutch cure*. New York: W.W. Norton.

Humphry, D. (1978). *Jean's way*. New York: Quartet Books.

Humphry, D. (1986). *Right to die: Understanding euthanasia*. New York: Harper & Row: Hemlock Society.

Humphry, D. (1991). *Final exit: The practicalities of self-deliverance and assisted suicide for the dying*. Eugene, OR: Hemlock Society.

Jamison, S. (1995). *Final acts of love: Families, friends, and assisted dying*. New York: G.P. Putnam's Sons.

Johnson, D. (1998, Nov. 26). Kevorkian faces a murder charge in death on video. *The New York Times*, A1, A18.

Kettler, B. (2000a, Jun. 25). A death in the family: "We knew she would do it." *Sunday Mail Tribune* (Medford, OR), pp. 1A, 8A.

Kettler, B. (2000b, Jun. 26). A death in the family: "I'm ready," she said. *Mail Tribune* (Medford, OR), pp. 1A, 3A.

Kevorkian, J. (1991). *Prescription—medicide: The goodness of planned death*. Buffalo, NY: Prometheus Books.

Liptak, A. (2002, Apr. 18). Judge blocks U.S. bid to ban suicide law. *The New York Times*, p. A16.

Lo, B., & Jonsen, A.R. (1980). Ethical decisions in the care of a patient terminally ill with metastatic cancer. *Annals of Internal Medicine, 92*(1), 107–111.

Luce, J.M. (1998). Withholding and withdrawal of life-sustaining therapy. In Hall, J.B., Schmidt, G.A., Wood, L.D.H. (Ed.) *Principles of Critical Care*, 2nd ed. (pp. 249–255). McGraw-Hill.

Macklin, R. (1993). *Enemies of patients*. New York: Oxford University Press.

Marker, R. (1993). *Deadly compassion: The death of Ann Humphry and the truth about euthanasia*. New York, William Morrow and Company.

Marker R. (2000). *Assisted suicide: The debate in the States*. International Anti-Euthanasia Task Force.

Meier L. (1986). Code and no-code: A psychological analysis and the viewpoint of Jewish law. In Meier L. (Ed.), *Jewish Values in Bioethics*. New York: Human Sciences Press, 35–45.

Meyer, J. & Murphy, K. (2001, Nov. 7). Ashcroft targets assisted suicide law in Oregon. *St. Louis Post-Dispatch*, A1, A10.

Mitchell, C. (2000, Aug. 28). When living is a fate worse than death. *Newsweek*, p. 12.

Pace, E. (1996, Aug. 19). Lester Cruzan is dead at 62; Fought to let his daughter die. *The New York Times*, p. B12.

Portenoy, R.K., Coyle, N., Kash, K.M., et al. (1997). Determinants of the willingness to endorse assisted suicide: A survey of physicians, nurses and social workers. *Psychosomatics, 38*, 277–287.

Quill, T.E. (1991). Death and dignity: A case of individualized decision making. *New England Journal of Medicine, 324*, 691–694.

Quill, T.E. (1993). *Death and dignity: Making choices and taking charge*. New York: Norton.

Quill, T.E. (1996). *A midwife through the dying process: Stories of healing and hard choices at the end of life*. Baltimore: Johns Hopkins University Press.

Ressner, J. (2001, Mar. 26). When a coma isn't one. *Time*, p. 62.

Saunders, D.J. (2001, Jul. 24). If disabled means expendable. *San Francisco Chronicle*, p. A19.

Shavelson, L. (1995). *A chosen death: The dying confront assisted suicide*. New York: Simon & Schuster.

Shaywitz, D.A. (2000, Sep. 19). The right to live. *The New York Times*, Op-Ed, p. A25.

Shoff, K. (2000, Dec.). "And you shall live by them . . .": Dad survived, thanks to guidance from experts in halacha. *The Jewish Observer*, p. 13–15.

Singer, P. (1994). *Rethinking life and death: The collapse of our traditional ethics*. New York: St. Martin's Press.

Smith, W.J. (1997). *Forced exit: The slippery slope from assisted suicide to legalized murder*. New York: Times Books.

————— (2000a, Dec. 18). Dead wrong but still kicking: the physician-assisted suicide movement loses again. *Weekly Standard, 6* (14), pp. 21–22.

————— (2000b). *Culture of death: The assault on medical ethics in America.* San Francisco: Encounter Books.

————— (2001, Jul. 23). "Futile care" and its friends: Hospitals and legislators want to decide when your life is no longer worth living. *The Weekly Standard, 6* (42), 27–29.

Solomon, A. (2001). *The noonday demon: An atlas of depression.* New York: Scribner.

Sulmasy, D.P., Linas, B.P., Gold, K.F., & Schulman, K.A. (1998). Physician resource use and willingness to participate in assisted suicide. *Archives of Internal Medicine, 158,* 974–978.

Vacco v. Quill, 521 U.S. 793 (1997).

Washington v. Glucksberg, 521 U.S. 702 (1997).

Wickett, A. (1989). *Double exit: When aging couples commit suicide together.* Hemlock Society.

Wortman, C.B., & Silver, R.C. (1989). The myths of coping with loss. *Journal of Consulting and Clinical Psychology, 57,* 349–357.

PART II

What Mental Health Professionals Can Do

CHAPTER 5

Soothing Fears that Progress in Medicine Will Lead to Financial Disaster

Advocates of physician-assisted suicide and euthanasia see themselves as level-headed realists who, in reaction to medical progress, are forced by compassion and fiscal integrity to make "hard choices."

I think that it is time to challenge this state of affairs and to see that some of the presumed realities that are driving people to the conclusion that managed dying is necessary are actually unrealistic disaster scenarios.

The argument in favor of physician-assisted suicide and euthanasia comes in two forms: (1) the fear of futile pain and suffering, and (2) the fear of financial disaster.

The pain and suffering argument emphasizes the subjective state of the patients. It is maintained that many patients are being kept alive and suffering in hopeless conditions and that continued medical progress will make this problem worse. The financial argument claims that the cost of maintaining these hopeless patients is going to skyrocket, absorbing more and more of the economy.

In the next few chapters, we will take up these arguments in detail and show that the implication of disaster is based upon false premises and exaggerations.

It will be very helpful to our analysis to separate the pain and suffering argument and the financial argument. Otherwise, we run into the following difficulty: When contemplating new hopeful research and treatment directions, enthusiasm is dampened by the fear that these directions are luxuries that we cannot afford. When discussing new ways of paying for research and treatment, enthusiasm is dampened by the fear that these treatments will not be successful and will only prolong suffering.

For the sake of the chapter on the financial arguments, then, we will avoid pessimistic assumptions about what could be achieved if finances are not a problem. In the chapter on improving and developing our treatments, we will assume that they can be successfully financed.

There have been many discussions in recent years of health care costs. Discussions of cost cannot take place in a vacuum; in order to understand the impact of health care costs, they must be discussed in context. When discussing government budgets, health care costs must be considered in the context of available public and private funds and in relation to other expenses. However, any discussion that focused only on the direct costs to be assumed by government in a particular calender year would be very incomplete. Costs must be discussed in terms of their consequences for the society as a whole over a long period of time.

Rashi Fein (1958), discussed this point very eloquently in his classic book *Economics of Mental Illness*. In analyzing the costs of mental illness, he distinguishes between the direct costs of running government-sponsored programs and the total cost to society of mental illness, which includes such things as the loss to society of the employment that the person would have been engaged in had he been healthy.

Fein indicates, "Once it is clear that we must deal with total cost, it is also clear that costs (in this sense) cannot be eliminated. Surely we all agree that direct costs can be decreased in a variety of ways, e.g., by elimination of existent programs or even obscuring of problems. This, however, does not eliminate total costs and may not (indeed, probably does not) reduce them" (p. 128).

Oddly enough, this more complete perspective turns out to be profoundly optimistic, and the choices we face are easier. How can this be?

Fein explains that if we ask the question "Should we bear the *direct* costs of mental illness" and don't consider the total costs, the question seems very "complex" because it seems to be partly humanitarian and partly an economic question (p. 128). This question seems to create a dilemma where economic considerations and humanitarian considerations are in conflict.

However, in fact, economic and humanitarian considerations are not in conflict. Fein explains that "When viewed from the perspective of total cost, . . . the problem becomes *simpler* . . . the question does not even involve humanitarian and ethical value judgements on which differences of opinion may exist . . . the answer is really quite simple: that increases in direct costs reduce *total* costs" (pp. 128–129).

Including a more complete perspective in the analysis not only makes the decision process easier, but the results can be better as well. Fein shows that a perspective including total costs can actually be profoundly more optimistic and more effective. He writes, "We may have the best of all possible worlds, a world in which the using of resources in a particular way does not come . . . at the expense of any other uses, but instead increases the total supply of resources available" (p. 129).

Unfortunately, those who are alarmed about health care costs do not take into account the indirect benefits of health care spending. Moreover, they are not careful about assessing the available resources. Instead, there is a trend of assuming that we are in a state of financial disaster.

There is not a comprehensive discussion of where more funds for health care could be derived. Instead, from the false assumption of financial disaster, it is presumed to be necessary to make the sorts of hard choices where humanitarian and economic considerations are in conflict. The hard choices are conceived of as a need to choose between the medical needs of the old and the young. From this perceived emergency and this perceived dilemma, many elaborately argued discussions emerge.

These dire assumptions are very much taken for granted in the writings of advocates of assisted suicide. They simply begin by saying that we cannot afford health care costs without first determining whether we are indeed in a state of emergency and whether we must in fact face these disagreeable choices.

The financial discussions of those who are fearful about health care costs often ignore considerations about the total costs to society of the illness which would result if the health care is not provided, not only the greater prevalence of illness and the loss of health and employment, but also the decline in the infrastructure of the health care system in terms of talented and trained personnel and equipment.

Rashi Fein eloquently asks, "What can society afford *not* to spend on mental illness and health?" (p. 138).

FALSE EMERGENCIES

The unfortunate assumptions of a *false emergency* which necessitate hard choices can be seen in the writings of Derek Humphry, cofounder of the Hemlock Society and author of the best-selling suicide manual *Final Exit*. He and Mary Clement write: "The United States is entering a crisis situation, the kind of emergency we have not dealt with before in this land of plenty" (Humphry & Clement, 1998, p. 320). They list greater and greater health care expenses over the years, italicized to convey a feeling of outrage. Finally they write, "Fiscal scrutiny is forcing the United States, as well as other technologically advanced nations, to figure out how much they want to spend on the older population" (p. 327).

We cannot allow this argument to go unchallenged. Not only is their conclusion socially unacceptable, but there are several major flaws in their reasoning.

Can we really claim to be in a crisis? Our society's sense of whether we can afford health care seems highly subjective. In 2000, only two years after Humphry and Clement's book was published, the projected surplus for the national economy over the next decade laid out by the Congressional Budget Office ranged from \$838 billion to \$1.9 trillion dollars (Stevenson, 2000, p. A22), and yet health care cuts continued as usual. In 2001, when the World Trade Center collapsed, medical personnel rushed to New York hospitals to volunteer their time. When Americans truly feel they know how to help, they respond generously. Humphry and Clement seem ready to sacrifice older people to resolve an emergency that doesn't exist.

Humphry and Clement's panic about the economy is no doubt derived from a whole trend in gloomy demographic predictions based on worries about the aging of the "baby boom" generation (Boskin, 1986; Longman, 1987).

As we have seen, in the years before the Karen Ann Quinlan case, fears of overpopulation were at a peak. Paul Ehrlich's 1968 best-seller, *The Population Bomb* (1971), set forth frightening disaster scenarios, in which overpopulation led to world-wide political and environmental catastrophes. This book proposed strategies for making it socially unacceptable to have large families and for rechanneling the energies of women into careers. Full page ads in the *New York Times* criticized the Pope for opposing birth control, announcing "Pope denounces birth control as millions starve" (Lader, 1971, p. 66). It is probably not an accident that the court cases creating a shield of privacy for decisions about birth control (*Griswold v. Connecticut*) and abortion (*Roe v. Wade*) took place at this time. These privacy cases provided precedents for the Karen Ann Quinlan decision.

It is a very great irony then, to see what happened to this baby boom generation. Having been convinced to seek their fulfillment elsewhere rather than parenting large, traditional families, this generation is now being told by these pessimistic demographers that they have failed to produce enough children to support themselves in their old age! They have been told in many recent books and articles that the ratio of working young people to older people collecting Social Security is going to drop; e.g., ". . . if we continue with the current system, we will soon face the prospect of two workers paying taxes to support each retiree—a scenario that would create an intolerable tax burden" (Carter & Shipman, 1996, p. 138).

Suggested solutions to this problem range from health care rationing to encouraging greater fertility and immigration (Longman, 1987, pp. 130–151)! Even the authors of these suggestions find them disagreeable, but they see no way out. Longman writes that he himself doesn't like the suggestions that he is making because he is afraid that he will be discriminated against when he is old and sick (p. 128).

In *Social Security: The Phony Crisis*, Baker and Weisbrot (1999) state very clearly that worries about the soundness of Social Security are based upon "a steady stream of misinformation" (p. ix). The owners are not alarmed about the ratio of workers to retirees. "It is often noted . . . that the number of workers paying Social Security taxes for every retiree drawing benefits will fall from 3.3 today to 2.1 by the year 2030. . . . It is thus argued that the system will become unsustainable without serious benefit cuts. But the decline in this ratio has actually been considerably steeper in the past. In 1955 there were 8.6 workers per retiree, and the decline from 8.6 to 3.3 did not precipitate any economic disaster" (p. 32).

Baker and Weisbrot explain that the assumptions leading to the calculation of a shortfall in 2034 assume a rate of economic growth that is much smaller than what we have had in the last few decades. They also explain that even if the projected shortfall came about, it would only require "an increase in payroll tax of one-tenth of 1 percent each year (split between employer and employee), beginning in 2011 and continuing until 2046. . . . This would still leave future generations with an after-tax wage that is 28.7 percent higher than today" (p. 24).

They also point out that the calculations suggesting that there will be a burden on the future taxpayer fail to take into account the good aspects of the higher ratio of older people to younger people: "These figures . . . neglect to take into account the reduced costs faced by the working population from having a smaller proportion of children to support . . . the future burden of caring for a larger elderly population will be offset to a large extent by the reduced costs of education, child care, and other expenses of caring for dependent children" (p. 32).

Recent articles indicate that even the pessimistic prediction of a shortfall has already been postponed a few more years until 2037 (Outlook improves, 2000, p. A1).

For Medicare as well, recent reports indicate more optimism. Medicare had previously been projected to run out of cash by 2001, but the newest estimate is that it will run smoothly until 2023 (p. A8). In fact, it has been estimated that Medicare will continue to collect more money in payroll taxes than it pays in benefits until 2010 (p. A8).

Baker and Weisbrot (1999, p. 59) point out that in many calculations of projected Medicare expenses, mistaken and pessimistic assumptions are built into the calculations. For example, they point out that many calculations of projected Medicare expenses assume that longevity will continue to increase but that even 30 years from now, the medical needs of a 60-year-old or a 70-year-old will be the same as they are now. These assumptions build right into the calculations the disastrous vision that every medical advance will bring us closer and closer to an excessive accumulation of debilitated, suffering people.

Clearly, these assumptions—that longevity will continue to increase at the rate that it has in this century, and that the debility that people experience at certain ages will remain the same—are not assumptions that can be taken for granted. In fact, there is evidence that these assumptions are false. Fries (1989) suggests that we may be witnessing what he calls a "compression" of morbidity. Because of better public education—better diets, exercise, and medical prevention—rates of heart attacks (p. 212) and lung cancer (p. 213), for example, have been greatly reduced. These sicknesses are occurring at later ages instead of earlier (p. 213). The data on primary prevention also fits his hypothesis. Changes in diet and exercise prevent sickness, but they do not alter longevity by much.

The big picture that emerges from this analysis is very encouraging. The fears of the prognosticators were based on the assumption that increased longevity would stretch out the years of being debilitated. Instead, we find, that healthy lifestyles are putting off our illnesses until it is almost time to die.

Califano (1994) reports that there has been an "almost 50% drop in the death rate from heart disease since 1960" (p. 132) and that the prevalence of chronic disability among the elderly has dropped (p. 135).

Just because people are living longer than the Social Security system designers originally expected doesn't mean they are going to be sick longer.

Even though there may be more older people proportionately than there are now, each person dies only once; they only have one final illness. Those that live into their eighties will not have the final illnesses in their sixties and seventies that previous generations who died in their sixties and seventies had. By living into their eighties, they are not burdening society any more than any other generation. In fact, their productive years are prolonged.

Baker and Weisbrot (1999) point out that although the rules of Social Security require them to make a 75-year forecast, an accurate forecast is truly not possible. They ask us to imagine a prediction of current realities made 75 years ago (p. 23). As of 1925, there was no polio vaccine, no respirators, no intensive-care units, no open heart surgery, no antipsychotic medication, no antibiotics! It would be ridiculous to make a budget according to a 1925 prediction. It is also ridiculous to get frightened because our current status does not fit the 1925 prediction.

It is almost inconceivable, given the medical progress that we have made in the last 75 years, that the next 75 years would not bring at least some unanticipated improvements. Our future tax rate may depend upon our future understanding of a few protein strings. If someone found a cure for Alzheimer's tomorrow, we would hear very much less about impending financial disaster.

The only way in which it would be conceivable that we wouldn't experience at least some medical advances in the next 75 years is if we shut off research. Oddly enough, there are actually enough people advocating this to make it a danger. Schwartz (1987) suggests that to contain costs, we should "forgo, at least in part, introduction and diffusion of innovative diagnostic and therapeutic measures" (p. 222). He discusses different methods such as limiting the "amount of money invested by the federal government in research on new technology" or tailoring reimbursement methods with the purpose of curbing "the development and diffusion of clinically useful technology" (p. 223).

The predictions of economic disaster that we are hearing currently are far from inevitable. We are all familiar with the argument that if two people were in a life-boat and only one could be saved, it would be permissible to try to save yourself rather than the other person. It is clear, however, that we are not currently in any such situation, and we may never be in such a situation.

When these pessimistic assumptions are examined, the best argument that can be made is as follows—if health costs continue to rise as fast as they have during a period of great medical progress even though no further medical progress is made, and if people continue to live longer but continue to get sick at a younger age, and if the economy grows at a much slower rate than it has, then, a few decades from now, we might have to raise taxes. This argument hardly justifies preparation for euthanasia!

FALSE DILEMMAS

Let's turn to a few examples of the kinds of dilemmas that are frequently posed about health care financing. Colen (1986) offers the following situation that he perceives as a dilemma:

We are spending $2 billion a year on dialysis for only about 60,000 people. Many of these patients lead normal, productive lives, but many do not. . . . just think for a minute of what even a single year's worth of that money could do to relieve famine in the drought-plagued areas of Africa, or what $2 billion a year could do to bring job training programs or mass transportation to our central cities. (Colen, 1986, pp. 24–25)

He offers another similar example that he perceives as a dilemma:

Do we really want to be expending our resources saving pound-and-a-half babies in an era when we are cutting back on childhood immunization and school lunch programs? (Colen, 1986, p. 23)

Humphry and Clement (1998) pose a similar argument:

Even now, however, people are beginning to question the common sense of keeping someone alive, at great societal and personal expense, who prefers to forgo the final hours or weeks of an intolerable existence. To what purpose? Might not money be better spent on preventive treatment, medicine for the young, educating the youth of the nation, or for that matter, the children in the patient's own family. Is there, in fact, a duty to die—a responsibility within the family unit—that should remain voluntary but expected nevertheless? (p. 313)

Colen's arguments and Humphry's argument have exactly the same structure. In each argument, the assumption is made that a health care expenditure must be opposed to some other particular expenditure. In each argument, it is implied that the funds saved from health care would be sufficient to make major progress with the other problem. In each argument, the other problem selected is some sort of heart-rending situation.

I believe that these comparisons that are offered as dilemmas are not, in fact, true dilemmas. There are I believe, at least three mistaken assumptions in these perceived dilemmas. First, as we have seen, it is unfair to assume that we are undergoing some sort of fiscal emergency and that the current amount of funds is insufficient or that the amount of funding is fixed. If taxes are raised, the dilemma disappears. The tax base can also be raised without raising taxes. If people spend slightly more, incomes will rise, and the amount of available tax funds will rise. As we have seen, the healthy rate of economic growth that we have been sustaining allows us to pay our health care expenditures and even to expand them. Only recently, Social security benefits were increased for people between 65 and 69 who wish to work (House passes break, 2000) and Medicare prescription benefits are being actively discussed.

Colen portrays the $2 billion dollars spent on dialysis as a terrible burden. If we use the 1980 census of 227 million and the 1990 census of 249 million (United States, Population, 2000) and interpolate, we can estimate the population of the United States in the year Colen published *Hard Choices* (1986) at 240 million. Dividing the $2 billion dollars by 240 million people, we find that this money could be raised with a contribution of only $8.33 per person. If taxes were raised by only $8.33 per person, or if the gross national product rose slightly, we could do both the dialysis and $2 billion dollars worth of famine relief.

Colen is only calling the choices hard because he assumes that the American public is simply not willing to pay for very much. He takes this as an immutable fact. He is not really so hopeless about the handicapped children and the premature baby as he is about the American public's willingness to help. For example, he says:

Would saving a baby with Down's syndrome or spina bifida . . . really be an issue if money were freely spent on the care of handicapped children and adults? . . . the same administration that is pushing so hard to save these babies has been cutting off funds to help pay for their care. (Colen, 1986, p. 24)

The unwillingness of the American public to pay more is a subject worthy of study. We should not simply take this as a given. The cynical climate that prevents people from contributing more for long-term care of the handicapped is not an unalterable feature of our culture, and it is probably based upon distrust of those spending the money. When the American public trusts a person or believes in a cause, they respond generously. Instead of simply assuming that the American public will not pay more for care of the handicapped, we should make it a goal to investigate their grievances and regain their trust.

Second, it is unfair to choose some sort of heart-rending issue to oppose to the health care cost. Even without an increase in tax funds, there are certainly many budget items that could be cut without choosing a heart-rending item. Given that the amount of public funds is not immutably fixed and can be raised with taxes, and given the wide choices of budget items that could be cut, we can weigh the health care against any items in the public budget or private budgets that we choose to weigh them against. Private funds could be spent on more taxes or more health care premiums instead of whatever they were being spent on before. For Colen's dilemma, the choice is not really between dialysis and famine relief. It could be a choice between dialysis and potato chips or dialysis and cigarettes. If each family foregoes a few bags of potato chips and uses these dollars for taxes or for health care premiums we could do both the dialysis and the famine relief.

Humphry's argument is equally invalid. He implies that the money saved on the grandmother's health care could be spent on her grandchildren's education. This is naive. When a patient opts to hasten his or her death, the health plan doesn't refund the unspent money to the family. The money will go to the health care administrator or to his office. Kassler (1994) writes that "Pennsylvania Insurance Department officials found that executives of Blue Cross plans . . . had spent $50,000 on a conference table, more than $234,000 on sporting events over four years, and $53,000 on club memberships in one year" (p. 29).

We can see that arguments like Humphry's are not serious financial arguments. These arguments are not coming from people who are committed to medicine or education for young people or mass transportation or any such thing. They are rhetorical flourishes.

Unfortunately, there are a lot of people in the medical field who believe this kind of argument. Macklin (1993, p. 148) describes an ethics conference that she attended with a group of medical students. A medical student referred to certain patients as being from the "margins" of society (p. 149). One such patient was a chronic alcholic and drug user. Another was mentally retarded and disabled. Some of the doctors-to-be argued that it was "the physician's obligation to save society money" (p. 150). Although some argued that the money spent on these patients could be better spent on prenatal care or family health clinics, when they were asked where the money would actually go if it were not used on these patients, they had no idea. In spite of not knowing where the money would go, many still thought they were obligated to be fiscal gatekeepers (p. 150). Macklin cites Arnold S. Relman, former editor of the *New England Journal of Medicine*, as arguing that savings in one part of our health care system are not necessarily reallocated to worthy expenditures elsewhere.

Third, it is unfair to assume that a large amount of money will be saved without making comprehensive specific calculations. We must question the assumption that money is even saved at all. This assumption is usually given without any accounting and without any proof.

Those in favor of euthanasia speak of saving people pain at the very end of their lives because they know this scenario elicits the sympathy of the ordinary voter. They claim that lives will be shortened by just a few days or hours. In this case, how can they claim that the amounts saved will be so huge as to solve all kinds of other problems?

On the other hand, if they admit that once someone like Jack Kevorkian is available, the people who find their way to his door are an assortment of depressed people in whose education society has already invested and who potentially have many productive years or even decades ahead of them, how can they claim that this is a saving? If we are to stick to a purely financial argument (instead of bewailing the unnecessary loss of these people's lives) it would only be fair to calculate the financial losses that their early deaths would entail.

Let us go over some examples of these kinds of arguments. Humphry and Clement do indeed claim that the savings from encouraging more patients to shorten their end of life medical care will be huge. They mention that Chambers, Diamond, Perkel, & Lasch (1994) found a $60,000 difference between the medical bills of Medicare patients with and without advance directives. They imply that this amount could be multiplied by the number of people, which they give as 2 million, who die annually in the hospital (Humphry & Clement, 1998, p. 321). If we multiply $60,000 by 2 million, we would estimate a saving of $120 billion dollars. This estimate seems excessive. Our entire national budget for 2001 is only $1.84 trillion dollars (Stevenson, 2000, p. A1).

The study cited by Humphry used only Medicare patients (Chambers, Diamond, Perkel, & Lasch, 1994). According to Dean Baker and Mark Weisbrot (1999), ". . . managed-care providers have been able to profit enormously by selecting, as much as possible, the healthiest senior citizens and leaving the rest . . . in the hands of Medicare" (p. 6). It therefore seems reasonable to suppose that the sample for the study had unusually high bills.

Emanuel and Emanuel (1994) conclude that "we must stop deluding ourselves that advance directives and less aggressive care at the end of life will solve the financial problems of our health care system" (p. 543). They estimate that the greatest amount that might be saved by reducing "aggressive life-sustaining interventions for dying patients" is $29.7 billion. Moreover, this saving wouldn't do anything to reduce the growth of health care spending over time (p. 543). The reasons for this are that it is not possible to tell in advance which patients will die. Since many who eventually die were expected to live and expected to benefit from aggressive interventions, advance directives would not reduce this kind of care. Moreover, the care for patients who are expected to die, even if they forego aggressive life-sustaining measures, is still expensive. Humane palliative care is very labor intensive (p. 543).

A recent study backs up the point made by Emanuel and Emanuel about the difficulty of predicting which patients are going to die. Christakis and Lamont (2000) found that doctors prognoses on life expectancy were accurate only 20% of the time.

Not only do those who advocate managed dying exaggerate the potential savings of managed dying, they also fail to discuss the financial losses resulting from such a policy. In fact, these losses are not often mentioned by opponents of managed dying either, perhaps because it is offensive to them to make the decision about managed dying on the basis of cost. Perhaps they fear that by entering such a discussion, they are accepting the premise that expenses should be the determining factor.

However it is important to reveal that Humphry's arguments are not just morally shortsighted. They are also economically shortsighted.

We cannot assume that the saving in health care services billed for particular patients who choose to write advance directives or commit physician-assisted suicide would be good for the economy. Is it good for the economy to have a number of unemployed nurses who collect unemployment insurance and don't make their usual purchases or pay their usual taxes? Is it good for a hospital to have a large number of empty beds? Is it good for medical suppliers to have a reduction in business?

Suppose Humphry had selected any other item that is bought and sold and that has increased over the last few decades. Suppose, for example, he chose leisure footwear and moaned about how money was being wasted on all those different kinds of sneakers. Suppose he suggested that we all stop buying sneakers. It would be clear that this would not be good for the economy.

His argument only has the illusion of being persuasive, because he mixes together the two issues of whether the health care expenditures are too expensive and whether they are desirable. He keeps making pitiful references to how the medical care is "unwanted." He implies that purchasing a few extra years for older people is foolish.

This is not valid economics argumentation. When claiming to be making a financial argument, it is not fair to tuck these value judgments into the argument. Evidently the American public does want this care because they are currently paying for it.

Moreover, if a sizable number of patients cut short their end-of-life care, how would hospitals react? The amount that is billed for particular medical services does not necessarily reflect exactly what it costs the hospital. The amounts billed for each service include a portion of the hospital's regular operating overhead.

Rashi Fein (1958) writes that one often hears about the cost per patient year in public mental hospitals and how additional patients "cost" this amount and extra discharges "save" this amount (p. 9). He writes, "It should be manifestly clear that certain expenditures . . . remain fixed regardless of small, and often, unfortunately, even of large, changes in numbers of patients, e.g., electricity, heat, water, psychiatric care, and nursing care, among others. Does an extra guest cost anything or does the hostess add more water to the soup?" (p. 10).

If there are fewer services for which a hospital can bill the insurance company, the hospital still has to cover its overhead, so it will just charge more for all the other patients' billable services. If the insurance company has a limit on coverage for each diagnosis, then these other patients will reach the limit faster if each service costs more. And if many patients elect to cut short their end-of-life care, the insurance companies may lower these limits for each diagnosis. It is hard to see how the hospital could profit from physician-assisted suicides. Anyone committing physician-assisted suicide to save the hospital or save society money will have died in vain.

Macklin (1993) writes:

We may know how much hospitals charge for a one-week stay in the neonatal unit, but do those charges reflect the actual cost of caring for a particular premature infant? Or are they derived from a more general cost-accounting scheme that produces large revenues for the hospital in some areas in order to offset unavoidable losses in other areas? A physician who decides that a particular patient can probably do without a computed tomography (CT) scan may feel virtuous by acting to save society money. But that act of rationing could result in a loss of money for the hospital or the radiology department, which is eager to maintain or increase the number of CT scans because third-party reimbursements pay for the expensive machine and thus enhance overall revenues. (p. 164)

Expenditures in certain areas do not only benefit the patient, they may benefit society in other ways. Eisner (1994) writes, "Medicare, whatever the excesses, inefficiencies, or lacks in our national health program, has certainly contributed not only to current health care but also to investment in the most advanced technology in the world and as we shall see, public spending and deficits, contrary to popular notions, may generally have contributed to more . . . not less investment in tomorrow" (p. 58).

In other words, if we cut Medicare or otherwise encouraged large numbers of terminally ill patients to decline life supports, there would be much less demand for certain medical equipment and fewer personnel trained to use this equipment. Then, younger, otherwise healthier individuals who needed these medical interventions and these trained personnel in an acute emergency might not get adequate treatment, and society would have a large loss from the unnecessary deaths of these patients.

What about the loss to society of the individuals who choose to shorten their lives who would have otherwise lived? What about some of the mothers that Kevorkian dispatched? We would have to count the cost of the child care that their widowers were required to pay. For those who still had marketable skills, we would have to count their lost earnings and lost taxes.

I can think of one case where hundreds of millions of dollars would have been lost to valuable research if a decision had been made for an earlier death. The actor Christopher Reeve was paralyzed from the neck down after falling from a horse. While he was still unconscious, his family gathered at his bedside. His mother "became distraught and began arguing strenuously that the doctors should pull the plug" (Reeve, 1998, p. 34). Other members of the family disagreed and they eventually prevailed. Even though he remained on a respirator, Christopher Reeve is a highly sought-out and highly paid, inspirational speaker, who has raised hundreds of millions of dollars for neurological research. If we are to give a fair financial accounting of the amount of money that would have been "saved" by terminating his life early, we would have to subtract these hundreds of millions of dollars and all his earnings and taxes from the amount "saved."

Wesley J. Smith (1997) gives an example of a man who was diagnosed as being in a persistent vegetative state and whose doctors "strongly urged the family to discontinue . . . life support, including nutrition." They instead sought a "second opinion," and discovered that he had been misdiagnosed; he had suffered a "severe brain seizure." A week later, he made a full recovery (p. 51) and resumed a productive life. The lost earnings of individuals like this, who remained in a coma just a little too long, but who could have lived, would have to be counted as losses.

Also, we would need to calculate the amount of time in health care institutions spent talking and writing about ethics and drafting policies and guidelines. All of this would be greatly abbreviated if we didn't depart from our traditional ethical framework. The salaries of many ethicists and administrators could be deducted as well as the amounts that would have been added to the economy by the scientific discoveries that we would have had if so many medical people weren't sidetracked into creating an enormous literature on ethics.

Moreover, every time policies change and open up new ethical frontiers, there are scores of new lawsuits. We would have to count the cost of these lawsuits also in the negative column. This is money lost as a result of ethical changes, not money saved. These losses won't show up as health care expenditures; they will show up in judicial expenditures, but they also come out of government budgets.

Moreover, we can count the losses that hospitals have when their most sensitive staff are distressed by having to work in settings where financial considerations have priority over patients. Reports of dissatisified medical personnel indicate that this could become a serious problem: Califano (1994) cites a report about a family practitioner who said he wouldn't become a doctor again because of insurance hassles, and a new physician who was discouraged from choosing medicine. Califano states, "Revulsion to this bottom-line fixation is leading some doctors to retire early, others to reconsider their profession, and some of the most talented candidates for a life in medicine to stay away from the field" (p. 35).

In any economic analysis, attention must be paid to other factors besides costs, such as precious limited natural resources. In the field of health care, it is legitimate to consider medical talent, scientific talent, and emotional sensitivity in patient care as precious natural resources. If we set up our health care system in such a way as to squander these talents instead of maximizing them, our health care will suffer even if our budget appears to be in order.

Young people make career decisions early in life and then stick with these decisions for many decades. There are currently talented and idealistic young people who are deciding not to become doctors because of all the ethical turmoil and financial hassles that they are likely to encounter in medicine. Even if we were to begin today to turn our health care system around and make it the kind of system they would choose to work in, we have already lost a number of good people whose absence will be felt over the next four or five decades. If we do not begin right away, we will lose still more talented young people.

Even Peter Singer, whose arguments on behalf of euthanasia have caused him to be greatly criticized, admits that financial arguments against caring for the gravely terminally ill do not hold water. His own mother, who suffers from Alzheimer's disease and can no longer recognize him or any of her children or grandchildren, is cared for by a team of home health-care aides. In justifying these expenditures, he said, "... it does provide employment for a number of people who find something worthwhile in what they're doing" (Specter, 1999, p. 55).

This is exactly the point. If we simply count dollars and cents, we can make silly mistakes. We must also count limited natural resources.

If some of our sensitive medical personnel leave their jobs, and the ones who remain are overloaded with work, can we count the cost to the hospitals of the ensuing malpractice suits when patients and families can't find a sensitive ear for their concerns, even for nondying patients? Califano writes, "... most malpractice lawsuits start with the plaintiff's dissatisfaction with the interpersonal process by which care is delivered; the way a doctor or nurse talks on the phone, delivers a diagnosis, or handles a patient or family's grief" (1994, p. 303).

Do we count the time lost from work for family members stressed from trying to communicate with the medical staff and the psychotherapy needed by the families to recuperate from this that comes out of their own medical plans? Do we also count the psychotherapy needed to recuperate from all the family schisms caused by having to argue about nearly impossible health care surrogacy issues?

The determination of managed care to cut costs puts all health care consumers on the alert. They read books and magazines and scan the Internet when one of their loved ones is ill. When they fear that the health plan of their relative is putting their loved one's life in jeopardy because of cost considerations, they are more likely to request second opinions and more likely to insist on every available option being pursued. If advocates of managed care thought that they could reduce unnecessary tests, they failed to estimate the losses incurred by the lack of trust between patient and physician.

It is highly unlikely that the amounts saved by managed dying would substantially offset all of these losses that are not being counted sufficiently.

Moreover, even if money were saved by shortening end of life care, that money would be more likely to go to corporate profits and lawsuits than to educating the children of the inner cities and feeding the children in the Third World.

UNINSPIRING GOALS

A point that seems very obvious has been totally lost in the analysis of costs presented by advocates of physician-assisted suicide and euthanasia. Any analysis of cost is incomplete without an assessment of what is gained and whether it is worth it. Saving money cannot be the predominant goal of our health care system. This makes no sense whatsoever.

Eisner, in his book, *The Misunderstood Economy: What Counts and How to Count It* (1994) explains that accumulated assets can be just pieces of paper. What is truly valuable are machinery and equipment (p. 36) and a "well-educated and well-trained work force" (p. 54).

The efficiency of a system can only be judged in terms of the important goals that it exists to achieve. A system that spends less is not to be commended if its technique of reducing expenses is to avoid doing its job. Saving money by shirking important tasks is destructive and, in the end, much more costly.

Rashi Fein points out that cutting costs is not . . . always desirable. He writes, "Any business firm . . . could eliminate its costs by . . . 'going out of business'. . . . Yet few do so. . . . What is desired is that costs be minimized *consistent with a given level of production*" (1958, p. 126).

Even if Humphry and Clement were correct that we could save $120 billion, would it be worth it? The sum of $120 billion divided by 252 million people, the approximate population of the United States in 1994 when Chambers, Diamond, Perkel, and Lasch published their study, is $476 per person. If for that amount we could have the peace of mind when a loved one goes to the hospital that no one was going to be rushing our loved one towards death to save dollars, this would be the best $476 per person that we ever spent. Using Emanuel and Emanuel's (1994) estimate that the amount to be saved by discouraging the continuation of end-of-life care was only $29.7 billion, the per person contribution would be only $118 dollars. If we also had to spend more to insure that the disabled are well taken care of, this would also be money well spent. Not only would the disabled be happier and their families happier, but also the large numbers of young people who ardently wish to have idealistic careers helping people would be happier.

What if all our budgets look good but everybody feels suspicious and frightened about their health care, sick people feel pressured to commit suicide, and idealistic young people feel embittered? Is that worth it?

I believe that this kind of talk about pseudodilemmas of health care financing has become so habitual that it is not even questioned. For some reason the kinds of financial arguments I have been discussing win easy acceptance and they are circulating around our society without much resistance. People believe that we are truly compelled to make terrible decisions, and enter without much resistance into discussions of what to do about these terrible decisions that we do not really have to make.

Unfortunately, this kind of rhetoric seemingly justifies a cynical culture in which good ideas for better treatments do not find ready support. Unfortunately our mental health facilities have withered and the perception in our culture that there are no funds available is a major stumbling block to improvement.

However, when we are not intimidated and examine the actual financial arguments, we see that they are not solid. There is much reason to believe that if we improve our strategies for treatment and improve our public image, we may find ourselves with enthusiastic backers and sufficient financial support.

REFERENCES

Baker, D., & Weisbrot, M. (1999). *Social security: The phony crisis*. Chicago: University of Chicago.

Boskin, M.J. (1986). *Too many promises: The uncertain future of Social Security*. Homewood, IL: Dow Jones-Irwin.

Califano, J.A., Jr. (1994). *Radical surgery: What's next for America's health care*. New York: Times Books.

Carter, M.N., & Shipman, W.G. (1996). *Promises to keep: Saving Social Security's dream*. Washington, D.C.: Regnery Publishing.

Chambers, C.V., Diamond, J.J., Perkel, R.L., & Lasch, L.A. (1994). Relationship of advance directives to hospital charges in a Medicare population. *Archives of Internal Medicine, 154*, 541–547.

Christakis, N.A., & Lamont, E.B. (2000). Extent and determinants of error in doctors' prognoses in terminally ill patients: Prospective cohort study. *British Medical Journal, 320*, 469–472.

Colen, B.D. (1986). *Hard choices: Mixed blessings of modern medical tech*nology. New York: Putnam.

Ehrlich, P.R. (1971). *The Population Bomb*. New York: Sierra Club/Ballantine Books.

Eisner, R. (1994). *The misunderstood economy: What counts and how to count it*. Boston: Harvard Business School Press.

Emanuel, E.J., & Emanuel, E.L. (1994). The economics of dying: The illusion of cost savings at the end of life. *New England Journal of Medicine, 330* (8), 540–544.

Fein, R. (1958). *Economics of mental illness*. Joint Commission on Mental Illness and Health, Monograph Series, No. 2. New York: Basic.

Fries, J.F. (1989). The compression of morbidity: Near or far? *The Milbank Quarterly, 67* (2), 208–232.

Griswold v. Connecticut, 381 U.S. 479 (1965).

House passes break for older workers. (2000, Mar. 2). *St. Louis Post-Dispatch*, A1.

Humphry, D., & Clement, M. (1998). *Freedom to die: People, politics, and the right-to-die movement*. New York: St. Martin's Press.

Kassler, J. (1994). *Bitter medicine: Greed and chaos in American health care*. New York: Carol Publishing Group.

Lader, L. (1971). *Breeding ourselves to death*. New York: Ballantine Books.

Longman, P. (1987). *Born to pay: The new politics of aging in America*. Boston: Houghton Mifflin.

Macklin, R. (1993). *Enemies of patients*. New York: Oxford University Press.

Outlook improves for Medicare, Social Security. (2000, Mar. 31). *St. Louis Post-Dispatch*, pp. A1, A8.

Reeve, C. (1998). *Still me*. New York: Random House.

Roe v. Wade, 410 U.S. 113 (1973).

Schwartz, W.B. (1987). The inevitable failure of current cost-containment strategies: Why they can provide only temporary relief. *Journal of the American Medical Association, 257* (2), 220–224.

Smith, W.J. (1997). *Forced exit: The slippery slope from assisted suicide to legalized murder*. New York: Times Books.

Specter, M. (1999, Sep. 6). The dangerous philosopher. *The New Yorker*, pp. 46–55.

Stevenson, R.W. (2000, Feb. 8). Clinton proposes budget that taps growing surplus. *The New York Times*, pp. A1, A22.

United States, Population growth and characteristics. (2000). *The Encyclopedia Americana*, International Ed., Vol. 27. Danbury, CT: Grolier, p. 531.

CHAPTER 6

Establishing a Productive Frame of Reference for Psychological Problems

Why are advocates of physician-assisted suicide and euthanasia so pessimistic about the emotional well-being of the sick and handicapped? Why do they think that the negative emotions of the sick and handicapped are beyond the range of normal comforting and also beyond the range of mental health treatment?

Our culture has embraced the idea of professional help for psychological problems. Professional consultation and therapy are frequently proposed as the solution for a wide variety of problems. However, our culture's very limited vision of therapy is contributing to pessimism about the dying and the handicapped.

Our popular culture is still spinning out the implications of the Freudian preoccupation with the experiences of the growing young person. Our culture, using its own unique interpretation of psychological theories, seems to believe that traditional morality, parental authority, and sexual repressiveness were at the heart of psychological difficulties, and is experimenting with a new kind of culture designed to avoid those difficulties. According to Sykes (1995), new curricula in some elementary schools train children to identify sexual feelings as early as kindergarten (pp. 167–169). Parents are taught that they should allow their children to develop on their own and not try to mold them according to their own ideas. Coming out of all this, we have a society whose image of mental health is the image of a young, sexually attractive and uninhibited individual, liberated from the influence of his or her parents.

The model of therapy held by our culture is a long relationship between patient and therapist, delving into the details of the patient's mental life in a way that is often uncomfortable because it requires the patient to face painful experiences that he may have avoided facing. This painful and expensive therapy is necessitated because the patient's childhood was not ideal.

Our culture has a long list of experiences that they believe every developing child needs, but unfortunately, so many children are not getting these needs met that there is a proliferation of potential candidates for therapy.

I believe that our culture's model of psychotherapy contributes to a feeling of panic about not being able to give everybody what they need. Not only are there so many candidates for therapy, but the therapy goes on indefinitely, and the outcome is far from certain. And during this long period of therapy, the patient is conceived of as belonging to a class of people from whom society cannot yet expect dependability because they are still forming themselves. Moreover, often the therapeutic relationship is burdened with some of the same problems of abuse as the parental relationship.

This generally accepted model of psychotherapy does not provide our general culture with any guide for handling psychological problems that occur outside the consulting room except to send more people for therapy.

The general public is understandably both infatuated and frightened by these ideas. Their infatuation with these ideas shows up on daytime television programming and in the tendency to sentence violent criminals to counseling. Their fear of these ideas shows up when it is time to vote for a higher budget for mental health. They are totally fascinated with the implications of rebelling against parents and sexual freedom. However, as parents and spouses themselves, they hardly want to be seen as oppressive or to be viewed as having a poor relationship. Moreover, as taxpayers, they hardly want to pay for this expensive therapy to be extended to all the misguided youth who are getting into trouble.

Moreover, and perhaps most important, they feel helpless as uninvolved bystanders who do not comprehend what is going on in therapy sessions. They are told that the patient, when he or she reconsiders his or her old problems, sees the problems in a new way, but what is this new way? What is more effective about it?

When families, friends, or neighbors try to help a distressed person, the popular psychology concepts they have learned often do not increase their effectiveness. When they encounter a problem, they may either retreat, feeling that only a counselor can deal with it, or flounder by encouraging the person to talk about past traumas or deep feelings.

Moreover, there is something intimidating about the vision of mental health held by our culture. Because of its focus on family relationships, that vision leads to a way of categorizing people and judging them. For example, often when someone's artistic contributions are discussed on radio or television, their accomplishments are weighed against their perceived personal failings as spouses or parents.

Society's hopes about helping all the people who need to be helped are lowered by this vision of therapy. But for no group is this pessimism as obvious as it is for the sick and the handicapped.

First of all, mental health, as conceived by our culture, seem impossible for a sick person to achieve. If mental health is conceived as independence from the family, how can a sick person who needs the physical and social support of her family, aspire to this goal? If independence is the ideal, not only must the sick person feel unable to achieve it, but also she may feel that she is preventing her children from achieving it. The principle that young people should be allowed complete independence from the family would weigh heavily in the thoughts of an old, sick, or handicapped individual. If she should need care from her children, the children's careers, relationships, and recreation—things that are perceived as important for the child's mental health—may suffer.

Quill (1993, p. 871) gives an interesting example of such a case (Brody, 1995, pp. 209–211). A 70-year-old woman with leukemia was transferred to a "home hospice program." She was expected to live only "a few weeks." However, she "did better than anyone had expected" and, two months later, she was stable and "relatively free" of symptoms (p. 209). Then "she began to focus on wanting to die," because of "her fatigue and her lack of a meaningful future" (Quill, 1993, p. 871).

However, the doctor and the hospice team discovered that her specific concern was that, because she was surviving longer than expected, she felt that her daughter was taking off too much time from work and that "her daughter had children who needed her." Because of this circumstance, she felt like a burden. After a "family meeting," she was apparently satisfied by a plan that she would go to a nursing home so that her daughter could return to work (p. 871). After that she no longer requested assistance in dying.

Not only is the mental health goal of independence inapplicable for the sick and elderly, also, the assumed method of therapy is impractical. Should a sick or dying person decide that in spite of the difficulty of achieving greater mental health at her stage of life, she nevertheless wants to try, the kind of therapy our culture imagines—many sessions with an understanding therapist with the opportunity to grow over a long period of time—would not be feasible. Nor would she be willing to undergo the pain of reliving all her painful experiences with so little time left.

Also, given our culture's intimidating tendency to judge people on how they handle difficult situations, the sick person feels exposed because she has a problem that she can no longer conceal.

In contrast to the way in which our culture is saturated with the popular concept of psychotherapy, our culture is almost entirely unaware of the powerful techniques of cognitive therapy, which have been shown to provide productive results in an increasing variety of psychological disorders (Beck, 1976; Ellis, 1962; Ellis & Harper, 1997).

Albert Ellis was a practicing psychoanalyst at the time that he developed

Rational-Emotive Therapy as an alternative to psychoanalysis. Ellis noticed that as his psychoanalytic patients were speaking about their problems, certain kinds of thoughts seemed to trigger anger and depression. The situation that the patient was reacting to did not trigger his negative emotions unless he drew certain conclusions. For depression, for example, the conclusion was a thought that had the following form: a person, either the patient or a significant other, was categorized as being hopeless. For example, "I am a failure." Or, "I am no good." Or, "my wife is impossible to get along with."

Ellis discovered that if the therapist, instead of simply listening, got actively involved and led the patient in a careful examination of the truth of these statements, the patient experienced great relief.

I once attended one of Ellis's famous Friday night workshops at the Institute for Rational-Emotive Therapy in New York. Ellis interviewed a woman from the audience. She talked about how her daughter was overly emotional and hard to get along with. She was preoccupied with the question of whether her daughter was so emotional because of a genetic resemblance to herself, or whether she herself had mistakenly taught her daughter to be like this. She was clearly horrified by the possibility that she had taught her daughter to be like this. Tears appeared in her eyes in reaction to this thought.

Ellis replied that it was, of course, both. Her daughter was overemotional just like her mother because of her genes and also because she had learned from her mother. But he directed the patient's attention in a completely different direction. Yes, her daughter was overly emotional, and that was where the mother must begin, but what was she going to do about it?

The effect on the mother of Ellis's question was astonishing. Her tears instantly changed to laughter. What was she laughing about?

Her previous preoccupation with the reason for the daughter's overly emotional behavior was suddenly seen not as a tragedy but as a silly distraction. She suddenly saw herself, not as a criminal on trial for a terrible accusation but as an ordinary mother whose daily business was to help her children get through the day despite their ordinary foibles.

The internal high drama that she was reacting to—am I or am I not one of those terrible mothers who ruin their children—was interrupted. The accusation of being overly emotional was taken as simply a description of a behavior that was somewhat undesirable but could change, rather than as a life-long condemnation to a tragic and hopeless condition. Ellis's reaction to it was more or less to say, what's the difference if the problem is genetic or if the mother caused it? For the moment, the mother was no longer caught up in this drama, and it was a great relief. She could put up with her daughter's emotions for the moment, and even hope for improvement, because it wasn't her daughter's behavior that triggered the mother's emotion, it was her *thoughts about* her daughter's behavior. Whenever her daughter behaved this way, she began thinking that she was a terrible mother.

Not only was the woman's emotional state reversed from despair to hope, but suddenly she was brimming with ideas about what she could begin to do about the situation. She hadn't even asked herself what to do about it before because she had had a terrible self-accusation that continually distracted her from moving in a productive direction.

Ellis's theory highlights the limitations of ordinary human thought. Ellis does not single out people who had problems in their childhood as being prone to this kind of self-accusation. He claims it is a common occurrence, almost universal. Nor does he claim that after therapy patients are free of these dramatic self-accusations.

Although Ellis makes it clear that we are all in perpetual danger of seriously irrational thinking, his theory is, nevertheless, profoundly optimistic. He believes that we can be taught to talk ourselves out of these negative thoughts.

It was very clear to the audience how the woman instantaneously switched from fear and despair to productive thinking. Anyone who had seen this would understand how, even though in America we have many people who are hurting emotionally, this could all be reversed if our culture was helping them rather than hurting them.

If the woman he interviewed decided to go for psychotherapy with Doctor Ellis, she would have been given much practice in talking herself out of these self-accusations, until finally, she could do it consistently on her own. Since these self-accusations had caused her to suffer a great deal and had also distracted her from working on her problems, she would also experience a greatly improved mood and improved circumstances.

Ellis called this therapy Rational-Emotive Therapy until recent years, when he changed the name to Rational Emotive Behavior Therapy (Ellis, 1993). Aaron T. Beck developed another similar therapy called cognitive therapy. (Beck, 1976). These two therapies are the source of the cognitive-behavioral approaches that so many psychologists and psychiatrists are using today.

The great strength of the cognitive approach to therapy is that it takes the mystery out of the therapeutic relationship. Cognitive therapy is a mentoring relationship in which the patient brings in problems and talks about how he is thinking about the problems and finds ways of thinking that make these problems seem much more manageable. Although the method and the purpose of the therapy are much clearer to the patient, the resulting improvements are just as deep and lasting as those of other kinds of therapy.

Traditional therapists had noticed the same kinds of self-accusations that Ellis noticed. But they didn't intervene to challenge these self-accusations directly. The process was very indirect. The patient explored his or her personal history and how he or she came to form these self-accusations. This process implied that it was not necessary to consider the self-accusation as reflecting the truth about the patient. However, during therapy, the self-accusation itself can be perceived as a problem. The patient may no longer think "why am I so emotional," but he may think "why am I always accusing myself of being so emotional?" Some patients are affected negatively by counseling because they start thinking "why did my family treat me in such a way that I accuse myself?"

Ellis's therapy frees the patient from both problems simultaneously. The patient doesn't have to think that being overemotional is an insoluble problem. He can work on it. Moreover, he doesn't have to think that accusing himself of being overly emotional is an insoluble problem. It is simply considered normal. It is considered part of normal everyday life to have to talk oneself out of a few irrational accusations.

Childhood memories come up in cognitive therapy, just as they do in traditional therapy, but the focus is different. Some people who depend upon a concept of therapy derived from popular sources believe, for example, that if the patient is angry at their parents for things that happened in their childhood, this anger is present at all times and has a continuous effect upon the patient. They believe that in order to release this anger, certain situations must be discussed in therapy in a certain way.

In cognitive therapy, the problem and the improvement are conceived of in a different way. The old anger from childhood is not present in hidden form. It is simply triggered over and over again because every time the patient thinks about his old grudges, he draws the same conclusions. It is not the memory of the situation contained in the grudge that causes the anger—it is the conclusion that causes the anger. When the patient learns good anger management, his conclusions will be different, and his emotions will be different.

According to Ellis, when you listen to an angry person, you will hear him frequently using certain words—*should, must, have to*. According to Ellis, an angry person has a list of *shoulds* that he thinks the world *must* conform to. He or she angrily compares the world as it is to her list of shoulds. Each time he says to himself, "he shouldn't have done that" or "she shouldn't have done that," he becomes angry.

Even a slight change in these thoughts makes a big emotional difference. If the patient, remembering what his parent did, thinks, "he shouldn't have done that," he will become angry. But if he thinks "I would have been happier if he hadn't done that," it takes the sting out of the experience. The "should" statement creates an irrational feeling that some order in the universe has been violated in a very dangerous way and that things just can't be right until this wrong is corrected. The emotion generated by the "I would have been happier" statement is less troublesome. It doesn't compel the patient to focus on the past. The patient is free to focus on improving the present and the future.

The patient who was harmed by a difficult childhood is harmed not just because there was so much to be angry about. He is also harmed because, in a relationship in which anger seemed so justifiable, he did not have the opportunity to learn how to manage his anger.

Fortunately, in cognitive therapy, it is not too late to learn how to manage anger. When patients in cognitive therapy think of their old grudges, they learn to apply their new anger management techniques to their old grudges. And these new techniques work.

Another related irrational thought that Ellis has highlighted and that is very useful in clinical work is related to anger, but it expresses complete desperation. The thought is "I can't stand it." This very commonly occurring thought allows people to just give up on whatever they are trying to do. Sometimes it can lead to irrational behavior.

The therapist's job is to point out that this thought is an exaggeration, that the patient has already been tolerating the annoyances or discomforts that he is talking about. Although he would greatly prefer not to have these problems, he can, in fact, stand it. Like Ellis's other interventions, this too provides relief. The statement, "I can't stand it," provides the irrational hope of some kind of escape. What, however, is the alternative? Because the patient knows there is no alternative, he is frightened by his own statement. He has always wondered, what if I can't stand what is happening? And now he thinks he is at that point. What can he do? The question is somewhat incoherent and it is a relief not to have to face the terror of complete confusion. Whatever the discomfort that led to the statement, it is at least a known quantity. He is not leaping into insanity or into the unknown.

Cognitive techniques, as contrasted with traditional therapy, can be taught in other situations, not just in therapy. They can be taught in brief therapy, not just in long-term therapy. They can be taught by friends to one another. They can be taught in groups. They can be taught by example. They can be taught by self-help books. They can even be taught by computer techniques (Olevitch & Hagan, 1991; Selmi, Klein, Greist, Johnson, & Harris, 1982).

Research reports with many different patient populations have supported the efficacy of rational-emotive behavioral and cognitive techniques (Beck, 1976; DiGiuseppe & Miller, 1977; Garety, Fowler, & Kuipers, 2000; Kingdon & Turkington, 1994; Wright, Thase, Beck, & Ludgate, 1993). In numerous studies, cognitive therapy has been shown to be as good or better than antidepressant medication for the treatment of depression (Murphy, Carney, Knesevich, Wetzel, & Whitworth, 1995; Simons, Murphy, Levine, & Wetzel, 1986; Wetzel, Murphy, Carney, Whitworth, & Knesevich, 1992).

The depression and anger that plague people who are diagnosed with terminal diseases or who become handicapped and have to rely on others for assistance is no different from the depression and anger that strike healthy people. It is true that under these kinds of circumstances a higher proportion of people succumb to depression, and there is an association between physical illness and suicide. For example, Dorpat and Ripley (1960) found that out of 80 suicides whose medical history was available, 70% suffered from "one or more serious physical diseases" and 51% had "expressed sadness, despair, or hopelessness" about their "illness or its consequences" (p. 351). Eleven percent had had major surgery (p. 355).

Historically, the understanding of this association was somewhat contorted, and the implications for prevention were unclear. Dorpat and Ripley wrote that "It seems likely . . . that suicide in these individuals came from the same internalized self-destructive trends which contributed to their psychosomatic illness" (p. 355).

In contrast, the cognitive approach to the psychological distress of the ill gives us a very direct explanation of the association between illness and suicide and offers suggestions for suicide prevention.

The circumstances—pain, disability, restricted life-style, isolation, the stigma, and the necessity of relying on others for assistance—provide the occasion for many people, even those without previous psychopathology, to draw the kinds of conclusions that lead to debilitating depression, anger, and suicide. Quite simply, the sick person has more problems about which to have a problem.

Although a person may have been very good at coping with ordinary problems before she became ill, she may have had irrational thoughts about sickness and disability that never revealed themselves because she was never sick or disabled before. For example, many healthy people use as their mechanism for coping with stress the statement, "Why am I getting upset about this problem? At least I'm healthy." This coping mechanism only works as long as you're healthy. If a person who uses this statement to cheer herself up becomes ill, she then needs to find a new way of coping.

The irrational thought, "I'm no good," can trouble people who are sick, at least at the beginning of their illness, before they have time to realize how many positive experiences they are still capable of. I once had a patient who developed a problem in his legs. He could no longer work, and he had to keep his legs elevated for long periods of time. He felt depressed because he accused himself of being useless to his family. Eventually, he found ways of being useful at home; for example, he could stand long enough to prepare meals for the family (Olevitch, 1995, p. 71).

The person with a new handicap needs time to discover all the ways that he can still be happy and useful and ways of coping with irrational thoughts for which he has not yet developed an answer. If, before he became sick, someone harbored negative thoughts about sick or handicapped people or had an ideology in which people must justify their existence by accomplishing work, these thoughts and ideas will need to be worked on once he becomes ill.

The thought that a handicapped person is "no good" is not a rational description of what he can and cannot do. It is a global judgment, full of negative emotion, that harms the person who is thinking it. It has the same irrational, negative, paralyzing quality as the mother's judgment of herself as a terrible mother.

When the cognitive therapist meets with a statement like this, he can query further. No good for what? The simple act of examining this statement gives relief to the patient. In the process of listing what he can and cannot do, the patient sees that he will be missing some activities, but this doesn't add up to a tragic, global judgment of being doomed. As he does an inventory of the skills and abilities that he still has, the "no good" judgment begins to seem unreasonable. He may be disappointed that he can no longer walk or dance, but he sees that he can still get from place to place, and he can still enjoy music. Disappointment doesn't freeze a person's productive thinking; he simply moves on to something else. But a global judgment of "no good" halts all productive thinking.

The above example illustrates why some people say that they learn so much from the experience of being sick. All through their lives, they may have believed a person was not good unless he or she were earning a full-time salary. They may have been haunted by the possibility that they would no longer be able to meet this standard. When they become sick and find other ways of feeling worthwhile, they realize that their old standard was unnecessary, and they feel liberated.

When I worked as a clinical psychologist on inpatient wards, I noticed that many patients felt very guilty about taking their disability pension or about not working.

I would talk to them about how people are not self-sufficient throughout their entire life. People don't work when they are growing up, and they don't work when they're older, and they don't work if they stay home with their children, and they don't work if they are sick or if the job market changes and they need to be retrained in different skills. I explain that pensions exist because most people in society don't want people to suffer just because they are sick. They themselves paid taxes when they were working and it is only fair that they should be able to collect their pension if they need it.

This kind of discussion seems to help with the misconception that working at a paying job is an essential part of being human and that someone is "no good" if he is not working.

Many patients who are unemployed nevertheless find socially useful things to do with their time, such as taking care of aging parents, encouraging their mentally ill friends, or doing volunteer work.

A few years ago, an issue of *Newsweek* magazine presented two very interesting articles. One was about the Dilbert comic strip, which was wildly popular because it focused on the absolutely insane things that go on in the American workplace (Levy, 1996). The strip, the article said, helped workers laugh at some of the crazy things that they had to spend their time on at work. The other article was about the difficulties of returning welfare mothers to work (Klein, 1996). When you put the two articles together, you really have to think about the question of whether paid employment is really any guarantee that you are spending your time in a worthwhile manner. Why try so hard to return these mothers to the workplace, where their time might be occupied with nonsense? These kinds of reflections help patients to not automatically equate paid employment with being worthwhile.

Ellis, particularly in his early writings, instructs patients that simply to be human is infinitely worthwhile. Thinking that you must do any particular thing to be worthwhile is irrational.

Unfortunately, some people are so handicapped that they put this belief to the test. What if you are so handicapped that you can't do anything at all?

The actor Christopher Reeve became paralyzed as a result of falling from a horse in 1995 (Jenish & Novak, 1999). As a result, he could not move his body or breathe without a respirator. In his book, *Still Me* (1998), he talks about how his wife still valued him and wanted him. In other words, even if someone is almost totally handicapped, he can still be a treasured companion to his spouse. Reeve also talks about how his small child still took pleasure in seeing him, and how important that was to him.

Jean-Dominique Bauby, a former magazine editor, suffered from locked-in syndrome after a stroke. He could communicate only by moving his left eyelid. He wrote a book about what it was like to be in his condition. A helper read him the letters of the alphabet and he selected the letters he wanted to use. In this book, *The Diving Bell and the Butterfly* (1997), he describes in a very touching way how his children visited him on Father's Day. He wrote, "Today is Father's Day. Until my stroke, we had felt no need to fit this made-up holiday into our emotional calendar. But today we spend the whole of the symbolic day together, affirming that even a rough sketch, a shadow, a tiny fragment of a dad is still a dad" (Bauby, 1997, p. 70).

Feeling worthless is not the only problem for people who are sick. Having to depend upon others can be a problem as well. The chronic psychiatric patients that I worked with in psychiatric hospitals often articulated very clearly that they felt ashamed of being dependent upon others. This feeling can be handled in a similar way to the feeling of the mother who felt she was a terrible mother.

The patient who is suffering shame about being dependent very often has developed the concept that there are two kinds of people: those who are independent and those who are dependent. They feel ashamed of being part of the less desirable group.

Discussion of the way in which the patient has categorized people often can show the patient that he is judging himself unnecessarily. Every human being is fully dependent upon others. You cannot make money selling a product unless somebody wants to buy it. You cannot support a family unless you have a family. You cannot say something interesting unless someone is there to appreciate it. You cannot be a boss unless someone follows your instructions. You can hardly do anything at all that someone else didn't teach you how to do. You can hardly do anything at all without things that were made or built by other people.

The patient has not entered a new, undesirable category of dependent people by becoming ill. He is simply becoming dependent in some new ways that he is not yet accustomed to.

Unfortunately, it is very common for people who have to rely on others for their activities of daily living to become angry that their needs are not met sooner or better. Nursing home residents may have to wait for a nurse before they can go to the bathroom or eat. Good anger management is very important for such people to get through the day. Once they think of the nurses as imperfect human beings who get distracted or forget things or have certain insensitivities, they don't mind as much having to ask or remind the nurse about what they wanted.

Having a long list of should—for example, how often your children should visit or how often the nurse should take you for a walk or what you should be able to do for yourself—would be a serious handicap in a nursing home. Life can be hell for someone who is always angry. But in the same home, under the same circumstances, with the same diseases, and with the same staff, you can find people with better anger management skills who succeed in remaining relatively cheerful and friendly.

People who have recently suffered a decline in their health or have recently heard a bad prognosis for their illness are afraid that they might come to a point where "I can't stand it" will be a reality.

It is reassuring for people who are worried about this to receive information from their doctors and nurses and also from other people who share their same illness. One patient said about a cancer support group "I thought this group would be a bunch of old ladies crying. In fact we spend much of each meeting laughing" (Surviving, 2000, p. 4).

Cognitive techniques of adjusting to illnesses and managing stress related to illness can be worked into the treatment plans of people with serious disorders without making them feel that they have been declared mentally ill and in need of psychotherapy. The patient's family can also benefit from cognitive therapy at the time of the patient's illness.

Any efforts of the mental health profession to inform the public about the successes of the cognitive approaches to therapy would help to repair the gap in popular knowledge. The cognitive frame of reference is highly suitable for the problems of the aged and the handicapped and is readily understandable to the public. It is not intimidating. Ellis makes it clear that these irrational thoughts are part of the normal human experience. It is not mysterious. It is not as expensive as traditional therapy. Moreover these concepts can be spread in other ways, not just by the traditional one-on-one therapy. Since the effectiveness of the cognitive approach does not depend upon the development of a unique, special emotional relationship with a therapist, it doesn't hurt to teach someone a few concepts even if you can't work with the person continuously. In fact, it helps. A person's education in cognitive self-management can be accomplished by learning a little bit from a lot of different people. Moreover, in order to learn about cognitive therapy, patients do not have to reveal embarrassing material about themselves. They can learn helpful techniques to cope with some of their easily discussable problems and apply them themselves to their more embarrassing problems. Because it is not embarrassing and not mysterious and not so time-consuming, the cognitive approach is not as painful as traditional therapy. Therefore it can be undertaken even by a terminal person who does not have long to live, since it is not a sacrifice for the sake of the future, but something worthwhile in the here and now.

It is very painful for me as a cognitive therapist to hear the advocates of physician-assisted suicide and euthanasia suggesting helping people die because of their "dignity." Feelings of shame about being helpless are so clearly and so effectively addressed by cognitive therapy that it is unthinkable to suggest that suicide is appropriate for these problems.

The cognitive therapies are a great tool, and it has now become urgent for the public to know more about these techniques.

The basic theory of cognitive therapy is very uncomplicated. A few kinds of thoughts—the categorizing thoughts (I am a failure, I am hopeless,), the *shoulds*, the *musts*, the *have tos*, the *needs*, and the *I can't stand its* are implicated in a huge amount of unnecessary human misery. Paying attention to the thoughts of a distressed person makes the interaction with him more productive.

The fact that cognitive therapies have been so successful is confirmation that the kind of thoughts targeted by cognitive therapy—Ellis called them irrational thoughts; Beck called them automatic thoughts—truly correspond to something very critical in the relationship between human thoughts and human emotions.

It is amazing and frightening to see that so many of the claims of the advocates of physician-assisted suicide and euthanasia are almost exactly the opposite of what cognitive therapy teaches. In cognitive therapy, we teach the patient that he can gain strength by contradicting his belief that he "can't stand it." Advocates of physician-assisted suicide and euthanasia believe that there truly comes a time in most people's lives when they "can't stand it" any more, and they encourage people to keep asking themselves if it's time yet.

In cognitive therapy, we teach people that the shorter the list of things that they tell themselves that they "need," the happier they will be. Ellis says all we really need is food, water, and air. Other than that, the rest are all wants rather than needs.

The advocates of physician-assisted suicide and euthanasia encourage people in their belief that they need a long list of things, and that when they can no longer have these things or do these activities, they truly have no more reason to exist.

In cognitive therapy we teach people not to make themselves ashamed by saying to themselves, "I should be more attractive or more able to take care of myself." Although it would be more pleasant to be healthy and attractive and able to take care of yourself, it is not an obligation.

The advocates of physician-assisted suicide take these shoulds and musts as facts. They agree that life isn't worth living if you have to be fed or toileted.

When cognitive therapy is used, and these irrational thoughts are contradicted, it makes the person stronger and healthier. The movement for physician-assisted suicide and euthanasia is the exact opposite of a support group. Instead of moving in a direction to console and inspire sick people, this movement has rhetoric that would have the effect of causing despair.

In the absence of public recognition of cognitive techniques, and with the widespread influence of assisted-suicide rhetoric, it is sad to see how sometimes intense efforts of families and friends are unsuccessful in preventing suicide.

Shavelson (1995, pp. 105–157) discusses the fascinating case of Kelly Niles, a man in his thirties who had been quadriplegic for two decades and had formerly seemed superbly adjusted to his situation. He had enjoyed the use of elaborate communication devices, had attended college, and had a wide circle of friends. His mother reported that his decline seemed to be related to a romantic disappointment. A close woman friend, Liz, had told him over a long period of time that they might possibly have a relationship in the future. Finally, she told him that they would not (p. 129).

His mother's reaction to his depression was to feel that she had followed the wrong strategy. She had always taught him that he could "become whatever he wanted," . . . Now she felt, . . . "It wasn't real, I made a mistake . . . he really *couldn't* have everything everyone else had, everything I had promised him" (pp. 114–115).

Having decided that she had made an error, she, his father, his attendants, his therapist, and his spiritual advisor all changed their goal to helping him accept his limitations. Unfortunately, Kelly became more interested in death (p. 130).

His family and helpers were swept into helping him plan his death even though they wished to avoid the legal complications of physically assisting him. They fantasized with him about how he could do it (pp. 120–121). They understood his frustration, and took his side in bemoaning the difficulties of society not allowing them to help (p. 121). As this process continued, he became angrier and angrier about his inability to die and their unwillingness to help him (p. 139). Finally, he succeeded in dying of starvation just as he finally persuaded his mother to help him (p. 150).

Kelly's physical limitations had been present for two decades. His lack of a relationship was also a long-standing problem that he had tolerated for most of his adult life with the exception of a one-year relationship that took place ten years before his suicide.

According to the theory of Rational-Emotive Behavior Therapy or cognitive-behavioral therapy, the difference between his earlier loneliness and his current loneliness was that he was telling himself something different about it.

Possibly, during his earlier years, he misinterpreted his mother's encouragement as meaning that he could definitely achieve certain specific goals eventually. This is problematic. Whether a child will marry or not, whether he has children or not, is not something that any mother can promise her child. Kelly may have never quite grasped the cognitive aspect of human happiness. He didn't understand that, even with his handicap, he could be as happy as anybody else, regardless of whether he attained certain specific goals or not.

Kelly's thinking probably followed the pattern we discussed earlier in Chapter 1, in which people assume that there are necessarily certain objective psychological consequences to certain external events.

When Kelly's support network switched to emphasizing his limitations, he may have misinterpreted his limitations as restricting his possibility for happiness. If he believed that being physically handicapped necessarily causes a certain amount of unhappiness and being romantically rejected a certain amount and then started adding these together—along with a social rejection he had experienced and some technical difficulties—it is easy to see why he might have become convinced that he was hopeless.

What his support network was telling him about accepting his limitations may have sounded like very bad news. According to our culture's popular psychology, one grows by experiencing pain that one avoided experiencing before. The new line they were taking with him may have given him the impression that the good part of his life was only good because he was kidding himself and now it was time to start suffering.

How could some knowledge of cognitive therapy have helped his devoted family, friends, and attendants who had seemingly tried everything?

First of all, they themselves might have had more success in their efforts to console Kelly. Secondly, had they realized the potential benefits of cognitive therapy, they might have obtained effective treatment for Kelly. The cognitive message is optimistic. You can tell the distressed person that his whole physical and situational dilemma does not have the power over him that he thought it did. His beliefs are paramount, and his beliefs, with practice, can be under his own control.

In cognitive therapy, you can indeed face your physical and social limitations, but without fear, because they do not determine your happiness. Nor does your love life. Your beliefs determine whether you are paralyzed by depression or free to carry on with the business of improving your life.

What were Kelly's beliefs?

First, he thought that Liz's rejection meant that he would never marry or have children. When a person becomes suicidal, he is not usually just unhappy about his present situation. He has also concocted what he believes to be an airtight case that his situation will never improve.

The cognitive therapist knows that the kinds of situations that people are usually so upset about, such as romantic relationships, are very quirky and impossible to predict. The very characteristics that bothered Liz about Kelly may have been attractive to somebody else. Moreover, if she was put off by some of his behavior, he might change sufficiently so that he could attract somebody else. Many very happily married people could spend hours telling you about all of the humiliating rejections that they had to undergo before they finally succeeded in finding their mates.

The very fact that Kelly is concluding something about his own future from Liz's rejection should make a cognitive therapist or a friend very confident that he must be making unsupported generalizations about himself in order to jump to this unjustified and gloomy conclusion.

When a woman says "maybe" over a long period of time about whether she feels that a certain man is for her, the "maybe" is often really a "no." The reality of the situation is that he was trying very hard with the wrong woman—a situation that also afflicts the able-bodied. As soon as he stops wasting his time with the wrong person, his chances of finding a relationship are much improved, since he may meet a woman who is much more interested in him than the previous woman was. Moreover, when he approached the task of finding someone without thinking that it was a life-or-death matter, he might be more successful.

It is important to help the patient realize that he might very well be wrong about his gloomy assumptions. There is no need to make overly rosy assumptions, just to cast enough doubt on the patient's "airtight" case to shake his certainty in his gloomy outlook. Patients are often amused when they see how weak their evidence is.

Even in cases of social rejection, which Kelly had experienced when he was asked not to return to a favorite restaurant (pp. 128–129), depression can be averted or minimized. When the victim of social rejection is helped to realize that it is not a sign of personal failure, he may still be sad but can take positive steps to rebuild his social life.

Secondly, Kelly had a belief system that was directly implicated in his suicidal ideation. He believed very strongly in a certain kind of afterlife. He wanted to die so that he could "cross over." However, his beliefs stemmed from academic study in Eastern religions rather than from growing up in a particular religion and learning it fully. If we conceive of each belief system as a tree, he had removed a branch—the belief in an afterlife—from Eastern religion, leaving behind the rest of the tree. He did not feel bound by the prohibitions against suicide that are usually part of such religions. Nor was he bound by the focus on achieving a relaxed, contemplative, all-accepting state of mind. He had grafted this branch—the belief in an afterlife—onto his own belief system—a secular, American, well-to-do focus on active skill attainment, physical mastery, and social achievements. Then he proceeded to actively try to enter the afterlife.

Kelly might have benefited from a discussion of how he was mixing together incompatible belief systems with dangerous results. If he was so certain that the beliefs he had borrowed about the afterlife were true, how was he so sure that he could disregard the beliefs about the sinfulness of suicide? If he thought it was all right to believe in whatever he felt like believing, what would be wrong with simply convincing himself that if he focused on learning about how to begin a truly successful relationship, he might eventually be able to achieve this?

Kelly could probably see that if he assumed he might be successful and remained hopeful for his whole life, he wouldn't have lost anything, even if his hopes were not fulfilled. On the other hand, if he invented his own version of an afterlife and sacrificed his life to hurry into it, he would have lost a great deal.

As long as Kelly's family, friends, and helpers believed in a one-to-one correspondence between external events and emotions, their encouragement was not fully effective and they placed no hope in finding effective therapy for Kelly. Because of their discouragement and their belief in the rhetoric of the assisted-suicide movement, they couldn't see his error in concluding that he was doomed to sorrow.

Kelly concluded that he would never have a relationship and that he would not be happy and that this meant that he was not worthwhile. His desire to become more worthwhile was very clear. He said, "When I cross over, I'll be moving forward in my life. If I had a mate, that would also be moving forward. . . . I'm ready to move" (p. 119).

Kelly might have been able to stop judging himself according to whether he was loved or successful and instead, get genuinely involved and interested in going about his efforts in a different way. He could have felt proud of himself for learning to wait, for pursuing goals patiently, or for understanding that human beings—even the able-bodied—make certain efforts but don't entirely control the results. He might have enjoyed the feeling of strength and hope, knowing that he didn't need love or have to have love and that he could stand it if he wasn't loved.

If the mental health professions are successful in transmitting to the public a Rational-Emotive Behavior Therapy or cognitive-behavioral therapy vision of psychological disturbance and the kind of satisfaction that people can achieve by pursing their goals patiently in a rational way, whether they achieve them or not, the friends and family of future patients like Kelly would possibly have a greater chance of success in breaking up a developing pattern of suicidal ideation, and if they weren't succeeding, they would see the need for treatment more clearly.

The cognitive model has an important implication that we need to be aware of. Because it focuses on how certain ideas cause emotional symptoms, it implies that as ideas spread, emotional distress can be contagious.

The traditional therapy model does not imply that emotions can be contagious except within the family. But the cognitive therapy model implies that distress can be contagious in larger groups as well, such as in schools or in society as a whole. Anyone who hears and accepts the assumption that if you're no longer independent you can't enjoy your life acquires new fears that he didn't have before.

As we saw in Chapter 1, the essence of psychotherapy is the recognition that the emotions of the human being are subjective in nature instead of objective. This recognition provides the basis for therapies that enable people to bring out their greatest psychological strengths in difficult situations.

Advocates of physician-assisted suicide and euthanasia are trying to have certain human situations certified as being so difficult that they require a whole new ethic. They are beginning with the terminally ill. They are trying to carve out a special area in our law and in our thought to deal with these special situations.

By doing so, they give credence to a model of human emotion based upon objective events rather than subjectivity. Terminal illness is only one of the many circumstances that they believe should be considered so objectively undesirable that the life of the person experiencing it is considered to be lowered.

Managed dying activists also are trying to carve out cognitive handicaps as being another special area that renders a human life less precious and worthy of protection. Wesley J. Smith eloquently titles his chapter on the danger of the slippery slope to the cognitively disabled "Creating a Caste of Disposable People" (Smith, 1997, pp. 36–67). The cases he discusses are cases of cognitively disabled people who were not terminal, people who could have lived with their feeding tubes.

This catalog of possible human situations, ranked according to desirability, can become a way of hierarchizing people. People who are in a bad situation are seen, from the perspective of this theoretical system, as being unworthy of protection against suicide. This point was clearly articulated in the brief submitted by Physicians for Compassionate Care to the U.S. District Court, which was considering Attorney General Ashcroft's November 6th ruling that to assist suicides in Oregon using controlled substances was a violation of federal law. The brief points out that patients who have been labelled "terminally ill are deprived of the protection against assisted suicide that other citizens enjoy" (Physicians for Compassionate, 2001).

Although this kind of thinking does not discriminate according to gender or race, it is a new form of discrimination. The aged, the handicapped, the sick are seen as lower forms of humanity and as having less of a claim to society's protection.

As we can see from history, there are times when irrational ideas do not remain hidden in each person's thinking. There are times when these irrational ideas take over and become the conventional thinking of the day. There have been times in history when someone's race or religion was a reason for large numbers of people to think that he was without value and without the right to live. Instead of being identified as cognitive distortions, the thoughts "he is no good" or "they are no good" become the basis for destructive societal policies.

Historically, these generalizations have been based upon race or religion. We have worked hard to try to protect our generation from racism and sex discrimination and all the things that put some people in a position inferior to others. However, this new ideology of hierarchizing people according to their health status is just as dangerous.

Wesley J. Smith (2000) has pointed out that this hierarchy of human worth based upon health status is entrenched in the thinking of many of the bioethicists who are on hospital ethics committees and who are influential in forming health policies that can exclude some patients from medical care.

We in the mental health field who have listened to the thinking of our patients with the concepts of cognitive therapy in mind know that the problem of how we think of the sick and handicapped doesn't just apply to the sick and handicapped. If we allow a category of worthless people, then everyone will constantly be wondering when they or their loved ones will begin to fall into this category.

This possibility has been dealt with humorously in a magazine piece about a middle-aged woman who talks to her sons about how she would like them to help her die if her mind ever goes. Suddenly she remembers how one of her sons becomes irritated when she calls him by his brother's name. She feels compelled to explain that she means when her mind goes totally. The eagerness of her sons to agree to her request and their nonchalance about the precise conditions under which this agreement would be activated begin to trouble her (Oppenheimer, 2000).

Ellis's focus on thoughts such as "I am no good" or "He is no good" implies that human beings have the following cognitive limitation: they are often on the verge of considering themselves or other people worthless. To give legitimacy to the idea that the lives of some people are indeed worthless is to create a major psychological public health hazard that will affect everyone.

As mental health professionals, we can make it clear that placing human beings in some sort of hierarchy according to their cognitive ability is not just a threat to the handicapped but to the mental health of the entire culture.

The kinds of ideas that are circulating in society greatly affect the kind of culture we will have and the kinds of problems we can solve. The principle that human beings are equal in worth energizes human beings and brings out their psychological strengths and their creative energies. Putting human beings in a hierarchy of worth leads to depression, stagnation, and social turmoil.

There is another aspect to the theory of cognitive therapy that has profound implications. If a person is not guided by shoulds and musts and have tos, what is the organizing principle of a healthy personality? Ellis and Harper (1997) tell us that "Intelligent people tend to require vitally absorbing activity to stay most alive and happy . . . complex, absorbing, and challenging occupations or interests" (p. 207).

Those who advocate blocking progress in medical technology because it creates new procedures that are too expensive (Schwartz, 1987) are not only harming those who would have benefited from the medical procedures. They are also harming a whole generation of young people who could find an exciting sense of purpose in pursuing these new discoveries.

The very problems that some are choosing to disregard would provide just what our young people need to sink their teeth into. What immense challenges there would be in finding ways to care for the sick and the handicapped. If life-sustaining devices are frightening—can we invent more comfortable ones? If nursing home personnel see their residents as less than human, are there ways we could reorganize long-care settings to bring out the best in our caregivers? If some people can no longer move or communicate—can we do neurological research to help them? If people are unprepared for being handicapped, are there ways that we could educate our young people to give them the coping skills that they will need in old age?

Current headlines are declaring that the genetic code has been cracked and that incredible medical progress is just around the corner. Doesn't it seem ironic that just at this time, we should be declaring that it is time to pull the plug on so many people?

Medical progress is not the cause of the current crisis. Nor are medical expenses. Our society is depressed in the same way that an individual is depressed. Depressed thoughts are circulating and no one is contradicting them.

It is time for the mental health professionals, who understand the cognitive distortions in depression, to challenge the statements about the impossibility of helping the sick and handicapped and the impossibility of paying for what they need. Just as a patient who is depressed can't seem to find the energy to put on his socks, society just can't find the energy to help the sick.

Questioning these depressing assumptions that are circulating in our society will generate new enthusiasm, new strength, and new ideas.

REFERENCES

Bauby, J.-D. (1997). *The diving bell and the butterfly*. New York: Knopf.

Beck, A.T. (1976). *Cognitive therapy and the emotional disorders*. New York: International Universities Press.

Brody, H. (1995). Ethical aspects of the physician-patient relationship. In D. Wedding (Ed.), *Behavior and Medicine* (pp. 201–213). St. Louis, MO: Mosby.

DiGiuseppe, R.A., & Miller, N.J. (1977). A review of outcome studies on Rational-Emotive Therapy. In A. Ellis and R. Grieger (Eds.), *Handbook of Rational-Emotive Therapy* (pp. 72–95). New York: Springer.

Dorpat, T.L., & Ripley, H.S. (1960). A study of suicide in the Seattle area. *Comprehensive Psychiatry, 1*, 349–359.

Ellis, A. (1962). *Reason and emotion in psychotherapy*. Secaucus, NJ: Citadel.

Ellis, A. (1993). Changing rational-emotive therapy (RET) to rational emotive behavior therapy (REBT). *The Behavior Therapist, 16* (10), 257–258.

Ellis, A., & Harper, R.A. (1997). *A guide to rational living*. North Hollywood, CA: Wilshire.

Garety, P.A., Fowler, D., & Kuipers, E. (2000). Cognitive-Behavioral Therapy for medication-resistant symptoms. *Schizophrenia Bulletin, 26*, 73–86.

Jenish, D. & Novak, P. (1999, Jun. 7). Man of steely determination, *Maclean's*, p. 61.

Kingdon, D.G., & Turkington, D. (1994). *Cognitive-behavioral therapy of schizophrenia*. New York: Guilford.

Klein, J. (1996, Aug. 12). Monumental callousness. *Newsweek*, p. 45.

Levy, S. (1996, Aug. 12). Working in Dilbert's world. *Newsweek*, pp. 52–57.

Murphy, G.E., Carney, R.M., Knesevich, M.A., Wetzel, R.D., & Whitworth, P. (1995). Cognitive behavior therapy, relaxation training, and tricyclic antidepressant medication in the treatment of depression. *Psychological Reports, 77*, 403–420.

Olevitch, B.A. (1995). *Using cognitive approaches with the seriously mentally ill: Dialogue across the barrier*. Westport, CT: Praeger.

Olevitch, B.A., & Hagan, B.J. (1991). An interactive videodisc as a tool in the rehabil-itation of the chronically mentally ill: A preliminary investigation. *Computers in Human Behavior, 7*, 57–73.

Oppenheimer, J. (2000, Sep. 5). My sons are all too eager to help me go. *Salon.* www.internationaltaskforce.org, International Anti-Euthanasia Home Page, up-dated Dec. 5, 2000.

Physicians for Compassionate Care. (2001, Nov. 8). Friend of the Court Brief on *Oregon v. Ashcroft et al.* www.pccef.org.

Quill, T.E. (1993). Doctor, I want to die. Will you help me? *Journal of the American Medical Association, 270*, 870–873.

Reeve, C. (1998). *Still me*. New York: Random House.

Schwartz, W.B. (1987). The inevitable failure of current cost-containment strategies: Why they can provide only temporary relief. *Journal of the American Medical Association, 257* (2), 220–224.

Selmi, P.M., Klein, M.H., Greist, J.H., Johnson, J.H., & Harris, W.G. (1982). An inves-tigation of computer-assisted cognitive-behavior therapy in the treatment of de-pression. *Behavior Research Methods and Instrumentation, 14* (2), 181–185.

Shavelson, L. (1995). *A chosen death: The dying confront assisted suicide.* New York: Simon & Schuster.

Simons, A.D., Murphy, G.E., Levine, J.L., & Wetzel, R.D. (1986). Cognitive therapy and pharmacotherapy for depression: Sustained improvement over one year. *Ar-chives of General Psychiatry, 43*, 43–48.

Smith, W.J. (1997). *Forced exit: The slippery slope from assisted suicide to legalized murder.* New York: Times Books.

Smith, W.J. (2000). *Culture of death: The assault on medical ethics in America.* San Francisco: Encounter Books.

Surviving and thriving with gynecologic cancers—together. (2000, Fall). *Barnes Jewish Cornerstones*, 3–7.

Sykes, C.J. (1995). *Dumbing down our kids: Why America's children feel good about themselves but can't read, write, or add.* New York: St. Martin's Press.

Wetzel, R.D., Murphy, G.E., Carney, R.M., Whitworth, P., & Knesevich, M.A. (1992). Prescribing therapy for depression: The role of learned resourcefulness, a failure to replicate. *Psychological Reports, 70*, 803–807.

Wright, J.H., Thase, M.E., Beck, A.T., & Ludgate, J.W., (Eds.). (1993). *Cognitive ther-apy with inpatients: Developing a cognitive milieu.* New York: Guilford.

CHAPTER 7

Refusing to Do Consultations That Justify Physician-Assisted Suicide

The Death with Dignity Act of 1994, put into effect in Oregon in 1997, stipulates that a capable adult Oregon resident who is suffering from a terminal disease likely to produce death within six months and who has voluntarily expressed a wish to die may make a written request for medication for the purpose of ending his or her life. It states that if "in the opinion of the attending physician or the consulting physician a patient may be suffering from a psychiatric or psychological disorder, or depression causing impaired judgment, either physician shall refer the patient for counseling. No medication to end a patient's life in a humane and dignified manner shall be prescribed until the person performing the counseling determines that the patient is not suffering from a psychiatric or psychological disorder, or depression causing impaired judgment" (Sect. 127.825).

"Counseling" is defined as "a consultation between a state licensed psychiatrist or psychologist and a patient for the purpose of determining whether the patient is suffering from a psychiatric or psychological disorder, or depression causing impaired judgment."

Fenn and Ganzini (1999) write, "psychologists have been grappling with how to fulfill their legally specified role in the process of physician-assisted suicide" (p. 235).

The mental health profession is understandably reluctant to accept the role that society would like us to play. As mental health practitioners, we would rather be called in on this problem much earlier rather than at the last minute.

We can see many problems leading to the desperate feelings of ill people, and many of these problems would be preventable with adequate mental health services. There is a limit on how far society can go in neglecting the needs of the sick and handicapped before these patients become desperate. We would much prefer to be asked to prevent the desperation of the terminally ill than to provide documentation to help them die.

There seems to be universal agreement that a greater focus on the mental health of the terminally ill would be extremely beneficial and might well prevent the perceived need for physician-assisted suicide.

Emanuel (1998) suggests a different way of handling requests for physician-assisted suicide. Instead of simply evaluating competency, Emanuel suggests for the practitioner a structured way of evaluating the patient and providing alternatives for the patients that will take care of the problems that are provoking the request for suicide. It includes evaluation for depression and other psychiatric conditions, discussion about goals for care including their fears, providing information to calm their fears, inquiry and treatment of their sources of suffering; for example their need for attention, need for a meaningful purpose, adjustment to a disability, problems in relationships, insufficient family or community support, spiritual support, full information about the kinds of palliative care and hospice care possibilities available, consultations with other doctors and specialists, and securing maximum relief of suffering by removing unwanted interventions (pp. 644–645).

Ganzini and Lee (1997) write that a "comprehensive role for the mental health professional" would be preferred by many psychiatrists. The frequency of "depressive syndromes"—present in up to "58% of terminally ill patients with cancer"—and the failure of general practitioners to identify depression and the " 'psychological autopsy' studies" showing that 80% of cancer victims "who committed suicide had depressive syndromes" implies that this syndrome is crucially important (p. 1825). Ganzini and Lee (1997) point out, however, that if the patient isn't referred for treatment until they ask for death, treatment may not be feasible, since antidepressants take weeks to become effective (p. 1825).

Ganzini and Lee, citing Block and Billings (1995), also point out that when "feelings of isolation, anger, fear of abandonment, and loss of control" are addressed, patients have a resulting decrease in the desire for death (p. 1825).

Sullivan, Ganzini, and Youngner (1998) wrote, "We encourage our medical colleagues to involve psychiatrists in the evaluation and care of the dying. Psychotropic medication, supportive therapy, and family intervention can ease suffering and promote autonomous choice" (p. 30).

Hamilton and Hamilton (1999) consider the taped comments of the first legal physician-assisted suicide patient in Oregon, and eloquently outline therapeutic strategies that might have helped the patient regain her desire to live.

In contrast, the kind of competency evaluation suggested by the Oregon Death with Dignity Act, where the job of the mental health professional is simply to decide whether the patient has a mental disorder that impairs judgment, has provoked much negative comment.

Fenn and Ganzini (1999) found that of 423 respondents in a survey of licensed psychologists in Oregon who were in clinical practice, one third of the sample (approximately 141) said performing the evaluation was "outside their practice area," and another 111 said they would "refuse to perform the evaluation." Only 164 were willing to perform the evaluation (p. 237).

The respondents suggested "standards for evaluations should include assessments at multiple points in time, extended waiting periods, mandatory psychotherapy or trials with antidepressants" (pp. 239–240). However, as Fenn and Ganzini point out (p. 240), many of the people in Oregon who applied for assisted suicide didn't survive the 15-day waiting period. Although many of the respondents said they felt comfortable with the evaluation if it could be prolonged, it is not clear if this is practical, given that the applicants wait until they are nearly dead before they request physician-assisted suicide.

Fenn and Ganzini also point out that near the end of life, there is no time to establish "a therapeutic relationship." The patient will be severely "debilitated" with "periods of cognitive impairment." The quality of the evaluation will suffer because the evaluator must do such critical work in a hurry and "in far from ideal circumstances" (p. 241).

Sullivan, Ganzini, and Youngner (1998) suggest that "While psychiatrists have skills relevant to the understanding and evaluation of patients' decisions, they should not have the social authority to use themselves as the measure of when it is right to die" (p. 26). They also suggest that competence assessment is not the way to resolve the tension in society about the acceptability of suicide (p. 26).

I believe that these concerns are very sound. I think we need to examine very carefully what exactly we are being asked to do and whether it is within the limits of our competence and whether our reports would be used properly or misused. This debate has taken place in a hurry, and I believe that there may be additional good reasons for questioning the principles involved in this proposed evaluation that have not yet been fully articulated.

The evaluation of competence is a traditional activity for the mental health profession. An adult is considered competent unless declared incompetent by a court. Incompetent means that they are unable to carry out certain activities that any other normal adult would be able to carry out. There is a very restricted list of activities for which the concept of incompetence is ordinarily invoked; for example, competence to stand trial and competence to handle money. These particular situations are based upon hundreds of years of experience with the kinds of things that mentally ill people do in traditional society when they are not restricted. For example, because of the multiple instances of psychotic people getting themselves into inextricable money difficulties, defaulting on commitments, getting evicted for not paying rent, and a multitude of other highly predictable problems that any case manager or any landlord could tell you about, society has evolved the following practice: When a psychotic person who possesses money is confused to the point where their finances are in danger, a guardian is appointed.

The effect of mental illness upon judgment is an abstraction that is not useful in a courtroom. Although mental illness invariably affects judgment in very important ways, some of these effects are subtle and hard to detect. Some of them appear only under certain unusual circumstances. An expert witness might be asked by a judge to comment more specifically upon whether the impairment in someone's judgment affects his ability to handle money or make certain other specific legal decisions.

The ability to handle money involves a specific set of skills and knowledge. There is a wealth of observable evidence that the evaluator can use. Moreover, there are normal standards against which he can compare the confused person. We have a good idea of how much money a typical individual might spend in a typical year on various items. It is easy to examine the patient's financial records and calculate how much the patient has been spending and how long it would take her to use up all her money. Does the patient know how much money she has? Does she know what her expenses are? Can she figure out how much she has left after her expenses? Can she restrain herself from an unwise purchase? We know what constitutes a mistake and what we are trying to avoid. These mistakes are highly visible and easy to determine.

The legal right to handle your own money if you are not declared incompetent does not mean that normal people are perfect in their ability to handle money. Normal people make mistakes with their money. Moreover, normal people who do not have the time, the skills, or the inclination to handle their own money can hire financial advisors to help them. The legal right to handle your own money is based on a rough societal estimate that handling money is considered to be largely within the capability of the normal adult. Even this right is not unlimited, however. The government protects even normal people against the consequences of foolish money decisions. For example, we are required to contribute social security tax so that we won't be foolish enough to leave ourselves without resources for our old age.

Now, in contrast, let us examine the competence to decide whether to live or die.

In contrast to the right to possess property and to dispose of property, normal people have never been considered by the law to be capable of deciding whether to dispose of their own lives.

As we discussed in an earlier chapter, society takes many steps to prevent people from making the decision to end their lives. They provide suicide hot lines, counseling, prevention programs, support groups, gun-control laws, barricades, restrictions on barbiturates, police protection, civil commitment, and psychiatric emergency rooms—to name only a few of the efforts society makes to prevent people from taking their own lives.

Therefore, in asking a mental health professional to write a report about whether a terminally ill person has a mental disorder that renders them incapable of making this decision, a critical logical step is being skipped. Normal people are considered capable of financial transactions, so we can ask if a mental disorder renders people incapable of making financial transactions. But if normal people have never before been considered capable of deciding whether to live or die, how can we ask whether a particular individual has a handicap in making such a decision relative to normal people?

Society's traditional and current position on this issue is that normal people are not considered capable of deciding to end their own lives. This is the position that the advocates of physician-assisted suicide would like to change. Society's position is also shared by the mental health profession. We typically try to prevent suicide whenever we can.

The burden of proof should be upon the advocates of physician-assisted suicide to prove the assertion that they are simply assuming and skipping over—that normal people have the ability to make good suicide decisions. Otherwise, the advocates of physician-assisted suicide and euthanasia are simply inventing a new specialty that doesn't exist—distinguishing between people who still have this assumed ability and people who have lost this assumed ability.

The trouble is, how could you possibly establish that this ability exists in the first place? Although there exists a tradition of hypothesizing that there are rational suicides, it is hard to see how evidence could be found to support this hypothesis.

The suicide rate in the United States is approximately 30,000 per year (U.S. Census Bureau, 2000, Table No. 138, p. 99). It is widely recognized that a very high proportion of these suicides have a diagnosable mental illness. For example, in a very current, authoritative collection, Moscicki (1999) cites this proportion as approximately 90% (p. 45). A classic study by Robins, Murphy, Wilkinson, Gassner, and Kayes (1959) found that an even higher percentage of suicides, 94%, were psychiatrically ill.

If 90% of the 30,000 suicides have a psychiatric illness, to find data on potentially rational suicides, you would have to focus primarily on the 3000 people per year who committed suicide without a recognizable mental illness. An unknown percentage of these people would have an undiagnosed mental illness. An unknown percentage of these people would have acted on an emotional impulse that didn't count as a diagnosable mental disorder but nevertheless affected their mental state in such a way as to impair their judgment.

Having whittled down the sample by these unknown percentages, how would you then establish that the remainder of the sample had made good suicide decisions? How could you possibly determine what kind of a subjective life a suicide victim could have experienced, if he had not committed suicide? Since this is unknowable, even in a single instance, it would obviously be impossible to compare the suicide decisions of people with varying degrees of judgment in order to determine which cognitive defects prevent good judgment about suicide decisions.

So we see that in practical terms, we cannot say that the mental health professions truly have in their possession any data about whether fully normal people can make capable suicide decisions, much less any data about whether impaired people can nevertheless make capable suicide decisions.

When we look at this assessment task from a theoretical point of view instead of a practical point of view, the results are not any better. We can see, from a theoretical point of view, that the ability to handle money is a fairly circumscribed set of skills. On the other hand, the ability to predict whether the whole rest of one's life will be worthwhile is not a circumscribed set of abilities. It involves anticipating all of one's future joys and sorrows and weighing them against each other.

No one considers suicide unless he is at a point where he is discouraged about the future. In a state of discouragement, it is hard for a person to see that the future contains positive surprises as well as negative surprises. Few people have insight into their own mood swings or their own discouraging self-talk. A person can retain the ability to enjoy things even though he has lost the ability to realize that there will still be much to enjoy.

No one knows what his future situation will be. There are always unexpected problems but also unexpected opportunities and sources of support. Many depressed people think they have no friends and then, once they recover, they suddenly rediscover a whole social network that they had allowed to wither. No one knows his future potential.

In a state of discouragement, it is most likely that a person will overestimate future pains and underestimate future opportunities.

Whether the person suffers from diagnosable depression is not the issue. The *Diagnostic and Statistical Manual of Mental Disorders* published by the American Psychiatric Association begins with an important disclaimer. First, the disclaimer states that the categories in the manual should not be taken as a permanent list of disorders. It states that the manual contains "a consensus of current formulations of evolving knowledge" (*Diagnostic and Statistical Manual*, 1994, p. xxvii).

Second, the disclaimer makes it very clear that the categories in the manual "do not encompass. . . . all the conditions for which people may be treated or that may be appropriate topics for research efforts" (p. xxvii).

Third, the disclaimer makes it very clear that the categories in the manual and the characteristics that are considered in applying the categorizations "may not be wholly relevant to legal judgments, for example, that take into account such issues as individual responsibility, disability determination, and competency" (p. xxvii).

The manual was intended for internal use in the mental health field. It was intended to help us standardize our research and treatment in such a way as to maximize scientific progress. It was never intended to be, nor is it in any way suitable to be, a guide to society about who needs treatment or about who is worthy of certain legal rights or privileges or protections.

Given the movement for physician-assisted suicide and euthanasia, we have unfortunately come to a time where the gaps in our manual suddenly have become critical to certain people. Patients needing the protection of being part of a recognized category are not getting this protection.

There are patients who suffer the miseries of hopelessness and suicidal ideation who do not meet the current criteria for clinical depression and for whom medication will not be effective. These patients are nevertheless not in a psychologically normal state of mind and need protection from harming themselves and can benefit from psychological treatment.

A 50-year-old woman in the Netherlands, known as Netty Boomsma, whose physician Boudewijn Chabot, assisted her in suicide because of what he saw as psychological misery was such a patient. Boudewijn Chabot did not feel that she was psychotic (p. 62) and also said she was "not depressed" (p. 69). He believed she did not have a "psychiatric illness" (p. 60).

He interpreted this lack of a diagnosis to mean that she was "not a patient" (p. 68). He did not insist that she accept the bereavement treatment suggested by one of the other doctors with whom he discussed the case (p. 65).

If Chabot had perceived her as having a psychiatric disorder, he might have hesitated before prescribing lethal medication.

In former times, clinicians used to speak of depression without vegetative signs—a condition in which the patient experienced hopelessness and helplessness but did not show loss of appetite or sleep disturbance. Currently, such patients are no longer considered to manifest clinical depression. The criteria for clinical depression were redesigned to make them more exact, and perhaps more predictive of who would benefit from antidepressant medication. In narrowing these criteria, no one ever intended to imply that those who had suicidal thoughts but did not meet the criteria were not in need of help. No one ever intended, by narrowing the criteria, to endorse the philosophic position that there is such a thing as rational suicide.

Nevertheless Chabot found his way to this position. Given his perception that his patient did not meet the full criteria for clinical depression, he concluded that her suicide was rational and could be assisted.

The most important question therefore is not whether the patient is suffering from a diagnosable psychiatric disorder that is included in our current manual. The question is, rather, whether he is impaired in the normal way that all humans are impaired, that he is suffering from some sort of reversible, temporary emotional upset that will pass. Hendin makes the point that the situation of facing death is itself terrifying to many people and that, with mental health treatment, they can face this without feeling that they need to take charge and commit suicide (pp. 181, 221–222). It is just as tragic if someone loses his life because of a temporary emotional state that is not in our diagnostic manual.

In fact, the very practice and legitimization of physician-assisted suicide could profoundly change the relationship between diagnostic categories and suicide. When suicide was highly stigmatized, someone who wished to commit suicide had to do it in complete isolation. Robins, Murphy, Wilkinson, Gassner, and

Kayes (1959) found that certain diagnoses—the depressed phase of manic de-pressive illness and chronic alcoholism—accounted for a large proportion of the suicides that they studied. Patients with these diagnoses experience periods of intense psychological pain, but have periods of good cognitive functioning. Be-cause of their high motivation and excellent cognitive capabilities, they were perhaps more able than other psychiatric patients to cope, in complete solitude, with the technical details of a successful suicide.

Destigmatizing suicide could change all this. When it is destigmatized and help is offered, it may attract new categories of psychiatric patients who, being more dependent upon others, couldn't carry out a suicide without support. It may also attract psychiatrically normal people who are simply upset about their illness and persuaded by appealing rhetoric.

These considerations make the following question even more compelling—why are we being asked just about diagnosable mental disorders? Why aren't we being asked about how the painful emotions can be reversed?

The focus on diagnosis can be very confusing in cases of physician-assisted suicide. Joan Lucas was a 65-year-old Oregon woman suffering from amy-otrophic lateral sclerosis (ALS) who died following the procedures of the Oregon Death with Dignity Act. Her psychological evaluation consisted of an MMPI mailed to her by a psychologist and filled out with the help of her children, who counseled her on how to answer some of the questions (Kettler, 2000, p. 8A).

Kettler wrote, "The psychologist formally confirmed what the doctors knew: Whatever depression Joan might have was directly related to her terminal ill-ness—a completely normal response" (p. 8A).

This psychologist missed the point. Whether it is a normal, that is, a fre-quently occurring response, to feel depressed in these circumstances is not the issue. The issue is not where did the depression come from, but what does it do to her judgment and is it reversible? Whether depression comes from a lifetime of psychopathology or from an expectable reaction to a devastating event, it can still distort judgment and it is still reversible.

The decision about suicide is irrevocable. If someone's competence to handle money is misjudged, there is often a chance to straighten this out. With suicide, there isn't another chance.

To summarize, the psychologist is being asked a question that is loaded with the theoretical assumptions that the advocates of physician-assisted suicide are hoping to put forward.

By answering the question in either direction—yes or no: this patient does or does not suffer from a mental disorder that impairs his judgment to make a suicide decision—either way, the psychologist is giving the advocate what he needs. The advocate wants to take these reports and show them to the rest of society. He wants to use them to bolster his claim that mental health profes-sionals agree that there is such a thing as a normal ability to make a good suicide decision and that this ability is only absent when judgment is impaired by a mental disorder.

A report saying that Mrs. X no longer has the ability to make a good suicide decision helps the advocates of physician-assisted suicide just as much as a report that says that she has this ability. Saying that she has a mental disorder that impairs her ability to decide implies that unimpaired people have this ability.

We are not being asked "is there anything that can be tried to help this person feel better?" There is a good reason we are not asked this question. The reason is that the answer is always affirmative.

We are being asked, instead, only whether the patient has a diagnosable mental disorder that impairs judgment. We can answer it *yes* or *no*. Everything else in our report might be disregarded. And if we say no, he does not have a diagnosable mental disorder, or no, he does have a diagnosable disorder but it doesn't impair his judgment, the person will die.

On the slippery slope, we are being asked to be the sled.

It is not sufficient to simply argue that mental health professionals who do not wish to do these evaluations can excuse themselves. Wesley J. Smith tells us about an Oregon suicide case that is very pertinent to this issue (Smith, 1999). Kate Cheney, an 85-year-old woman with terminal cancer, was turned down for assisted suicide by one doctor at her health plan, but her daughter insisted that the mother have a new doctor. The second doctor referred her to a psychiatrist for evaluation. The psychiatrist found that Cheney had a loss of short-term memory, and that she did not have the capacity required to weigh options about assisted suicide. Also, it seemed that Cheney's daughter was more invested in the suicide than Cheney. The patient herself was not pushing for it. The psychiatrist therefore concluded that assisted suicide was not appropriate (Barnett, 1999; Physicians for Compassionate Care, 2000; Smith, 1999).

Cheney's daughter sought another opinion, which the health plan again authorized. A clinical psychologist also concluded that Cheney had "memory problems" and agreed that "familial pressure" might be occurring. Nevertheless, the psychologist "approved the writing of the lethal prescription." An "ethicist/administrator" gave the final permission (Smith, 1999, p. 12).

Smith (1999) concludes "A major selling point of assisted-suicide advocacy is that close personal relationships between doctors and patients will prevent 'wrongly decided' assisted suicides. But Oregon proves the utter emptiness of this promise. Kate Cheney and her family were not deterred in the least by a psychiatrist's refusal to approve her self-poisoning. They simply went to another doctor" (p. 13).

As long as the mental health profession does not take a stand as a group that these evaluations are outside our competence, patients can simply shop around for an evaluation until they find one to their liking, the same way that they shop around for a lethal prescription. Out of 26 patients who died of physician-assisted suicide in Oregon in 1999, 8 received the lethal prescription from the first physician they asked, 18 from the second, and 8 from the third or fourth

(Sullivan, Hedberg, & Fleming, 2000). Compassion in Dying, an assisted-suicide advocacy group, reported that they gave referrals to 78% of the Oregon patients who died of physician-assisted suicide in 2000 (Oregon's 3rd annual, 2001, p. 2).

One reason why some therapists might be in favor of doing these consultations is that they visualize terminally ill patients in uncontrollable pain and they wish to help them.

Data from Oregon shows that, in fact, intolerable pain was not the reason for the physician-assisted suicides that occurred. A study of interviews with the physicians of the 70 patients who used physician-assisted suicide in Oregon between 1998 and 2000 revealed that inadequate pain control was only even mentioned as a concern in 17 cases (Sullivan, Hedberg, & Hopkins, 2001, Table 1, p. 606). Moreover, it was clearly noted that even in these 17 cases, although the patients were concerned about inadequate pain control, they weren't necessarily experiencing pain. Other concerns were much more frequently cited. For example, 58 cited loss of autonomy and 54 cited a decrease in ability to participate in activities.

Suppose mental health professionals act as if they consider the question "does this patient still have a normal capacity for making suicide decisions in spite of their mental illness" a reasonable question and begin doing these consultations. Suppose then, the Oregon law changes, and instead of being restricted to terminal illness, physician-assisted suicide is allowed for any patient with an uncomfortable disorder, whether he is terminal or not. If mental health professionals then decide that they no longer wish to do the consultations, they might be accused of refusing for political reasons, because they are against physician-assisted suicide.

The time to take a stand on the issue of whether these consultations make sense is now, while the law stands as it is.

Given what we know as therapists about human limitations, how can we stand by and allow society to give people decisions that they very likely cannot handle?

The theory of cognitive therapy implies that the human mind is quite limited in its rationality. Patients in cognitive therapy are taught to expect that they will fall into emotional generalizations and that they must remain on the alert, always ready to argue with their own assumptions to determine if they are perceiving reality accurately.

In cognitive therapy, the patients are often given homework assignments. They are taught how to record their own moods and behaviors and examine them in the way a behavioral scientist would. They are taught to record their thoughts to see if they are generalizing inappropriately.

The patient is taught what scientists and journalists already know—that human objectivity is an achievement that requires considerable exertion.

According to Ellis, there is a biological tendency to fall into emotional exaggerations. When a person feels angry at another person, he doesn't have a realistic model of the other person in mind. He doesn't see him as an imperfect human being with many great qualities and a few annoying quirks who is being insensitive at this particular moment about a specific issue. He sees him, instead, in a dramatic, emotional way, as always or almost always doing mean or stupid things. After the passage of some time, he might forgive the other person and remember his good qualities.

When a person has just been diagnosed with a terminal illness, he doesn't see himself as suffering a serious inconvenience, he sees himself as completely no good or worthless. He may feel that he won't be able to stand being sick. However, after a while, he may discover that he still can enjoy many aspects of his life and that the symptoms might not be as bad as he anticipates.

I have so far simply applied the limitations in the judgment of healthy individuals to the situation of being sick. It is also possible, however, that medical illnesses render human judgment even less capable than usual. Cassell, Leon, and Kaufman (2001) found that when hospitalized medical patients were given judgment tasks that are used to study childhood cognitive development, the sicker patients showed levels of judgment comparable to children younger than 10 years of age.

The traditional religious world view held that certain decisions were beyond the reach of human intelligence and were up to God. In our modern culture, there is an emphasis on removing any remnants of religion from our laws. But what if certain decisions are indeed beyond the reach of human intelligence? Will we make them anyway? Should we just blunder through instead of admitting that we need some sort of protective limit?

In many instances laws do protect citizens from making erroneous decisions. We don't publish long pamphlets about all the things you should consider when you get in the car to judge how fast to drive. We don't suggest evaluating the driver's mood and the weather conditions and the traffic conditions before deciding. The law simply says, observe the speed limit or you'll get a ticket. We also decide for people whether they should use illegal drugs and whether they should make some provision to educate their children. Given that we have discovered over time that people make much better decisions when they get concrete guidance from the law in many practical matters, does it truly make sense to give people this brand new freedom to decide to end their lives?

Some mental health professionals might wish to do these consultations because our usual tactic has been to try in every way to enhance our prestige in society by doing more and more. However, I do not think that these interventions are going to enhance our prestige. I was once chatting with another psychologist about methods for attracting more patients to a private practice. I asked him whether he had been giving free lectures. He said he had done this, but he had found from experience that the only consequence of giving these free lectures was that he got a lot of invitations to give other free lectures.

I think that if we do questionable consultations, the consequence will be that we will be invited to do other questionable consultations. I think that, on the other hand, if we refuse to do these consultations, advocates will have a much harder time winning acceptance for physician-assisted suicide.

Sullivan, Ganzini, and Youngner (1998) write, "... it may be more difficult politically to endorse or legalize physician-assisted suicide without the psychiatric safeguard. But the societal debate about assisted suicide will be more honest and revealing" (p. 30). They point out that by requesting these evaluations, society shifts the burden of a "troubling moral decision" (p. 24).

With the option of physician-assisted suicide closed off, the increased sympathy of society for the pain and emotional suffering of the patient might begin to have benefits. There might be increased desire on the part of society to provide the patient with the kind of help he needs to prevent his desperation. Our agenda with the terminally ill should not be just to extract them from their final dilemma, but to prevent the dilemma in the first place.

We could imagine a medical setting where the involvement of mental health professionals was a part of treatment whenever there was a terminal diagnosis. We can imagine an intensive care unit where mental health professionals were constantly there, helping the patients and the staff and the family. This can only come about if we insist as a profession that not enough is being done to help the sick and the disabled.

If we are to be leaders in this area, we cannot agree to provide an excuse note for the medical profession and the hospital administrators and the HMOs on a case-by-case basis from all the things that they didn't do for the patient.

It would be naive of us to assume that we can protect our clients by agreeing to do these evaluations and then judging them to be incompetent. Incompetent patients are in danger as well because of surrogate decision making. Patients have already died because they were considered incompetent to reverse their previous health directives.

An interesting case was published in the *Hastings Center Report* (An alert and incompetent, 1998). A woman who had written a living will stipulating that she did not wish to be on life supports was hospitalized, and she was dependent upon a respirator to breathe. She nevertheless adjusted and had a good relationship with the nursing staff and enjoyed watching television programs. Her old friends who knew about her living will insistently called the medical staff's attention to these directives. The patient was asked if she wanted the respirator removed and she said "no." But the catch is, they didn't consider her competent any more. After much discussion, it was decided to transfer her elsewhere and remove the respirator. "On the day of the transfer the patient and nursing staff cried" (An alert and incompetent, 1998).

Our job is to teach society to be more sensitive to human suffering. Possibly we can see the urgent sympathy for the critically ill as an expansion of awareness of individual feelings. The awareness of suffering has increased enough to make people uncomfortable and make them want to remove the suffering instantaneously. Now we must teach our culture to be not only sensitive but also patient and willing to invest the time and energy and resources necessary to provide good health services and support services in a less stressful manner. We have to insist that the current, insensitive way of treating sick people, combined with a new strategy of allowing physician-assisted suicide, will inevitably lead to all kinds of psychological problems and all kinds of unnecessary suicides. To provide justification for these unnecessary suicides in the form of a psychological report would be a complete abandonment of our treasured goal of a society organized in such a way as to maximize the psychological functioning of all of its members.

REFERENCES

An alert and incompetent self: The irrelevance of advance directives. (1998). *Hasting Center Report, 28* (1), 28–30.

Barnett, E.H. (1999, Oct. 17). Is Mom capable of choosing to die? *Oregonian,* G1, G2.

Block, S.D., & Billings, J.A. (1995). Patient requests for euthanasia and assisted suicide in terminal illness: The role of the psychiatrist. *Psychosomatics, 36,* 445–457.

Cassell, E.J., Leon, A.C., & Kaufman, S.G. (2001). Preliminary evidence of impaired thinking in sick patients. *Annals of Internal Medicine, 134,* 1120–1123.

Death with Dignity Act, Oregon Revised Statutes, Section 127.800–127.897 (1998).

Diagnostic and Statistical Manual of Mental Disorders, 4th ed., *DSM IV.* (1994). Washington D.C.: American Psychiatric Association.

Emmanuel, L.L. (1998). Facing requests for physician-assisted suicide: Toward a practical and principled clinical skill set. *Journal of the American Medical Association, 280,* 643–647.

Fenn, D.S., & Ganzini, L. (1999). Attitudes of Oregon psychologists toward physician-assisted suicide and the Oregon Death with Dignity Act. *Professional Psychology: Research and Practice, 30,* 235–244.

Ganzini, L., & Lee, M.A. (1997). Psychiatry and assisted suicide in the United States. *New England Journal of Medicine, 336,* 1824–1826.

Hamilton, N.G., & Hamilton, C.A. (1999, Spring). Therapeutic response to assisted suicide request. *Bulletin of the Menninger Clinic, 63*(2), 191–201.

Hendin, H. (1997). *Seduced by death: Doctors, patients, and the Dutch cure.* New York: W.W. Norton.

Kettler, B. (2000, Jun. 25). A death in the family: "We knew she would do it." *Sunday Mail Tribune* (Medford, OR), pp. 1A, 8A.

Moscicki, E.K. (1999). Epidemiology of suicide. In D.G. Jacobs (Ed.), *The Harvard Medical School guide to suicide assessment and intervention.* San Francisco: Jossey-Bass, pp. 40–51.

Oregon's 3rd annual assisted suicide report: More of the same. (2001). *Update, International Task Force on Euthanasia & Assisted Suicide, 15* (1), 2.

Physicians for Compassionate Care. (2000, Apr. 25). Pain Relief Promotion Act (HR2260): Written testimony of Physicians for Compassionate Care to United States Senate Judiciary Committee.

Robins, E., Murphy, G.E., Wilkinson, R.H., Gassner, S., & Kayes, J. (1959). Some clinical considerations in the prevention of suicide based on a study of 134 successful suicides. *American Journal of Public Health and the Nation's Health, 49*(7), 888–899.

Smith, W.J. (1999, Nov. 8). Suicide unlimited in Oregon: The result of legalizing physician-assisted suicide. *The Weekly Standard, 5* (8), 11–14.

Sullivan, A.D., Hedberg, K, & Fleming, D.W. (2000). Legalized physician-assisted suicide in Oregon—The second year. *New England Journal of Medicine, 342,* 598–604.

Sullivan, A.D., Hedberg, K., & Hopkins, D. (2001). Legalized physician-assisted suicide in Oregon, 1998–2000. *New England Journal of Medicine, 344,* 605–607.

Sullivan, M.D., Ganzini, L., & Youngner, S. J. (1998, Jul.–Aug.). Should psychiatrists serve as gatekeepers for physician-assisted suicide? *Hastings Center Report, 28*(4), 24–31.

U.S. Census Bureau, *Statistical abstract of the United States: 2000,* 120th ed. Washington, D.C.

CHAPTER 8

Insuring the Integrity of Informed Consent

Medical treatment involves very difficult experiences that most people do not wish to undergo. Doctors ordinarily avoid treating their own relatives and children because they may be swayed by the anticipated suffering into making the wrong decision. Just as it is hard to make a decision to put a relative into a painful situation, it is even harder to make this decision regarding yourself. The anticipated pain can override all the other considerations and short-circuit the decision-making process. In today's managed care environment, time to counsel the patient is often not available. The patient's decision may be guided by his irrational fears rather than by good information.

Highly skilled health counseling, liaison work, and emotional support is unfortunately necessary to get many people to do the difficult, scary things that they have to do to save their lives.

Massad (2000) wrote a touching piece in the *Journal of the American Medical Association* about his efforts to treat a woman's cancer. The patient "did not seem relieved" when he explained that her cancer was small and that she had an "excellent chance for cure." Instead, she just "shook" while he explained "treatment options" and cried when he asked for a decision. He told her to think it over and come back in a few days, but she failed to return. She "would not come to the telephone" when he called. Her daughter explained that her mother's friends had convinced her that cancer treatment just increases suffering. So she didn't return for immediate followup, as she was supposed to. Instead she simply waited until "her pain began to gnaw at her more intensely than her fear" and then returned for treatment. Her chances for being cured were no longer as good, but she endured her chemoradiotherapy and seemed "surprised" that her symptoms improved.

Massad discusses the lack of understanding, lack of resources, and lack of trust that keep some women from preventive care. Some women with a low educational level don't understand "what a cervix or a cell is." Some women won't schedule Pap smears because they can't afford child care or because they are in danger of losing their jobs if they "take time off." Some uninsured women, having been treated rudely, simply do not trust doctors. Massad describes how he tries to overcome this dangerous lack of trust and information by careful listening and explaining and relating. He particularly notes the difficulties of getting African-American patients to trust doctors (pp. 409–410).

Finkel and Rosman (1996), in a fascinating book chapter, describe a study in which "the American Medical Association sent a team of interviewers and investigators" to "provide a report" for a local coroner in a rural area where 6 people over the age of 60 committed suicide "in an 8-month period" (p. 88). Four out of the 6 had serious misconceptions about their illnesses and treatment. A 78-year-old man with emphysema and pneumonia who had required oxygen for the prior three weeks believed that "he needed rehospitalization" but his physician disagreed (p. 89). A 72-year-old-woman, after a successful masectomy, had an unrelated "bowel obstruction" that involved using a colostomy temporarily. She "believed that her physician and her husband were lying to her." She believed that she was really "dying of cancer" (p. 90). A 71-year-old man had "abdominal pain . . . for 4 months." He thought he had cancer and "refused to see his physician." The family urged him to see the doctor, but he "shot himself in the head." Autopsy showed that he had no cancer, only diverticulitis (p. 90). A 69-year-old woman with Parkinson's disease, although she was functioning very well, developed "a preoccupation that her life . . . was over." She talked about having "terminal Parkinson's disease" (p. 91).

Once, in a public psychiatric hospital, I worked with a woman whose initial checkup while in the hospital revealed a mass on her lung. She at first refused the recommended biopsy. Her communication skills were not good. English was not her native language, and she had been mentally ill for much of her life. Moreover, she spoke very softly, and it was difficult to hear her. I had to spend quite a few hours with her to help her communicate with her doctors, but it was rewarding. When I took the time to decipher what she was saying, I began to understand that she actually had some very intelligent questions. For example, she was worried that by piercing the mass with the biopsy needle the doctors would release cancer cells into her body. When I told them her question, they explained to me that there were actually medical studies on this very question. Fortunately, the studies had shown that there was no greater likelihood of tumors occurring in the path of the biopsy needle, as you might expect if her concerns were valid. When I explained these studies to her, she was reassured. Any residual anxiety was taken care of by the kindness of the medical staff. The psychiatrist, a very warm and kind woman, personally walked the patient into the medical wing of the hospital, holding her hand. Her malignant tumor was removed early enough to save her life, and she perceived herself as very fortunate that she had come into the psychiatric hospital and had a checkup just at the time she really needed one.

This kind of labor-intensive counseling, liaison work, and emotional support is necessary to help many people with the difficult, frightening things that they must do to save their own lives. Given the complexity of the human body and various medical treatments and possibilities, and given the reduced time that current physicians have to interact with patients, it should not be surprising that misunderstandings are common. Whether the patient underestimates or overestimates the dangerousness of his symptoms makes no difference—either way, he is in danger. A correct understanding of the medical significance of his condition is really critical for his health care.

The glorified rhetoric about patient autonomy as a solution to health care dilemmas has completely obscured the actual difficulties of informed patient consent and compliance. If indeed we are serious about the practicalities of helping patients to make good health care decisions, we should be gearing up for a tremendous educational effort.

Hall (1980) writes rather humorously about the incredible misconceptions that large numbers of patients have about the human back. For example, many patients believe that they have a "slipped disc" when there is really no such thing (p. 5). Many patients believe that their back has "gone out" when there is no physical reality to this concept (p. 5). Many people believe that an injury that occurred decades before their visit is responsible for their pain even though they had no pain until recently (p. 9). Some are afraid that the pain in their back is going to spread to the rest of their body (p. 10). Hall comments on this belief: "That would be a terrifying prospect if it were real" (p. 10).

Hall also comments that patients can become frightened because of their doctor's statements. For example, the doctor might say, "I can't help you," leaving the patient to think that he is a hopeless case, whereas what the doctor actually meant was, "I'm a surgeon—and you don't need surgery" (p. 21).

Mazzullo, Lasagna, and Griner (1974) discuss the surprising frequency of misinterpretation of instructions given with prescriptions. In their study, 67 patients were asked to interpret instructions on 10 prescription labels. There was no label that was consistently interpreted. The instruction to take medication "with meals" is often given with medications that should not be taken on an empty stomach. Unfortunately many patients thought this meant to take it some time before their meal. The use of the word "for" was also found to be confusing. Although patients easily understand that "for pain" means to reduce pain and "for sleep" means to increase sleep, when the word "for" was used in conjunction with something that they didn't know much about, they were confused by it. For example, many believed that a medication "for fluid retention" was to be taken when they needed to retain more fluids.

Eraker, Kirscht, and Becker (1984), in a comprehensive review of the literature on medical compliance, note the magnitude and pervasiveness of noncompliance as a problem in medical practice. Estimates of noncompliance for short-term medication range as high as 92%. Estimates for chronic conditions average about 50% (p. 259).

Eraker, Kirscht, and Becker point out that patients derive powerful but scientifically erroneous health beliefs from nonmedical sources such as cultural standards, parents' beliefs, and previous experience. They also misinterpret medical information. In order to counter these beliefs, the physician can provide information, but the process of convincing the patient to accept the information may involve turning to others that the patient finds more credible than the doctor, for example, to testimonials from other patients (p. 260).

Satisfaction with the doctor-patient relationship plays a large part in whether patients comply with medical advice. Factors such as impersonality, waiting time, and length of the session affect patient attitudes.

Efforts to improve patient compliance by devoting more time to patient education have been extremely promising. A study in which a group of physicians were given one to two hours of tutorials on compliance difficulties experienced by patients with hypertension resulted in the physicians spending a higher proportion of their time on patient education and resulted in better blood pressure control for patients of those physicians (Inui, Yourtee, & Williamson, 1976). Consultations with a pharmacist before patients left the hospital led to a 75% reduction in noncompliance (Eraker, Kirscht, & Becker, 1984, p. 263).

As physicians in managed care struggle to handle more patients and cut back on their patient education, it is clear that negative consequences in terms of greater patient noncompliance can only increase.

Also, since patient autonomy has become the predominant popular value in medical care, the question of compliance is no longer being framed in the same way. The principle of personal autonomy emphasizes that only the patient can decide whether the inconvenience of following the medical regimen is outweighed by the possible benefits or not.

However, we may still ask whether the patient truly understands the decision that he is asked to make. Does he really understand the benefits to be gained? Is he being given sufficient professional support to be able to carry through with a difficult, disagreeable regimen?

I was with an elderly relative in the hospital when the cardiologist came to see her. He suggested she should consider a transfer to a different hospital for an angiogram and possible angioplasty. After listening to his brief presentation, we had a very vivid impression that these procedures were risky for someone her age but very little idea of how likely it was that she might benefit. We were naturally terrified.

If not for our discussion with a second cardiologist, I doubt whether we could have summoned up the courage to go ahead with it. He described the angiogram as a low risk procedure that could yield valuable, and very possibly lifesaving, information that we really shouldn't be without, no matter which treatment strategy we were pursuing. He explained that even if she couldn't have a bypass, the information about which artery was blocked and to what extent would be valuable.

The third cardiologist, the one who did the angiogram and the successful angioplasty, told us that by opening up her arteries, he was going to improve her quality of life.

The very same procedure seemed aggressive to me during the first session, low risk and possibly life saving during the second, and palliative in the third.

After spending a number of hours on three separate days in a waiting room where cardiologists emerged and gave the families the results of the angiograms and angioplasty procedures that their relatives had gone through, I realized even more what a poor idea of the benefits I had gleaned from the conversation with the first cardiologist. We were apparently in a very distinguished heart institution where it wasn't at all a rare event to be able to open up an artery.

Each of the doctors contributed something to our understanding of the risks and benefits of her treatment. If we had stopped after talking to the first cardiologist, we would not have been sufficiently informed.

The concept of patient autonomy should be used as an ideal to inspire us to improve patient education and provide the extra expert consultations and the extra supports that help patients commit to and carry through on difficult medical regimens. It should not be used as an excuse to easily accept patient refusals, especially refusals in the absence of sufficient information and support.

Another time, I went with another elderly relative to another cardiologist. He presented the angiogram as low risk, and my relative agreed to do it. He commented that at her age, if she declined, he wouldn't argue with her. Thinking that this indicated some substantial risk at her age, I asked him why. He commented that an elderly person might find the procedure inconvenient, and since she had already had the opportunity to live a full life, she shouldn't be pressed.

When my relative heard him assuming that a person of her age might decline because they were done with trying to live, she jumped in and said, "but I want to live even longer."

I think this cardiologist was doing a great job of conveying respect to an older person and making sure that she understood that it might be dangerous not to find out more about her heart functioning—all without scaring her—but I wondered whether this idea that older people refuse treatment because they're not sufficiently interested in living longer could be an obstacle in patient-doctor communication for other physicians.

To me, this experience suggests that we need more research on the issue of why elderly people sometimes hesitate or decline procedures that might have helped them. Are they done with trying to live? Or are there other reasons? They may be declining because they are so used to declining anything that isn't part of their usual routine. They may be declining because they're afraid the procedure will kill them. They may think the doctor is mistaken. They may have difficulty believing that they need the procedure. They may think the doctor just recommends the procedure routinely whether or not it is needed. They may fear some aspect of the procedure. They may not understand the benefits. They may think that if they really needed it, the doctor would have ordered them to do it instead of asking them.

There are no standards for how much a patient needs to comprehend before making a decision. A doctor charting that he discussed certain options with the patient doesn't mean that the patient understood them.

So far, we have been discussing a patient making decisions to follow or not to follow specific instructions given by his physician about a specific medical condition that the patient already has.

Given the high rate of misunderstandings and poor decisions even under these ideal circumstances, let us now contemplate the likely quality of patient decision making when patients undertake to make decisions about a wide range of hypothetical medical interventions that might be suggested for the wide range of medical conditions that they might possibly develop in the future.

When someone applies for a driver's license, because of the potential lethality of the automobile, we require that he take a written test and a road test to insure that he knows how to handle a car safely. When patients write a living will, do we give them any test to see whether they understand the range of different medical uses for the life-sustaining equipment that they are saying that they don't ever want? Why not? Do we put them in touch with other patients who have been on life supports? Why not? Do we rule out medical phobias before we permit patients to make decisions about what treatments to undergo? Why not? Do we check to see whether the patient has been frightened by their own previous medical experiences or by the medical experiences of her friends or family? Why not?

Not only are patients likely to be overly frightened about medical treatments, unfortunately, they are also likely to be naive about the limitations of advance directives and living wills and the incredible difficulties that arise in trying to interpret these documents and the unnecessary deaths that have occurred because of these problems. Are patients required to be tested to see if they understand the risk they are taking in leaving such directives? Why not?

Let us first discuss some of the risks that patients take when they write living wills and then discuss the fears that drive them to write living wills in spite of these risks.

The International Anti-Euthanasia Task Force in Steubenville, Ohio, now changing its name to the International Task Force on Euthanasia and Assisted Suicide, has a fact sheet about living wills (1996) called "The Living Will: Just a Simple Declaration?" that explains some of the difficulties inherent in living wills.

A living will is "a signed, witnessed document" instructing a physician "to withhold or withdraw medical interventions from its signer if he or she is in a terminal condition and is unable to make decisions about medical treatment"

(p. 2). Unfortunately, most people are unaware of the incredibly wide range of ways in which a living will can be interpreted.

According to this fact sheet: " 'Terminal illness' is often defined as 'an incurable or irreversible condition that will cause death in a relatively short time' " (p. 3). But many incurable conditions can nevertheless be "controlled for many years," during which "productive life" is possible. A "relatively short time" can be interpreted as "days, weeks, months, or even years." According to some definitions, terminal illness could even include "severe arthritis" or "mental illness" (p. 3). Statements about death being "imminent" are equally ambiguous (p. 5).

The inability "to make medical decisions" is just as difficult to interpret. The "attending physician" decides whether the patient is able to make medical decisions. He or she is the one "responsible for the patient's care at a given moment," (p. 3) and he or she may not know the patient. Moreover there might be a few attending physicians in the course of a day, "any one of whom" (p. 4) might decide that the patient was incapable of making her own decisions.

The attending physician might decide that the patient is "unable to make decisions" for many reasons. The patient could have a "hearing impairment" that "causes difficulty" in communication. Or the patient might just be "under stress" or confused because of "a medication error." Unfortunately, the patient might be mistakenly deemed "unable to make decisions" simply because the patient is "disabled or elderly" (p. 3).

It is easy to find accounts about the difficulties of interpreting the patient's wishes from her oral or written statements made before her illness. Eisendrath and Jonsen (1983) present the case of a Mrs. T., a 65-year-old woman undergoing preventive surgery. She indicated that if she experienced "a severe and disabling stroke" her living will should be "carried out." The living will stated that if there was "no reasonable expectation of my recovery from physical or mental disability," she should be "allowed to die" (p. 2055). After her surgery, she did indeed have a stroke. She was responsive only to pain, and was receiving "assisted ventilation." When it is anticipated that a patient will be on a ventilator for a short time, the tube goes into her mouth. This is very uncomfortable and cannot be maintained for a long period. If it is anticipated that she will need assisted ventilation for a longer time, a tracheotomy is done, and the tube can be inserted into her neck instead. This is much more comfortable.

Mrs. T developed pneumonia and a tracheotomy was performed. At this point "certain staff members" began to question the continuation of treatment, given her living will. Even after her respiratory status improved somewhat, her brother became concerned about her neurologically impaired state and "implied that he might begin litigation" if she was "allowed to continue living" this way.

The ethics committee met and her "neurological status was meticulously reviewed." Psychiatric consultants concluded that her living will "had not been the result of any discernible psychiatric illness." The conclusion was that at this point her prognosis was uncertain. It was "impossible . . . to predict to what extent . . . the deterioration, dependence, and hopeless pain" that she was worried about would materialize. They followed the rule of "in cases of doubt, favor life."

Within ten days, Mrs. T once again "became capable of written and verbal communication". She "began speaking short phrases." Her "ability to speak" continued to improve dramatically. She was later "asked about . . . the living will." She felt that she had not been in a condition in which such a document should have been invoked. Even the brother who had threatened litigation wrote a thank-you "note to the medical . . . staff" stating he was "glad that the staff had stood firm in providing . . . maximal therapeutic efforts."

This case occurred in 1983. It was a very close call. Mrs. T. came close to dying because of her living will. She put herself in a situation where her life depended upon the quality of the ethics committee. It is not clear whether most ethics committees today continue the rule of favoring life in cases of doubt.

Wesley J. Smith gives several examples of patients who died because of their advance directives. He writes that "Martha Musgrave, a seventy-three-year-old woman . . . who in 1993 decided to undergo a hip replacement" signed an advance directive "along with the other usual admission documents." She evidently didn't think it was that important, because she usually talked over any "important decision" with her daughter, but she didn't mention the advance directive to her. She was doing well but then "suffered a cardiac arrest caused by an unexpected embolism." Because of her living will, "the staff assumed that . . . she wanted to die if faced with a grave medical condition." Even though the complication that she was suffering was treatable, they did nothing. They didn't even call her daughter until after she died (Smith, 1997, pp. 215–216).

A "nursing home resident" was the victim of a similar death. She was given "the wrong medication," but because she had a "living will instructing that she not be resuscitated," they "assumed she would not want to be treated" and let her die without telling her about "the mishap" or asking her whether she wanted treatment (p. 216).

Smith described the incident of Marjorie Nighbert, who had given her brother "the authority to make her health–care decisions." When she had a stroke, she was having trouble learning "the techniques used by stroke patients to eat and drink." To prevent aspiration, the doctors placed "a gastronomy (feeding) tube in her abdomen." She had "stated in conversations that she would not want to use a feeding tube," so he felt compelled to have it removed, even though she wasn't terminally ill. Even after twenty days, she hadn't died. The staff was "sneaking food to her." She was verbally requesting food and water. In spite of this evidence that she didn't wish to die, her "temporary guardian" felt she didn't "have the capacity to revoke her advance medical directive" and the judge "ordered the starvation to continue." Her brother was "emotionally distraught" (Smith, 1997, pp. 216–218).

Macklin (1993, pp. 4–6) also gives an example of a patient with a "treatable illness" who died because of an advance directive. A 97-year-old woman who had been very independent had had some "difficulty in swallowing" for the past two years, and "her nutritional status became compromised." Then she got pneumonia and was hospitalized. The medical staff suggested giving her "artificial nutrition" through a tube "inserted into her nose . . . or else through a catheter . . . in her neck." The improved nutrition would help her fight off the pneumonia. Because she was so ill with the infection, it was not possible to communicate with her. Her children, however, refused the feeding tube because their mother "had signed a living will" and told them about it 11 years earlier refusing " 'heroic measures or invasive procedures' to prolong her life" in case of a "terminal illness." At the "medical conference," the doctor was concerned about "the interns and residents" who would feel guilty for not feeding this woman. They were extremely frustrated at not being allowed to treat a "treatable illness" in an otherwise functioning person. The patient had stated in her living will that she did not want "heroic measures." Macklin writes, "This points to a classic problem that has plagued the traditional living will. Is a feeding tube a heroic measure . . . ?" (p. 6).

Macklin points out clear questions that could be asked about the application of her document to the situation. Was a nasogastric feeding tube "heroic?" Was her condition a "terminal illness?"

Macklin concluded that it was proper to honor her directive and let her die. But one wonders why they didn't put in the feeding tube, treat the infection, and, if she survived, then ask her what to do.

Rita Marker tells an amazing story about how in different circumstances, people take different positions on the issue of whether a feeding tube is "heroic" or not (Marker, 1993, pp. 88–89). Mary Hier was a 92-year-old woman with no physical illness except that she had needed a feeding tube for years. She had, however, been "in mental institutions for more than half of her life" and believed "that she was the Queen of England." When this "tube became dislodged" and needed to be replaced, "a Massachusetts court ruled that" having the feeding tube reinserted was a "highly intrusive and risky procedure" that she "would have refused if she were competent." In "the same newspaper" there was a story about a 94-year-old woman, Rose Kennedy, who had "minor surgery to correct a nutritional problem." These two women needed the same surgery, but for one, it was described as "minor." For the other it was described as "highly risky." Fortunately, other people intervened on Mary Hier's behalf and the feeding tube was reinserted, and she lived for years, still believing that she was the Queen of England.

Unfortunately there are certain medical procedures—the insertion of feeding tubes and respirators—which over and over again trigger these same conflicts.

What is it about these procedures that is so terrifying that people would rather die than undergo them? Are these fears rational or not? Are these procedures really worthy of the terror that they inspire? Could it be that in our culture, so infatuated with independence, we are overly frightened of procedures that leave a person in a clearly dependent state?

There are already many recognized phobias related to physical illness and medical treatment; for example, injection phobia, cancer phobia, hospital phobia, and dontophobia. Normally with phobias, we do not stop to argue about whether the patient's choice to avoid the feared situation at all cost is a manifestation of personal autonomy. We design treatments to help the sufferers of these phobias return to everyday life.

What if a new fear arises in our society about which we have no tradition? Wouldn't it make sense to have some discussion of whether or not the fear should be considered a phobia?

Are people who sign advance directives requesting that they be allowed to die rather than be put on life supports aware that in recent years, there have been prominent examples of people who managed to continue many worthwhile activities even while they were dependent upon a respirator? Senator Jacob Javits, in his later years, continued to practice law and make public appearances using a respirator (*Life sustaining technologies*, 1987, pp. 223–224). More recently, Christopher Reeve, a well-known actor, best known for his portrayal of Superman, has made many public appearances with his respirator. He is a highly paid public speaker, inspiring many people, and he has raised millions of dollars for neurological research (Jenish & Novak, 1999). Research findings indicate that 87% of patients with muscular dystrophy who are ventilator-dependent report positive emotions and life satisfaction (Bach, Campagnolo, & Hoeman, 1991)

Stephen Hawking is yet another example. Hawking is a physicist who suffers from amyotrophic lateral sclerosis (ALS). Although he has used a respirator since 1985, he has continued to write books and scientific papers and give presentations. He has a computer program that can be controlled by head or eye movement. He can write what he wants to say and then send it to a speech synthesizer. He said:

Using this system, I have written a book, and dozens of scientific papers. I have also given many scientific and popular talks. They have all been well received. I think that is in a large part due to the quality of the speech synthesizer. . . . The only trouble is that it gives me an American accent. However, the company is working on a British version. . . . I have had motor neurone disease for practically all of my adult life. Yet it has not prevented me from having a very attractive family, and being successful in my work. . . . I have been lucky, that my condition has progressed more slowly than is often the case. But it shows that one need not lose hope. (Hawking)

Abramson (1996), cited in Binner and Klinkenberg (1998), tells of an ALS patient, Lance, whose achievements were also extraordinary. Abramson, who had known Lance when he was a medical intern, was visited by Lance and his wife years later, after Lance had been suffering from ALS. Abramson writes:

When I saw Lance I barely recognized him. He was propped up in a wheelchair, markedly wasted, his arms were strapped to the sides, and a ventilator was supplying oxygen . . .

he was unable to greet me with a handshake, a smile, or a nod of his head. . . . I was astonished to learn that his life was rich. He worked actively and fully almost every day as an emergency room physician. He explained that he had lost use of his muscles, but his brain functioned perfectly well. He was able to process the histories and physical examinations performed by nurse practitioners, arrive at a diagnosis, and then provide therapy through his nurse assistants. . . . Lance faithfully read all current medical literature assisted by equipment that turned pages. (Binner & Klinkenberg, 1998, p. 8)

Interestingly enough, earlier in his life, Lance had said, "Never let them tube me. I wouldn't want to live if I was restricted in any way" (pp. 7–8). Later on, of course, he changed his mind (p. 8).

Are people who sign advance directives given information about the risks of signing advance directives and about the ability of patients on life supports to adapt to these supports? Why not?

Guardians also may be influenced in their medical decisions by lack of understanding, personal experiences, and medical phobias. Robert Wendland's wife, in a television interview, used the term "brain dead" to describe him, even though he could throw a ball and engage in other activities. By doing so she clearly demonstrated a lack of understanding of certain important medical concepts.

Some guardians assume that there is no possibility of improvement for a patient in a persistent vegetative state. Are guardians aware of how often this condition is misdiagnosed? Many patients, as many as 38% or 42% (Andrews, Murphy, Munday, & Littlewood, 1996; Childs, Mercer, & Childs, 1993), are actually visibly responsive, which means that they can communicate using small movements of the eyes, shoulders, or fingers.

Are guardians aware that even those patients who are indeed in a persistent vegetative state have a chance for improvement? Andrews, Murphy, Munday, and Littlewood (1996) found that of 23 patients who were indeed in a persistent vegetative state, 13 eventually came out of this state and only 10 remained vegetative. Levin et al. (1991) report that out of 84 patients in a vegetative state for whom follow-up data was available, 41% became conscious by six months, 52% by one year, and 58% within three years. Childs and Mercer (1996) conclude from this data that even after one year, the incidence of improvement is 14%. Even patients still in the vegetative state have been shown to have some covert cognitive processing that can be studied with positron emission tomography (Menon et al., 1998).

Are guardians required to demonstrate competence or knowledge about the consequences of agreeing to or refusing the medical treatments they are considering? Why not?

REFERENCES

Abramson, N. (1996). Quality of life: Who can make the judgment? *The American Journal of Medicine, 100*, 365–366.

Andrews, K., Murphy, L., Munday, R., & Littlewood, C. (1996). Misdiagnosis of the vegetative state: Retrospective study in a rehabilitation unit. *British Medical Journal, 313*, 13–16.

Bach, J.R., Campagnolo, D.I., & Hoeman, S. (1991). Life satisfaction of individuals with Duchenne Muscular Dystrophy using long-term mechanical ventilator support. *American Journal of Physical Medicine and Rehabilitation, 70* (3), 129–135.

Binner, P.R., & Klinkenberg, D. (1998). *Quality of life: Meaning and measurement: A report prepared for the Department of Mental Health Outcome Coordinating Office*. St. Louis: Missouri Institute of Mental Health.

Childs, N.L., & Mercer, W.N. (1996). Brief report: Late improvement in consciousness after post-traumatic vegetative state. *New England Journal of Medicine, 334*, 24–25.

Childs, N.L., Mercer, W.N., & Childs, H.W. (1993). Accuracy of diagnosis of persistent vegetative state. *Neurology, 43*, 1465–1470.

Eisendrath, S.J., & Jonsen, A.R. (1983). The living will: Help or hindrance? *Journal of the American Medical Association, 249*, 2054–2058.

Eraker, S.A., Kirscht, J.P., & Becker, M.H. (1984). Understanding and improving patient compliance. *Annals of Internal Medicine, 100*, 258–268.

Finkel, S.I., & Rosman, M. (1996). Six elderly suicides in a 1-year period in a rural Midwestern community. In J.L. Pearson & Y. Conwell (Eds.), *Suicide and Aging: International Perspectives* (pp. 87–96). New York: Springer.

Hall, H. (1980). *The back doctor: Ten minutes a day to lifetime relief for your aching back*. New York: Berkley books.

Hawking, S., www.hawking.org.uk/text/disable/disable.html.

Inui, T.S., Yourtee, E.L., & Williamson, J.W. (1976). Improved outcomes in hypertension after physician tutorials: A controlled trial. *Annals of Internal Medicine, 84*, 646–651.

Jenish, D., & Novak, P. (1999, Jun. 7). Man of steely determination. *MacLean's*, p. 61.

Levin, H.S., Saydjari, C., Eisenberg, H.M., Foulkes, M., Marshall, L.F., Ruff, R.M., Jane, J.A., & Marmarou, A. (1991). Vegetative state after closed-head injury: A traumatic coma data bank report. *Archives of Neurology, 48*, 580–585.

Life sustaining technologies and the elderly. (1987). Office of Technology Assessment. U.S. Congress. The living will: Just a simple declaration? (1996). International Task Force on Euthanasia and Assisted Suicide, P.O. Box 760, Steubenville, OH, 43952.

Macklin, R. (1993). *Enemies of patients*. New York: Oxford University Press.

Marker, R. (1993). *Deadly Compassion: The death of Ann Humphry and the truth about euthanasia*. New York: William Morrow and Company.

Massad, L.S. (2000). Missed connections. *Journal of the American Medical Association, 284*, 409–410.

Mazzullo, J.M., Lasagna, L., & Griner, P.F. (1974). Variations in interpretation of prescription instructions: The need for improved prescribing habits. *Journal of the American Medical Association, 227* (8), 929–931.

Menon, D.K., Owen, A.M., Williams, E.J., Minhas, P.S., Allen, C.M.C., Boniface, S.J., Pickard, J.D., & the Wolfson Brain Imaging Centre Team. (1998). Cortical processing in persistent vegetative state. *Lancet, 325*, 200.

Smith, W.J. (1997). *Forced exit: The slippery slope from assisted suicide to legalized murder*. New York: Times Books.

CHAPTER 9

Promoting Palliative Care in Medicine and Mental Health

The movement to permit physician-assisted suicide and euthanasia has called our attention to the subjective comfort of the critically ill. It has become apparent that for a variety of reasons, the alleviation of pain and suffering has sometimes not been a priority for physicians. Nor has it become routine to call in mental health professionals for medically ill patients who are in distress.

Although many people have envisioned a great cooperation between medicine and the mental health professions, this cooperation has yet to be established. It is now needed more than ever, because new medical treatments push patients to their psychological limits and cause them to undergo psychiatric symptoms that are often not recognized or treated. Psychological weaknesses cause otherwise normal people to fail in the difficult endeavor of maintaining their health and treating their illnesses, an area of life in which they may face tasks more difficult than in any other area.

Perhaps in the next few decades, we will have more success in building this important alliance. In medicine, there is now a growing recognition that it is critical to maintain patients' alertness and cooperation and focus on their subjective comfort and that it is critical to maintain communication with the family. In the mental health field, cognitive techniques, which are effective, feasible in a medical setting, easily understandable, not stressful, not stigmatizing, and time limited are more readily available. Given these changes in both professions, we may now have a chance to establish a much wider range of cooperation between medicine and the mental health professions than has ever existed before.

In medicine, the realization that subjective experiences of the patient are critical is beginning to effect changes in medical practice. Until now, according to Perry G. Fine, M.D., medical schools have spent little time on pain management and encouraged residents to attend to other things instead. Pain control was not regarded as credible or respected since it involved getting into the "pool of suffering" rather than maintaining objectivity (Phillips, 2000, pp. 428–429).

Patients, when they are ill, can describe their symptoms in very misleading terms. Medical personnel need to plan their treatment according to the correct diagnosis, not the patient's report. The patient's reports about pain are among the most subjective data that doctors have to handle. Patients with the very same illness range widely in the amount of discomfort that they report. Moreover, even with the same level of discomfort, some patients tolerate it very well while others become obsessed with their sensations. It is perhaps for this reason, that the medical community has only recently begun a major effort to alert medical staff to the pain of the patient.

Moreover, poor pain management has, in the past, been attributed to doctors' fears of causing addiction in the patient and also doctors' fears of prosecution for the overuse of narcotics.

Fortunately, however, many investigators believe that pain control can be achieved for almost all patients, even for terminally ill cancer patients (Levy, 1996).

Cundiff, a physician who studied in English hospices in 1979, writes, "Most practicing physicians in the United States have not seen first-rate cancer pain management and the optimal control of the physical symptoms of cancer and AIDS. Like me before my hospice tour, *they don't know that they don't know how to do it*" (Cundiff, 1992). Hendin (1997) gives beautiful case examples of how pain and suffering in terminal patients can be alleviated (pp. 206–208, 210–211).

There have been several recent attempts to call the attention of physicians to the patient's pain. There was an almost successful attempt to pass national legislation to make it clear that pain is a legitimate purpose for prescribing narcotics. Moreover, the Joint Commission on Accreditation of Healthcare Organizations is shifting its "pain management paradigm" to encourage adequate pain control. Pain management will become a "patient rights issue," and also an "education and training issue." Quantitative aspects of pain will be systematically assessed on a 10-point scale. As designated by the Department of Veterans Affairs, pain should be regarded as the "fifth vital sign," monitored along with "blood pressure, pulse, temperature, and respiratory rate" (Phillips, 2000, p. 428).

New pain management guidelines that went into effect in January 2001 emphasize an "interdisciplinary approach, individualized pain control plans, . . . frequent reassessment of pain, use of pharmacologic and nonpharmacologic strategies" (p. 429). Pain assessment is incorporated into recommended procedures and goals. Patients receive education about pain management. Pain management is addressed in the discharge planning process, and incorporated "into the organization's performance measurement" (Phillips, 2000, p. 429). About 20 percent of hospitals now have some sort of palliative care program, and the American Board of Hospice and Palliative Medicine is certifying physicians in the specialty of hospice and palliative medicine (Adams, 2001).

As medicine reaches for higher standards regarding the patient's subjective comfort, this may create an opportunity for the mental health professions to make great contributions in the area of health care. I would like to briefly touch on just a few of the many areas in which our future mental health research and practice may have great practical implications for medicine.

One way in which we can contribute is to learn more about the treatment of psychiatric symptoms that arise in normal people during medical treatment. An example would be a common phenomenon, well known on the intensive care unit (ICU) which ICU employees call *ICU psychosis.*

Easton and MacKenzie (1988) report that ICU psychosis is a reversible, confusional state that usually occurs between the third and seventh day on an ICU and generally disappears within 48 hours after discharge. They report that 12.5–38% of conscious patients experience this phenomenon. In their own sample of 10 patients, 50%, or 5 patients, recalled that they thought they were going crazy. They responded hesitantly for fear of being labelled mentally ill, and they thought they were the only ones to experience this problem. The patients reported 27 delirious experiences, of which only one was pleasant—most were scary, terrifying, or very frightening. For example, one patient reported that he thought he was in a supermarket, tied inside a playpen. He tried to get attention, but he was ignored. Another believed that the ICU was a "front for dealing drugs" and they were trying to make him part of "a drug ring."

Even higher rates of ICU psychosis have been reported. In a study of 25 trauma patients in an ICU, 22 felt as if they were being "held prisoner" and 14 remembered "feeling that they were trying to escape" (Schnaper & Cowley, 1976, p. 886). Freyhan, Gianelli, O'Connell, and Mayo (1971) reported that 51% of open heart surgery patients had "psychiatric complications" (p. 186).

One can only imagine the feelings of the family as they witness the distress of these patients. If they survive the intensive care unit and go home, possibly they tell the family later about their delirious experiences, but possibly not. If they don't tell, or if they die and no one ever hears about it, the family might attribute some of the terror that they witnessed to the medical procedures. They think that the patient is upset about all of the pain and all of the tubes; whereas, instead, he might be upset because he thinks he has been captured by terrorists. It's amazing to think that the patient would actually be much less upset if he realized that he was seriously ill, possibly dying, and being treated in an intensive care unit.

A few decades ago, however, a number of hopeful articles were written. Lazarus and Hagens (1968) reported a research investigation in which preventive strategies were followed at one hospital but not at another. A "psychiatrist became a member of the team" (p. 1191) at Milwaukee County General Hospital. Each patient had an interview two to three days before surgery. In this session, the psychiatrist reviewed the patient's view of his illness, corrected any misconceptions if he could do so in a therapeutic way, and found out "how the patient was dealing with" his anxiety about his current symptoms and his "reaction to the prospect of surgery" and the future. He checked for depression and got information about "characteristic modes of handling anxiety" . . . "any psychiatric history," and his, "current life situation" (p. 1192). He tried to "help the patient realistically appraise the situation and strengthen his confidence in the hospital and the physician's treating him" (p. 11). He made himself available to the patient and also made a social worker available for the family.

Moreover, the nurses were given a completely different set of instructions from those they usually followed. Apparently the nurses "had assumed" that it was better not to converse with the patients because they were "so uncomfortable." The psychiatrist encouraged them, instead, to rapidly "establish . . . a positive, supportive," relation with the patient to help reestablish "reality, identity, and self-esteem." They were to make sure the patient knew the time and what was going on and to avoid interrupting his sleep (p. 1192).

Although "11 out of 33" patients in the control group experienced psychiatric reactions, in the experimental group, only 3 out of 21 did (p. 1192). Of these three cases, one was "a chronic schizophrenic," one had neurological problems, and the third, because of scheduling problems, didn't have the initial interview with the psychiatrist (1193).

Lipowski (1974) expands upon the idea of the liaison psychiatrist, an idea that had not yet come into practice at the time he wrote the article and, I believe, is still not established as the norm.

In spite of this hopefulness in the literature a few decades ago, the high rates of ICU reactions have probably remained stable. The most recent edition of the *Diagnostic and Statistical Manual of Mental Disorders* (2000) reports that "the point prevalence of delirium in the hospitalized medically ill ranges from 10% to 30%. In the hospitalized elderly, about 10% to 15% are reported to exhibit delirium on admission and 10% to 40% may be diagnosed with delirium while in the hospital. . . . Up to 80% of those with terminal illness develop delirium near death" (*Diagnostic and statistical*, 2000, p. 138).

It is fascinating that the symptoms that often cause this whole problem of health care surrogates are often psychiatric symptoms rather than medical symptoms. A delirious patient, or a patient sedated because of delirium, cannot make decisions.

Boland, Goldstein, and Haltzman (2000) believe that the term "ICU psychosis" is misleading, because it suggests that confusion in the ICU is inevitable. This idea can "delay proper medical attention" (p. 300). The treatment for delirium, they emphasize, is to "identify and then treat the underlying cause" (p. 300).

The "most common cause of delirium" is medications (p. 300). The authors recommend that when at all possible, medication should be switched to one that is "less lipophilic (therefore less penetrating into the brain)" (p. 300). If a medication must be given, it should be given at the smallest dose that is effective ". . . determined either through clinical titration or through the use of serum drug levels" (p. 300).

Boland, Goldstein, and Haltzman also point out that patients can be screened to identify those most likely to suffer delirium and be treated prophylactically (p. 302). High-risk patients can be seen right "after surgery (. . . before problems develop)" (p. 303), and that neuroleptics are very effective in treating delirium. They also mention environmental influences such as having a window in the room, which apparently cuts the rate of delirium in half by helping the patient to distinguish between day and night (p. 303).

Other nonpharmacologic methods of managing patients to reduce delirium suggested by Boland, Goldstein, and Haltzman include having a clock in the room, offering explanations, restraining the patient as little as possible, controlling pain, showing empathy, and enhancing communication. They cite a study by Stovsky, Rudy, and Dragonette (1988), in which it was shown that "patient satisfaction" after cardiac surgery could be enhanced by showing the patient a "communication board" that they would be able to use after surgery when they would be unable to speak because of endotracheal tubes (Boland, Goldstein and Haltzman, 2000, p. 308). The board had pictures and captions such as "I am cold," "I am hot," "Raise my head," "I have to urinate," "What time is it?" and "Where is my family?" (Stovsky, Rudy, and Dragonette, 1988, p. 283).

Shuster, Chochinov, and Greenberg (2000) also point out that careful attention to delirium can be very productive. They say that it is a "challenge to overcome therapeutic nihilism" (p. 321). They emphasize that "As many as one-third of cases of delirium seen in the terminally ill are reversible" (p. 321). Given this information, it is unfortunate that "The stigma associated with psychiatric evaluations or the assignment of a psychiatric diagnosis inhibits the use of psychiatric services even in hospice settings" (p. 317).

They also point out that a lot can be done for the family:

. . . the distress experienced by the family of an agitated, delirious patient is usually obvious. Family education, including an explanation of the process of delirium in layman's terms, a description of the planned interventions, and an explanation of how the symptoms of delirium are related to the underlying terminal illness can provide great relief to the family. (p. 321)

There is every reason to believe that if we improve our monitoring of medication dosages that cause delirium, improve patient and family education, explore techniques of maintaining continuous communication with the patient, explore extensively which aspects of the ICU experience have the most impact on the patient's emotional state, and experiment with greater flexibility in the

ICU to the patient's emotional state, we may be successful in maintaining much greater patient comfort and true cooperation between doctor and patient.

Of all of the painful aspects of being in an ICU, some affect emotional state more than others. There is reason to believe that immobilization in particular can cause psychotic reactions. Mendelson and Foley (1958) and Mendelson, Solomon, and Lindemann (1958) report the phenomenon of vivid hallucinations in polio patients immobilized in respirators. Furthermore, in the literature on sensory deprivation, it was found that immobilization and prolonged recumbency can elicit hallucinatory experiences, even when the subjects are not deprived of visual and auditory stimuli or social contact (Zubek, Aftanas, Kovach, Wilgosh, & Winocur, 1963; Zubek & MacNeill, 1966; Zubek & MacNeill, 1967).

It is not surprising that keeping patients mobile might have clinical applicability. Commenting on a special ward for Acute Care for the Elderly at Barnes-Jewish hospital, Maria Carroll, a geriatric nurse, said, "We frown on bed rest for our patients . . . it's important to keep people moving . . . older patients tend to have less confusion when they are stimulated" (Elderly patients, 2000).

Continued research on these kinds of issues, isolating the factors that are critical to well-being, will do much to dispel the attitude that medical treatment and patient comfort are incompatible goals.

Another way we can contribute is by exploring new ways of providing preventive mental health treatment for the kinds of patients who, if untreated, would cause difficulties in medical facilities.

There are many patients who have enduring psychiatric conditions who are, nevertheless, not welcome at mental health facilities. Although their functioning in the outside world is notably poor and although they make repeated attempts to enter inpatient mental health facilities, they are rejected. The first reason for rejection is a practical one. The patients do not meet the criterion for admission that has become so common in our current budgetary drought—they are not immediately dangerous to themselves or others. The second reason is more theoretical. The patients do not have disorders that can be treated with medication, so they are not considered to be in need of inpatient treatment.

How ironic it is that even though an important goal of mental health treatment is subjective comfort, the palliation of emotional discomfort has not been a goal for mental health treatment any more than it has been for medicine! I have felt this most keenly as a psychologist working with nonpsychotic psychiatric inpatients. These patients had often suffered intense psychological discomfort, and although they were not expected to have major benefits from medication, they often felt relief when they were treated with supportive psychotherapy and other services, such as occupational therapy, available at mental health facilities. However, these patients, when repeatedly discharged, caused much trouble in the community, doing anything from breaking the rules at homeless shelters to jumping from bridges.

This gap in the mission of mental health treatment has not just caused problems in the community. It has actually caused problems for medicine as well, because when these kinds of patients are rejected from mental health facilities they end up in medical facilities, where they cause sufficient stress and confusion to put considerable pressure on the sagging ethical infrastructure in our hospital wards.

For example, we once treated a patient who had, over the years, repeatedly pretended to be retarded and been admitted to various facilities for the retarded and had then been ejected and sent to mental health facilities. Wherever he went, he always had an extensive workup for his congenital nystagmus and extensive new reports were written about his ever-lengthening psychiatric history.

Like many of the patients who carry on this kind of pattern with medical personnel, his story was long and fascinating. It would indeed be difficult to justify keeping such an individual for longer therapy in the hopes of curing his psychiatric condition; however, as palliative therapy, it would be extremely critical. These kinds of patients suffer terribly when they are turned out of one psychiatric facility after another. Each time this happens, their grudges are enhanced. With a palliative focus in mind, we might adopt a different goal of simply making this patient feel better for a while.

When a patient discovers that he can feel pretty decently for a period of time, he learns how to keep it up. Cognitive goals and palliative goals are highly compatible.

I believe that when we forcibly and repeatedly reject suffering patients whose conditions we cannot correct and don't accept the goal of palliation as a legitimate focus at our mental health treatment facilities, we are disappointing the taxpayer as well as the patient. The taxpayer isn't just concerned about psychiatric patients whose diagnoses are found in our manuals and who can be helped with medication. They want our help with all those mixed-up and miserable individuals who complicate life in our communities. Out of compassion, they often try to help these people on a personal basis. They often fail at this endeavor, and they want somewhere safe where they can bring the patient for more help.

Macklin (1993, pp. 106–107) gives an example of "an 18-year-old boy with end-stage kidney failure" who would go off of his "prescribed diet" by eating "bags of potato chips followed by quantities of coca-cola and beer," skip his "dialysis session," and then be brought to the emergency ward unconscious by "a friend or relative." The nurses on the medical ward raised the issue of commitment to a psychiatric ward, but the "consulting psychiatrist" found no basis for this.

The position of the consulting psychiatrist does not stand up to reflection. His position was that commitment was not justified because the patient wasn't suicidal. The patient wanted "to continue living"; he simply didn't think he was in danger, because people had rescued him in the past, and he believed they would continue to do so.

This response from the psychiatrist did not help the medical team at all. The implication that the patient will learn his lesson by not being rescued is non-sensical, because he would die.

The medical staff, understandably angry, wondered if they could "refuse . . . to provide dialysis" to him, but they decided to continue. However, this case caused them to develop an argument that justified refusing life-saving treatment.

Macklin gives other similar examples as well. In one case, a man who had been alcoholic for 30 years was refused admission to an intensive care unit even though a specialist said his "condition might be reversible" and needed "a full evaluation" in intensive care (pp. 118–119). He was referred three times and refused three times.

Macklin also discusses refusal of heart surgery to drug abusers who reinfect their heart valves over and over again because of their drug usage. The medical staff feel pushed to the position that these patients shouldn't be treated (pp. 119–120).

These kinds of struggles cause some medical personnel to elaborate and to harden their positions about refusing treatment. In turn, these positions may hurt other patients.

The refusal of mental health facilities to provide treatment for psychiatric conditions which seem intractable may be reconsidered in the light of the idea of palliative care. With our current insistence on a curative focus, we usually make the following mistake. We ask how many years of intensive psychotherapy or inpatient rehabilitation it would it take before an addict or an impulsive or self-destructive personality could be turned into a model citizen. Then we decide that this is impossible and we provide the barest minimum medical maintenance and case management.

With the new palliative focus, we could ask an entirely different question. What ongoing supports could we provide to keep these people happier? Just as we are recognizing that pain control is a legitimate medical need, we can recognize that feeling happier is a legitimate psychiatric need. Can we keep our disabled people happier so they won't make themselves so sick and wreak havoc in our medical facilities?

When I first started as a psychology intern, there were indeed patients on the ward who were mentally ill but had been committed not because of their mental illness but because they failed to follow their prescribed diet and had uncontrolled diabetes or other conditions. The justification for their commitment was that they were unable to care for themselves. They often were very grateful for the care that they received. Once their medical condition was under control, their mental status improved enough for them to learn more about how to take care of themselves or to be referred to a group home. I believe that these were worthy and life-saving interventions. I hope that the new focus on patient autonomy doesn't prevent commitment of such patients.

A new kind of focus on palliative care in both medicine and mental health with a generous combination of patient education and cognitive support would go far to help individuals afflicted with various combinations of medical and psychiatric symptoms. For those who are worried about expenses, I think the savings from such a focus would be substantial. When inappropriate constraints are put on medical personnel, forcing them to reject obviously distressed people, the inevitable consequence is that medical staff have to spend a considerable amount of their paid work time arguing with each other about which patient to reject. Far from being a sign that modern life is just so complex and difficult, it is, rather, a sign that we have set people up to struggle with each other and we are paying both sides to argue for most of the day. In my opinion, the greatest number of wasted health care dollars are spent on these arguments. If, instead of trying to avoid the work of taking care of our sick, we commit ourselves to it generously and use good patient education and cognitive support and organize our facilities to do more instead of less, we will inevitably begin to reap and to accumulate benefits of decreased conflict and stress and increased health.

Needless to say, there are many other areas of research that may also bear fruit in terms of alleviating the desperation felt by doctors, patients and families. The devotion of our time and energy to the interface between medicine and mental health will not be in vain. If we make the efforts to do research in this area and to establish the partnerships that we need to establish to pursue our findings and translate them into practical reality, we will be rewarded with a medical system that will be vastly more powerful in bringing health.

REFERENCES

Adams, D. (2001, Aug. 20). Movement toward collaboration in clinical palliative care. *American Medical News, 44*(31), p. 26.

Boland, R.J., Goldstein, M.G., & Haltzman, S.D. (2000). Psychiatric management of behavioral syndromes in intensive care units. In A. Stoudemire, B.S. Fogel, & D.G. Greenberg (Eds.), *Psychiatric care of the medical patient*, 2nd ed. (pp. 299–314). New York: Oxford University Press.

Chevlen, E.M., & Smith, W.J. (2002). *Power over pain: How to get the pain control you need.* Steubenville, OH: International Task Force.

Cundiff, D. (1992). *Euthanasia is not the answer: A hospice physician's view.* Totowa, NJ: Humana Press.

Diagnostic and Statistical Manual of Mental Disorders—Text Revision. DSM-IV-TR. (2000). Washington, DC: American Psychiatric Association.

Easton C., & MacKenzie F. (1988). Sensory-perceptual alterations: Delirium in the intensive care unit. *Heart and Lung, 17,* 229–235.

Elderly patients deserve special treatment. (2000, Autumn). *To Your Health!* (pp. 2, 8). Barnes-Jewish Hospital.

Freyhan, F.A., Gianelli, S., Jr., O'Connell, R.A., & Mayo, J.A. (1971). Psychiatric complications following open-heart surgery. *Comprehensive Psychiatry, 12,* 181–195.

Hendin, H. (1997). *Seduced by death: Doctors, patients, and the Dutch cure.* New York: W.W. Norton.

Lazarus, H.R., & Hagens, J.H. (1968). Prevention of psychosis following open-heart surgery. *American Journal of Psychiatry, 124,* 1190–1195.

Levy, M.H. (1996). Pharmacologic treatment of cancer pain. *New England Journal of Medicine, 335,* 1124–1132.

Lipowski, Z.J. (1974). Consultation-liaison psychiatry: An overview. *American Journal of Psychiatry, 131*: 623–630.

Macklin, R. (1993). *Enemies of Patients.* New York: Oxford University Press.

Mendelson, J., Solomon, P., & Lindemann, E. (1958). Hallucinations of poliomyelitis patients during treatment in a respirator. *Journal of Nervous and Mental Disease, 126,* 421–428.

Mendelson, J.H., & Foley, J.M. (1958). An abnormality of mental function affecting patients with poliomyelitis in a tank-type respirator. *Transactions of the American Neurological Association, 81,* 134–138.

Phillips, D.M. (2000). JCAHO pain management standards are unveiled. *Journal of the American Medical Association, 284,* 428–429.

Schnaper, N., & Cowley, R.A. (1976). Overview: Psychiatric sequelae to multiple trauma. *American Journal of Psychiatry, 133,* 883–890.

Shuster, J.L., Chochinov, H.M., & Greenberg, D.B. (2000). Psychiatric aspects and psychopharmacologic strategies in palliative care. In A. Stoudemire, B.S. Fogel, & D.G. Greenberg (Eds.), *Psychiatric care of the medical patient,* 2nd ed. (pp. 315–327). New York: Oxford University Press.

Stovsky, B., Rudy, E., & Dragonette, P. (1988). Comparison of two types of communication used after cardiac surgery with patients with endotracheal tubes. *Heart & Lung, 17,* 281–289.

Ulett, G.A. & Han, S.P. (2002). *The biology of acupuncture.* St. Louis, MO: Warren H. Green, Inc.

Zubek, J.P., Aftanas, M., Kovach, K., Wilgosh, L., & Winocur, G. (1963). Effect of severe immobilization of the body on intellectual and perceptual processes. *Canadian Journal of Psychology, 17,* 118–133.

Zubek, J.P., & MacNeill, M. (1966). Effects of immobilization: Behavioral and EEG changes. *Canadian Journal of Psychology, 20,* 316–336.

Zubek, J.P., & MacNeill, M. (1967). Perceptual deprivation phenomena: Role of the recumbent position. *Journal of Abnormal Psychology, 72,* 147–150.

CHAPTER 10

Taking a Personal Position against Physician-Assisted Suicide

Given that the currently underground practice of physician-assisted suicide is a threat to the lives of our patients and given that the rhetoric of the movement—such as the myth that, as a suicidal woman, Martha Wichorek, put it, there is a stage of life called "miserable existence," when you cannot do anything for yourself or others (Kaplan & Leonhardi, 2000, p. 268)—is a threat to the psychological health of the general public, one might expect that the mental health professions would display a strong negative reaction to physician-assisted suicide.

Society has not called upon the mental health professions to handle this matter except in a very limited and extremely frustrating way. We are not being asked whether it is true that there is a stage of life that is purely miserable. We are not being asked how to enhance the lives of the physically ill or the cognitively impaired. We are not being asked to do more for the untreated mentally ill. We are asked, instead, to relieve the guilt of society by giving them the assurance that we have identified certain limited categories of patients who will not be permitted to make end-of-life decisions because their judgment is impaired by mental illness. We certainly might expect our professions to protest this situation.

However, it turns out that substantial numbers of psychologists and psychiatrists are in favor of physician-assisted suicide. Of Oregon psychiatrists, 56% favored the law in Oregon permitting physician-assisted suicide (Ganzini, Fenn, Lee, Heintz, & Bloom, 1996). Of Oregon psychologists, 78% favored it (Fenn & Ganzini, 1999). Given this support for physician-assisted suicide by mental health professionals, it is not surprising that our professional organizations have reacted in a very limited way and have not mobilized against this threat.

The American Psychiatric Association took some steps to oppose physician-assisted suicide. The majority of the members and consultants to the ethics committee of the American Psychiatric Association believe that physician-assisted suicide is incompatible with the physician's role. The American Psychiatric Association joined with the American Medical Association (AMA) in campaigning against the Death with Dignity Act in Oregon (Karel, 1998) and in a brief urging the United States Supreme Court not to allow physician-assisted suicide (Psychiatrists break from APA stand, 1997). However these actions were very controversial within the membership since they weren't deliberated as fully as they would have been if there had been an official position paper. Although the American Psychiatric Association ordinarily follows the ethics of the AMA there was an initiative to delete the requirement that members follow AMA ethics. Some thought that this proposal had the purpose of paving the way for an independent, more favorable position on physician-assisted suicide (APA Board debates, 1998, p. 5).

The National Association of Social Workers made a statement in 1993 offering a basic framework in case physician-assisted suicide were legalized, which allowed members to be "present for the assisted death" but not to "deliver the medications" (Miller, 2000, p. 266).

In June 2000, a report was presented to the Board of Directors of the American Psychological Association by the Working Group on Assisted Suicide and End-of-life Decisions (Report, 2000). After summarizing the arguments from both sides, they decided that it was premature for the American Psychological Association to take a position. They believed there is not sufficient data to be definitive about the sequelae of assisted suicide. They recommended research on the effects of assisted suicide on individuals with terminal illness, family members of those dying of assisted suicide, health care providers, and society in general. After much debate, the Council of the American Psychological Association made a public statement endorsing this position (Thomas, 2001).

This seemingly neutral position is, in fact, not neutral at all. In order to collect more data on the effects of physician-assisted suicide, these deaths would have to continue to occur for an indefinite period of time. As we all know, research proceeds at a very slow pace, and even after hundreds of studies there is often no consensus about the implications.

Advocates of physician-assisted suicide are not waiting for the data to come in. They are busy helping people find lethal medication, counseling people who are interested in suicide, setting up suicide Web sites, rewriting medical textbooks, producing television programs, creating test cases, drafting legislation, initiating referendums, crafting hospital policies, and even writing books on bioethics for children. Perhaps most importantly, they have created slogans and concepts that make physician-assisted suicide seem attractive and passed these concepts around in every conceivable way.

Given the kinds of deaths that have already occurred—for example, the deaths of Kevorkian's victims such as Judith Curren and Rebecca Badger, the deaths of those who followed the instructions in Humphry's (1991) suicide manual, *Final Exit* (Marzuk et al., 1993; Marzuk, Tardiff, & Leon, 1994), the deaths of cognitively impaired patients whose feeding tubes were disconnected even though they never explicitly requested this, the deaths in Oregon of patients whose psychological evaluations to determine if they were competent to request physician-assisted suicide were superficial—it is difficult to see what kinds of additional evidence we might have to wait for.

There is certainly enough evidence to begin trying to persuade our fellow mental health professionals and the rest of our culture that there is much to be gained by avoiding physician-assisted suicide.

I believe it is important to enter into discussions with those who are leaning toward favoring physician-assisted suicide. The ultimate goal is to make them aware of the evidence and the research that is already available.

The ideal discussion is not a competition but a collaboration. The movement for physician-assisted suicide is a social experiment in which we are all involved. Both sides have predicted dangers. Advocates fear that people will be forced to undergo unnecessary pain and emotional suffering. Opponents fear unnecessary deaths of psychologically vulnerable people who may feel as if they are a burden, or incompetent people whose guardians may choose to hasten their death when they might have had a chance for survival. If one side prevails but the other side's danger predictions were actually correct, we will all suffer.

Therefore, we must make sure that the considerations that society uses in making this decision are factual and pertinent. If we allow irrational fears, guilt, confusion, ridicule, or intimidation to sway us, we may all suffer for it.

There are many kinds of people who are currently advocating physician-assisted suicide. Let me first give an example of the kind of advocate with whom we cannot share our information until we reassure and comfort her and, indeed, take up the causes that she is upset about and commit ourselves to helping her.

Colt (1991, pp. 351–354) tells the story of Billie Press, whose father suffered a great deal before he died. After his retirement, her father had been relatively happy living with her family. However, he had a stroke and heart attack at 85. A "second stroke left him paralyzed on his right side, unable to walk, and incontinent" (p. 352). The family couldn't afford home health care and put him in a series of three nursing homes, where he was not well taken care of. He "developed bedsores," and Billie would find him "lying in his . . . feces." His teeth had been neglected, and they "rotted and fell out" (p. 352).

Finally the family found a better nursing home, but he had "pain from osteoarthritis" which was poorly controlled. Worse still, in the morning he "was strapped into a wheelchair and left . . . face to the wall . . . aides checked on him only once every four hours" (p. 352). He had no one to talk to. They didn't "put on his glasses or his hearing aid" and his radio was untuned, so that it played only static (p. 353).

He started to talk to Billie about helping him die, but she was afraid of being arrested or losing her teaching license. Her father said, "Sweetheart, you mustn't do it then. . . . I must suffer to the end" (p. 353). Three years later he finally died. Colt writes:

More than a decade later, she continues to wrestle with her frustration at not having been able to help him die, and she finds it difficult to talk about his death without bursting into tears. . . . she worries that one day, like her father, she might be hopelessly debilitated and want to die but be unable to do anything about it . . . she has joined the Hemlock society . . . she says . . . 'For me, the bottom line is that people should have choices. And when the quality of life is gone—whether because of terminal illness or extreme age-one of the choices should be the option of leaving this life . . . Why did my father have to go on suffering for two and a half more years when he wanted so much to end it?' " (p. 354)

I would characterize Billie Press as being traumatized by the experiences she witnessed. She is experiencing the recurrent, painful, intrusive recollections characteristic of victims of post-traumatic stress disorder.

Ellis (1994) characterized the post-traumatic stress victim as thinking in absolutes. If the patient thinks that she hates the terrible events that happened and hopes that they will never occur again and thinks of ways to try to prevent them, she will feel appropriate feelings of shock, and fear but also feel determined and vigilant. If, however, the patient thinks that the events that occurred must absolutely not ever happen to anybody ever again and if it does happen it means she is totally inadequate for not stopping it, she will continue to feel overwhelming stress.

It is clear why Billie Press is attracted to the Hemlock society. Death is the only guarantee that a problem will absolutely not occur. It is also no wonder that Billie Press can't worry right now about Kevorkian's victims like Judith Curren and Rebecca Badger. It's no wonder that she isn't worried about Herman Krausz, a Canadian man whose doctors terminated his respirator against his will even though he wanted to live longer (Smith, 2000, p. 137). These other people's deaths must seem very remote to her.

We cannot, however, be swayed by her intensity. When we think about public policy, we unfortunately cannot immediately solve the problem so that it absolutely never occurs again. We can only take action in such a way as to begin to reduce the problem and then continue our commitment until it finally disappears.

We also cannot be swayed by the way in which she is framing the problem. We don't have to agree with her that people should have the right to die, but we can absolutely agree with her that we must do everything we can to make sure that nursing home patients are not strapped to a chair facing a wall and left with no one to talk to all day. That will be our method of preventing suffering.

We might hesitate to say this because we are afraid of giving Billie Press more pain than she is already suffering. We are afraid to say that her father's intense suffering could have been prevented—that his pain could have been better controlled, that his psychological needs could have been attended to. We want to avoid having her become painfully enraged at the nursing home.

However, giving her this kind of information will actually help her. She is so sure that these miseries are inevitable that she has committed herself to promoting the right to die. Unfortunately, this has not relieved her own stress. There is no right to die in our society. She still worries every day that she will have to go through these same miseries when she gets older.

It will be reassuring to her and others like her that although illness and old age are inevitable, the feeling of misery is not. If we emphasize that we are only recently realizing that we can do more about this misery, it will prevent her from feeling unnecessary guilt and rage. For Billie Press and for other advocates who are making pessimistic assumptions about the relief of suffering, we have many reassuring arguments.

Those who are concerned that dying patients may be suffering from intractable pain may be surprised to learn that pain is more treatable than people think (Cundiff, 1992; Chevlen & Smith, 2002). They may also be surprised to learn that pain isn't usually the reason for physician-assisted suicide requests (Smith, 1999, p. 13; Sullivan, Hedberg, & Hopkins, 2001). Out of 70 patients who used physician-assisted suicide in Oregon between 1998 and 2000, only 17 even mentioned inadequate pain control as a concern, and these patients weren't necessarily in pain (Sullivan, Hedberg, & Hopkins, 2001). Those concerned about the pain of dying patients may also be pleased to hear about the new initiatives designed to make pain control a required part of acceptable medical care (Phillips, 2000).

Those who are afraid of emotional suffering may be genuinely happy to hear about the great effectiveness, wide applicability, lower expense, and nonintrusiveness of cognitive techniques of psychotherapy. We must, however, convince them we are committed to actually making these techniques available to more people.

Those who are inexperienced with the terminally ill may be relieved to hear that the vast majority of terminally ill people don't want to die (Chochinov et al., 1995). They may be relieved to hear that most oncologists don't see the need for physician-assisted suicide (Emanuel et al., 2000).

Those who are horrified by life supports may be genuinely surprised to hear that many people on life supports have a positive quality of life (Bach, Campagnolo, & Hoeman, 1991).

Those who have been convinced that shortages of funds make health care improvements impossible may be genuinely pleased to hear the kinds of things that Eisner (1994) a distinguished economist has to say. It may be greatly reassuring to realize that the fear of national debt has occurred many times in history but debt has not led to disaster. It may be reassuring to realize that the national debt could just as well be called the national assets, because it consists of debts that we owe to ourselves such as bonds (Eisner, 1994, p. 100). It may be reassuring to realize that what we call medical expenses could be conceptualized instead as a thriving part of our economy where eager consumers pay for wanted services and employ millions of people. According to Kassler (1994, p. xi), the health care industry gained nearly 800,000 jobs in 1991, and by 1992, there were over 10 million health care jobs, not including workers in insurance, pharmaceuticals, or medical equipment and supplies.

It may be reassuring to realize that many of the so-called cost cutting ideas are actually wasting money and could be eliminated. Kassler (1994, p. 12) writes about the dubious record of utilization review (UR) companies. She points out that "Looking at UR scrutiny of cataract operations under Medicare, the inspector general of the U.S. Health and Human Services Department found that in 1990 UR firms possibly eliminated $1.4 million in unnecessary cataract surgery but at a cost of $13.3 million paid out to the UR industry."

This means that if we stop allowing economic arguments to discourage us, we can improve our health care facilities. It may be reassuring to realize that if we commit ourselves to providing better health care, we are not making a sacrifice—it will actually improve the health of our society and our economy and reduce a great deal of stress.

For health care in our country, we have a situation in which it is the best of times and the worst of times. For certain cases, an inspiring combination of medical talent and institutional support produce beautiful results. For others, undertreatment or mistakes occur. We are not aiming at the impossible when we commit ourselves to improving health care. We are simply aiming at delivering good health care more consistently.

These optimistic arguments may somewhat ease the fears of Billie Press. However, she will not be able to give up her struggle until she is convinced that something is actually being done so that in the future, people like her can find a way to take good care of their relatives—both physically and psychologically.

Not all advocates of physician-assisted suicide are feeling Billie Press's desperation. Some are excited about what they think is a great modern development. They are assuming that the problem of guidelines can be worked out, and they are eager to begin the job. Some of these advocates come across in a fairly intimidating manner. With these we must reason differently.

Let me give an example of the kinds of arguments I would characterize as intimidating. In November of 1998, the opening statements in debate about physician-assisted suicide were published in *Psychiatric Services*. Hartmann argued in favor of the legalization of physician-assisted suicide (Hartmann & Meyerson, 1998). Hartmann suggests that psychiatrists can play a useful part in our "American and international debate" by identifying what he calls "some psychological obstacles to discussion and to help clear some ground so that these emotion-laden areas can be open for reasonable discussion" (p. 1468).

Hartmann is seemingly making an innocuous opening remark about the tone of the discussion that he hopes will take place. However, as his argument continues, it becomes clear that his ground rules for discussion have been confused with his agenda for action. He rejects "laws simply criminalizing physician-assisted suicide" because they "do not help clear such ground . . . they also foster passionate premature closure rather than reasonable discussion, acknowledgment of complexity, learning, and evolution of varieties of decent, balanced, and caring solutions" (p. 1468).

Hartmann is using the term "discussion" in two different ways. When he says at the outset that he wishes "reasonable discussion," it seems as if he means discussion about whether to allow physician-assisted suicide. But when he implies that to oppose physician-assisted suicide is to oppose discussion, it becomes clear that he is referring instead to the sort of discussions about policies or guidelines which would have to take place if and only if physician-assisted suicide were to be allowed.

Hartmann's argument is intimidating because he plays upon the assumption within the mental health field that it is always good to discuss things openly. Ordinarily, no mental health professional would want to be characterized as not being open to discussion.

The ad hominem argument against opponents becomes even clearer as he goes along when he explains what he means by "premature closure." He states "we often wish away conflicts by leaning unreasonably on authority and what seem to be familiar or simplifying solutions" (p. 1468). As examples of these simplifying solutions, he gives "thou shalt not kill," the Hippocratic Oath, the constitution, the Bill of Rights, and the reliance on tradition (p. 1469).

He says, in effect, *I am in favor of physician-assisted suicide and a lot of good people are in favor of it and we are ready to get down to work in developing guidelines, but these opponents won't let us.* He characterizes those who oppose physician-assisted suicide as basing their opposition on an emotional unreasoned attachment to authority. He makes this even more explicit: "At a level that I think is always in conflict with our most adult selves, we all still sometimes have wishes to have good parents. Much of the strength and irrational appeal of authoritative guides or governments, and of many or most religions, have their roots in this psychological area" (pp. 1468–1469).

I would not describe his argument as intimidating if he showed how the opponents' position was unreasonable, but he has not done that. He has simply equated the opposition with some bad labels—childish, clinging, tied to anti-quated views—just by saying so.

The intimidating quality of his argument is also evident in his dismissal of the slippery slope. Hartmann writes, "Watch out for the slippery-slope metaphor. In physician-assisted suicide, it is usually a dishonest slope sitting queasily on a conceptual swamp" (p. 1470).

A discussion of possible dangers of a new policy is a part of any responsible public policy decision. A discussion of the slippery slope argument should include some discussion of the serious problems that have already occurred and what it would take to prevent these problems. If physician-assisted suicide were legalized and if there were some undesirable consequences, how undesirable would they have to be before Hartmann would want to revoke the legalization? What would have to happen? By what mechanism could the legalization be revoked? Advocates of physician-assisted suicide are very silent on these issues.

Hartmann also uses intimidation when he mentions Hendin's (1997) book *Seduced by death: Doctors, patients, and the Dutch cure.* Hendin, who is a world-famous psychiatric authority on suicide and executive director of the American Suicide Foundation, went to the Netherlands to study the Netherlands' practice of physician-assisted suicide and euthanasia. His book is one of the most important sources for anyone trying to understand what is going on there and what it means. Hendin, after studying available information from the Dutch government and interviewing prominent Dutch doctors, concluded that there were many very serious problems in the way that their policies on physician-assisted suicide and euthanasia are working. He reported, for example, that Dutch doctors are actively suggesting euthanasia to patients (Hendin, 1997, p. 52), that guidelines are not always followed (p. 177), and that many Dutch people are frightened of being put to death without being consulted (p. 99).

Hartmann dismisses Hendin's book by making reference to some unnamed Dutch psychiatrists who "do not think Hendin's book is accurate or fair" (p. 1470). He mentions some American names without saying what they said. We are led to understand that some important people consider this book not worth our attention. We are not told what particular points they disagree with or why. How can we be convinced by such an argument?

Another confusing tactic is that instead of writing in favor of "legalizing" physician-assisted suicide, he writes against "criminalizing" it. He makes it sound as if it is currently legal and the move to "criminalize" it is something new. This is completely false. In *Washington v. Glucksberg*, the syllabus for the U.S. Supreme Court opinion contained the following statement: "An examination of our Nation's history, legal traditions, and practices demonstrates that Anglo-American common law has punished or otherwise disapproved of assisting suicide for over 700 years; that rendering such assistance is still a crime in almost every State; that such prohibitions have never contained exceptions for those who were near death" (*Washington v. Glucksberg*, p. 702).

I believe that these kinds of intimidating arguments can have the effect of silencing opposition. There are probably many mental health professionals who are personally opposed to physician-assisted suicide but who do not speak out because they do not wish to be perceived as closing off discussion or as clinging to antiquated views. By ridiculing so many sources of previous ethical wisdom, Hartmann may make many readers uncomfortable and ashamed to speak up.

An odd thing about these innuendos is that when you really think about them, they don't make sense. If the opponent of physician-assisted suicide is clinging, as Hartmann says, to tradition, it could be said that Hartmann, rather than generating anything completely new and modern, is, like Kevorkian, an admirer of ancient customs as well. Kevorkian dedicated his book (1991), "To those enlightened doctors in ancient Hellenistic Alexandria and medieval Cilician Armenia. They dared to do what is right."

Although advocates of physician-assisted suicide would like to be seen as the modern ones, some of them are nostalgic about antiquated medicine. They want us to return to a time before respirators and feeding tubes. Many of them are terribly distressed about new medical procedures, because they involve new medical expenditures (Schwartz, 1987).

Advocates of physician-assisted suicide present themselves as being permissive, whereas those who oppose it are seen as authoritarian. One could easily argue that advocates of physician-assisted suicide are trying to institute themselves as the new authority. Advocates of physician-assisted suicide see themselves as permissive about a wish to die. But what about the wish to live? Can't this too be suppressed if authorities proclaim that it is selfish under certain circumstances? There is a strong human desire to fight death and to live as long as possible, but now, there are those who believe that this desire is undignified.

Wesley J. Smith discusses the writings of Hardwig, who has actually postulated that there is a duty to die if continuing to live will burden the family (Smith, 2000, p. 153). If this perspective is put forward authoritatively, people may be convinced. We know that people are very suggestible. In some cultures in the past, women willingly jumped into their husbands' funeral pyres. Moreover, fear of burdening their families affected many of those in Oregon who requested physician-assisted suicide (Smith, 1999, p. 13; Sullivan, Hedberg, & Hopkins, 2001). As the policy of physician-assisted suicide becomes more established, sick people may be feeling even more pressure to die. In 2000, there was a "significant increase in the number of patients who were concerned about being a burden to family, friends, and other caregivers" (p. 605).

Stanley Milgram found that people are much more obedient to authority than he had supposed. He designed an experiment in which the subject was asked to be a teacher and to deliver electric shocks to someone designated as the learner. He thought that only a small minority of subjects would deliver what they thought were severe shocks but this was not the case. Unfortunately, 65% of the subjects kept on pulling the lever that they thought was delivering severe shocks even after they heard the subject screaming, just because the experimenter said it was his responsibility. Milgram wrote, "A substantial proportion of the people do what they are told to do, irrespective of the content of the act and without limitations of conscience, so long as they perceive that the command comes from a legitimate authority" (Meyer, 1970, p. 278).

If patients get the impression that the choice to die is backed by the authority of the church or the government or the medical profession, that they are being told that their life is over and it is time to die, they may acquiesce, but this doesn't mean that dying was what they desired.

Moreover, the emotion-laden frame of reference in which one opinion is labelled permissive and the other authoritarian may simply be inappropiate. We cannot assume that assisted suicide is the sort of issue about which one person should hesitate to influence another. This is not a discussion between a teenager and his father about some aspect of personal self-expression. This is a life-and-death public health policy decision which will affect everyone.

A change in public health policy should be conceptualized as a major ecological decision. In the scientific field of ecology, we have learned the importance of caution when intervening in complex environments. We recognize that although we understand many of the factors influencing living things, we do not understand all of them and we cannot experiment haphazardly.

Our ethical ecosphere is made up of materials from many sources. It has not protected mankind perfectly, but it has allowed those of us in the Western world, to experience an environment of unparalleled personal freedom and abundance. Some advocates of physician-assisted suicide seem not to appreciate the caution necessary in tinkering with the basic infrastructure underlying our protections, even if some of it came from religious sources that are currently out of favor. For example, Timothy Quill (1993, pp. 40–41) talks about a family who did not call an ambulance when their mother slipped into a coma, because she didn't wish to go to a hospital. Instead, they waited until they were sure she was dead. They were shocked when the police interrogated them and when the funeral home would not accept the body without a death certificate. They had perceived this event only in a freedom-to-die context. They seemed totally unaware that a whole host of procedures is in place in our society to protect us from homicide. If no questions were asked about a dead body, anybody could poison his relative and claim that the relative was ill and didn't wish to be treated.

Our laws, like the interdependent species in our environment, have accumulated gradually and protect us in many ways that we are unaware of. For example, Judge Kleinfeld, who presides over the 9th Circuit Court of Appeals and who wrote a dissenting opinion in an important right-to-die case, believes that if there were a right to die, it might be difficult to justify suicide prevention activities. He noted that in cases of murder, the prosecutor might be in the position of having to prove lack of consent (Kleinfeld, 1997).

Stating that those who wish to protect people from assisted suicide are leaning unreasonably upon authority is intimidating to mental health professionals, who like to think of themselves as preserving individual freedom. Instead of calling good protections authoritarian, we can see them in a context of ecology and behavioral psychology. We have to set up our environment in such a way that dangers are not accessible. We don't leave a loaded gun in a preschool classroom. This isn't authoritarian. It is commonsense management stemming from our understanding of the behavior of preschoolers. Adults are also in need of wise protective policies that reduce the probability of accidents.

Hartmann's references to religious authority also have an intimidating tone. It is true that many times in the past, religious fervor caused problems with scientific progress, but it is clear that antireligious fervor can also cause problems. To a small minority of advocates of physician-assisted suicide, the current focus on the pain and suffering of dying patients is a golden opportunity to score points against religion. This is an emotional preoccupation of theirs, but, like any emotional preoccupation, it can be a distraction from the actual pros and cons of the issue at hand. They would like to blame patients' pain and suffering on the religious scruples of those who oppose managed death for religious reasons. We can take this up only briefly here, but suffice it to say that, first of all, many people oppose physician-assisted suicide on secular grounds. Second, many religious people favor physician-assisted suicide. Third, if we really had to take an account of the pain and suffering of patients in terms of a score sheet between religious and secular values, I don't think secular values would score the easy victory that the advocate seems to expect. It is true that possibly the forces of religious values keep us from "pulling the plug" precipitously, but aren't our secular values responsible for some of the pain and suffering as well? Isn't the decline of the family partly responsible for the isolation of the elderly and the sick? Isn't the buy-out of our hospitals from their religious roots into private hands responsible for the bottom line mentality that causes so much misery?

When we begin talking to people about physician-assisted suicide, we will have to bear in mind that the person we are talking to may have already been exposed to these kinds of intimidating arguments. He may have already accepted without question certain assumptions of the advocates. He may have accepted without proof that we are in a state of financial catastrophe and that those who try to provide more for patients are unrealistic. He may believe the claim that physician-assisted suicide and euthanasia are already going on and that they haven't caused any problems. He may have accepted that important people think it's safe to experiment with physician-assisted suicide, and therefore it's safe. Having accepted the authority of those who say it's safe, he may not feel that he needs an answer for the slippery slope arguments. He may, unfortunately, feel that slippery slope arguments are not coming from rational people and therefore don't need to be answered.

In a discussion, there can be an effect of group dynamics even if only two people are present. If you bring up slippery slope kinds of arguments—negative consequences of physician-assisted suicide—especially the kinds of slippery slope arguments that the person has heard before, the person you are discussing this with may feel that by allowing himself to get into a discussion about such matters, he is being disloyal to the group who trust the authority of those who say physician-assisted suicide is safe. For example, although it makes sense to search out historical precedents for the proposed changes in public policy, if you bring up the Nazi euthanasia program in conversation with some people, your opinions may be discounted.

How can we overcome these difficulties? Although Hartmann says he is seeking open discussion, it seems that there are certain topics that only opponents are eager to discuss. How can we engage advocates of physician-assisted suicide in an important discussion in which critical issues are truly brought up and perceived by both sides?.

The fact that physician-assisted suicide has been prohibited for so long is not persuasive to the advocate like Hartmann. The advocate believes that many societal problems are due to traditional ways of thinking about things and that once we are free of traditional assumptions, we can begin over again and do much better. Therefore any arguments bringing up traditional medical ethics or religious values are simply irrelevant to the advocate. Those values have prevailed before and now it is his turn to try something else, he thinks.

Unfortunately, even bad consequences of physician-assisted suicide that occurred recently are dismissed by him as being part of the past. The fact that some of Kevorkian's victims were not appropriate candidates for physician-assisted suicide by anybody's standards doesn't make him concerned because he feels that Kevorkian was an exception and that this occurred in the past when physician-assisted suicide was illegal and therefore couldn't be regulated. He truly believes that only by giving physician-assisted suicide a chance can we see what it will really be like.

We must, therefore, find, among his modern values, something that we can use for our discussion. Luckily, the advocate, like any person believing in modernism, places a very high value on getting at the absolute truth. He will be pleased to discuss rational issues about the feasibility of physician-assisted suicide and, hopefully, when he hears some of the problems that he hadn't known about, he may lower the priority level of his assisted-suicide advocacy plans.

It will bother him that the advocates of euthanasia concealed the problems of physician-assisted suicide, implying that it was an easy way to die; for example, in the television commercial for the referendum in Oregon which portrayed a daughter dying peacefully from pills, when in fact, her mother had to give her a lethal injection (Marker, 2000, pp. 5–6). He may change his mind when he finds out that many of the patients attempting physician-assisted suicide didn't die and experienced convulsions, vomiting, or other complications. An editorial in the *Oregonian* (Death without dignity, 1997) said that the failure rate of lethal prescriptions was 25%. Groenewoud et al. (2000) reported that 18% of physician-assisted suicide cases showed complications and required a physician's assistance.

He may not realize that organizations supporting physician-assisted suicide really have euthanasia on their agenda (Marker, 1993, p. 67).

Perhaps he didn't realize just how ineffective guidelines are. If he assumed that there would be protective guidelines, he may be surprised to find out that in Oregon an 85-year-old woman named Kate Cheney, who had enough symptoms of dementia to cause one psychiatrist to reject her competency to decide on assisted suicide, was able to shop around until she found a psychological evaluation that favored her request (Smith, 1999, pp. 12–13).

If he imagined that a psychological evaluation would consist of a series of caring interviews, he may react when he finds out that a woman died in Oregon after a psychological evaluation that consisted of an MMPI sent in the mail and filled out with the help of her children (Kettler, 2000, p. 8A).

Perhaps he didn't think about the difficulties of assigning the role of gatekeeper for physician-assisted suicide. Many managerial and professional occupations have higher suicide rates than the general population. Zoccolillo, Murphy, and Wetzel (1986) found that the lifetime prevalence of depression among medical students was three times greater than in the general population. Even when complicating factors such as gender and age are taken into account, rates of suicide among physicians appear to be elevated (Boxer, Burnett, & Swanson, 1995; Rose & Rosow, 1973). If we were indeed choosing gatekeepers for physician-assisted suicide, would it be logical to select a group with a high suicide rate?

No matter who would be in the position of gatekeeper, we must take certain problems into account. Perhaps the advocate is not familiar with the implications of cognitive therapy that people very commonly make emotional judgments about other people and that this tendency to categorize and rate human beings has special implications for the situation in which one person is in a position of power over another and possibly making life-or-death decisions about the other person. In such cases, the person in power may be easily persuaded to regard the other person in an oversimplified way that allows him to abuse the other person. Zimbardo experimented with college students, in a realistic mock-prison situation which was supposed to continue for two weeks. He found that those subjects given the role of guard treated those who were prisoners so badly that he elected to terminate the experiment early (Zimbardo, 1974).

Perhaps the advocate didn't realize how many medical patients have a completely distorted view of their medical condition or of their chances for survival with treatment (Massad, 2000). Perhaps he wasn't thinking about the possibility that patients may be attracted to physician-assisted suicide on the basis of phobic avoidance of medical treatment and illness rather than a desire to die.

Perhaps he didn't realize that legalizing physician-assisted suicide is the equivalent of removing environmental barriers that are highly effective in reducing suicides. He may not realize that many of the controls we impose—restrictions on gun ownership and barbiturate usage—truly have important effects on the suicide rate (Colt, 1991, pp. 335–336; Loftin, McDowall, Wiersema, & Cottey 1991).

Perhaps he still believes that society's permission to cause death deliberately can be clearly contained by the policy of personal autonomy because he hasn't read about the medical futility policies that are being developed that might deprive people of their lives who have not asked to die (Smith, 2000, pp. 131–

132, 137). Wesley J. Smith's, *Culture of Death: The Assault on Medical Ethics in America* (2000), is making Americans more aware of this problem, but he may not have heard about it yet.

He might begin to question the desirability of a movement to encourage large numbers of people to write advance directives when he finds out how some people have died unwillingly because of their directives (Smith, 1997, pp. 216–218).

He may be unaware of just how difficult it is for physicians to predict who is going to die and when. Christakis and Lamont (2000) reported that only 20% of predictions about how long patients had to live were accurate, and this was in a hospice sample. In a hospital sample, where the very question of whether they would live or die might be open, it might be even harder for doctors to predict accurately.

Perhaps with these kinds of information we can persuade him that, although helping people to die might seem desirable and is clearly a temptation for patients, families, and doctors, it is simply not feasible to achieve this without undesirable consequences. Perhaps we can convince him that the experimentation that he believes in has not been suppressed. There has in fact already been experimentation with physician-assisted suicide and the preliminary results do not look good. In an experiment where life is at risk and the preliminary results do not look good, is it wise to continue the experiment?

Lonny Shavelson is also an advocate of physician-assisted suicide. Like Billie Press, he has witnessed the pain of the dying, but unlike Billie Press, he is totally familiar with all the physical and psychological problems associated with physician-assisted suicide.

Shavelson has had more time than most other people involved in the physician-assisted suicide debate to develop and to think about his position. Physician-assisted death goes back three generations in his family. His grandmother, after surviving in an oxygen tent for ten months and calling for help incoherently night after night, died after her doctor gave her an injection (Shavelson, 1995, p. 7–8). When he was 14, his mother began to introduce him to the idea that at some point in his life she would want him to help her die (p. 9). He writes, "As a child, I thought this was a common family arrangement" (p. 9).

As a doctor and a journalist, he wrote a book called *A Chosen Death: The Dying Confront Assisted Suicide* (1995), in which he reports in detail five cases in which families and friends either assisted or were prepared to assist in suicide.

We don't have to tell Lonny Shavelson that most people requesting physician-assisted suicide don't do so because of pain. His cases illustrate this very well. A woman named Renee didn't want to take a chance on what her death would be like (p. 29). A lonely man, Gene, was afraid of in what condition he would be "if he had another stroke" (p. 76). A young man, Kelly, believed, "it will be better for me there" on the "other side" after I "cross over" (p. 118). A cancer patient, Mary, felt that she and her family had already "said what we've had to say" (p. 196) and it was "ridiculous and humiliating for me to lay here dying for days" (p. 197). The patient Pierre's depression lifted and he no longer asked for suicide (pp. 54–56).

Moreover Shavelson does not automatically dismiss concerns that poor and disabled people may be hurt by physician-assisted suicide.

Why, then, is he still in favor of physician-assisted suicide? First, to him, the issue of whether to allow physician-assisted suicide does not involve a choice between assisted suicide or no assisted suicide. Instead, he considers it a choice between suicide assisted by physicians and suicide assisted by friends and family.

To him, the request of the dying for help in dying is so compelling that he has accepted it as an obligation that must fall on somebody, and he begs for this burden to be removed from the shoulders of friends and family.

In commenting upon his situation with Renee, who had taken an overdose but had not yet died, he wrote, "At my side should have been two physicians, or an ethics review committee . . . to keep my personal judgment from running astray" (p. 104).

With regard to his own family, he wrote, "I pray that if my own father or mother repeatedly cries out for relief, it will not fall on me to . . . administer the pills, inject the medicine, or use a plastic bag to end their suffering" (p. 232).

He quotes a son who explained that he would have helped his mother die, "But it would be the most painful thing for the rest of my life—what a horrible thing for a son to have to do" (p. 232).

I think the most important point to focus on for those who make Shavelson's argument is that it is not necessary to assist in suicide. The assumption that assisted suicide is a necessity is a mistake. Even though Shavelson's mother recovered over and over again from her Crohn's disease and her depression, he assumes pessimistically that eventually she would see no hope and ask for "relief" (p. 10).

Earlier in his life, when he himself was struggling with depression, he put her requests aside (p. 10). To look at it optimistically, if he continues to put her requests aside, perhaps she will continue to recover. The doctor who injected his grandmother didn't take into account the long-term effects upon the expectations of her daughter and her grandson.

In cognitive therapy, people learn to escape and to help others to escape from the tyranny of emotions and from the belief that responding to emotions is a necessity. When you tactfully decline a request, based on irrational *have tos* or *musts* or *I can't stand its*, not only do you protect yourself but the other person as well. Having her request denied doesn't lead to the disaster she had feared, but instead, enables her to shift gears. She, herself then realized her emotional response wasn't necessary after all.

Oddly enough, it turns out that many of the assisted suiciders are committing suicide not because they really feel that they have to but because they want to pave the way for others who they believe might have to. Having tried all possible medical techniques their doctors can think of and having said goodbye to all their friends, they don't mind sacrificing a few extra days at the end for the cause just in case somebody who comes along later is really in intolerable pain.

When Shavelson explained to Mary that it seemed that she was lucky and from what her doctors had said, her death was expected to be relatively comfortable, she said she wanted to commit suicide anyway "to further the Hemlock cause because I have believed in it" (p. 184).

We see how the number of people who die by assisted suicide can grow far in excess of the number who are in pain, since each person who commits suicide and arranges for publicity—even though she knows she didn't really have to die early—believes she is helping some other person who might be in for more pain and distress than she is.

The second reason why Shavelson favors the legalization of physician-assisted suicide is that he believes that ". . . in a strange twist," it "could actually improve healthcare for the poor, disabled, and minorities" (p. 136).

Shavelson argues that the patient could be asked whether his care was adequate (p. 137). If it was not, a review committee would recommend that he receive further treatment or assistance (p. 137).

As an ideal example of how this process might work if physician-assisted suicide were legalized, he cites the case of Lawrence McAfee, a respirator patient, who sought permission to discontinue his life support. As he presented his case to the court, he made an "impassioned plea" about the circumstances of his life (pp. 137–138). As a result, McAfee got "full-time attendant care" and became a resident of "a group home where there was access to a bathroom and kitchen." This change in status apparently satisfied him, because although he was granted permission to discontinue his life support, he did not (p. 138).

Shavelson gives a sad example of a man, David Rivlin, who was respirator dependent and "confined to a nursing home" (p. 134) but whose request to the court was simply considered as a point of law—did he, or did he not, have the right to discontinue his life support (p. 137)? The law clearly gave him the right to do it and he did. His situation at the nursing home was clearly distressing to him, but nothing was done about it (pp. 134–135).

Since the possibility of someone opting to die by turning off his life supports did not in this case impel society to improve his situation, why is Shavelson so confident that the prospect of someone dying by physician-assisted suicide would be any more compelling? The eloquence of Lawrence McAfee is unusual. Most patients, especially if depressed, would be unable to make such an impression.

The five cases Lonny Shavelson presented in detail were all of extraordinary individuals with a close circle of friends, family, and helpers who shared a frame of reference that dictated a close analysis of whether the patient was going through a passing mood or was entering some sort of stage of readiness to die. They sat by the hour and discussed the patient's latest utterances. He believes that the legalization of physician-assisted suicide would add some oversight and more muscle to this support team and create the potential to offer better health care and better living conditions as an option.

Shavelson, having worked so closely with such unique, talented, and sensitive individuals, might not have the awareness of just how superficially procedures can be carried out when they are perceived as bureaucratic hurdles rather than as respected safeguards. Hendin reports that in the Netherlands, guidelines were seen in this manner (1997, p. 91).

I wish Shavelson had witnessed, as I did, a session in which a home health nurse came to measure my mother's blood pressure. She spent only a few minutes on the blood pressure. For the rest of the time she breathlessly whisked my mother through an evaluation which, on paper, may have appeared dazzlingly comprehensive. It included everything from fire safety to hurricane preparedness. She clearly had to rush off to other appointments, and, as I watched, amazed at her rapidity, I wondered what she would have done if my mother had wished to read the fine print on the thick pile of documents that she was handing her at an ever-accelerating pace for her to rapidly sign and hand back.

Instead of strengthening the preventive efforts of family and friends by providing a respected source of comprehensive considerations and financial supplements for life improvements, the legalization of physician-assisted suicide might, instead, make it possible for a patient like Shavelson's mother to completely evade her well-meaning family and friends. She would no longer have to rely on them. She might receive encouragement from suicide advocacy organizations, and with their help, she might easily locate a willing physician. She could even receive her prescription by mail. Her psychological testing could be done by mail as well. The protective procedures could be expedited because everyone involved might regard them as an unwanted obstacle.

Shavelson's belief that the review committee would offer the patient options to improve his support situation is based on the assumption that the idea of the patient losing his life unnecessarily would impel the committee to make these investments. Ironically, the very thrust of the physician-assisted suicide movement might undermine the sort of concern Shavelson is hoping to mobilize. The physician-assisted suicide movement tells us that we were wrong to automatically place the saving of life as a top priority. It tells us that only the patient can place a value on his own life and that, by creating barriers to suicide, we are violating his privacy and autonomy. Because of this massive theoretical shift, the committee charged with protecting patients from unnecessary suicides might be more worried about violating the patients' autonomy than about saving their lives.

The other mental health professionals that you have an opportunity to talk to about this issue have heard the kinds of arguments that Billie Press, Hartmann, and Shavelson are making and have been moved by these arguments, as any sensitive person would be. They are acutely aware of the effects of depression on judgment and want very much to protect people with reversible depression from committing suicide. On the other hand, they are moved by the plight of those who might be in intolerable pain. However, they haven't had the time to examine the issue thoroughly enough to be able to make a judgment about what would be best. They haven't had the time to integrate these fearful images with their day-to-day clinical experience of what people are really like and how their suffering can be relieved.

Moreover, they have perhaps given way to the rhetoric about reducing health care costs. They may believe—as did Billie Press and Hartmann—that no improvements in health care are possible and that therefore the misery of patients is a fact that must be accepted. They know, from their clinical experience, that cutting services does a lot of harm, but they don't feel they can do anything about it. They don't question the assumption that cutting services is necessary. They are unprepared to handle in a conversation the huge arrays of financial data that a serious answer to these questions might entail, so they give the advocates the benefit of the doubt and don't challenge them.

I believe that once we start to confront these arguments, we will easily win. As a cognitive therapist I believe that ideas make a difference. I believe that the first step for us is to change our attitudes. The idea that nothing can be done to enhance the lives of patients because of a lack of finances should seem shocking to us. We should vigorously challenge every aspect of this idea.

People claiming that we cannot afford better treatment should not easily silence us, as they have in the last few decades. Anyone suggesting that we neglect the basic health and psychological needs of patients and caregivers should be politely and pleasantly confronted with all of the indirect problems that this neglect will cause, and the expenses of these indirect problems should be calculated as part of the cost of their proposal.

The hardest part is recovering from the intimidation. It is intimidating to begin an argument that might include vast arrays of financial data. But the fact of the matter is that these vast arrays of data would be just as daunting for those who are assuming that we urgently need to reduce expenditures. They haven't presented any studies of how exactly the finances would work out. Their financial arguments are pure speculation.

It doesn't make sense that neglecting health care services would help our society. If we neglect any person's health, we can expect a worsening of his health condition, which would then require even more expensive treatment, or emotional distress, which causes further problems. By treating Billie Press's father better, her symptoms could have been avoided.

If we provide mental health professionals with examples that they can use in discussions with those who want to cut health care costs, perhaps we can help them feel confident enough to tackle this issue.

Kirschner (2000) gives an example of how trying to cut expenses can lead to disaster. He looked at the managed care treatment documentation of Kip Kinkel, a 14-year-old who killed his parents, two students, and wounded 25 others at an Oregon high school. Having been referred for serious problems, he was seen for "only nine visits over a six-month period." The therapist carefully explains that he didn't do a full psychological evaluation or work with the teen on his "use of explosives," and because it was not in his "contract" and that he wasn't " 'mandated' to consult with Kip's parents about the purchase of a . . . handgun." (p. 16)

It doesn't make sense to accept the idea that something good is occurring when we fail to do something that is needed. It costs money to refuse treatment. You need someone to write policies to justify the refusal. You need someone to watch and make sure nobody gets any services that the policy says should be refused. You need a whole staff to handle the complaints and the appeals and the lawsuits.

Another example of how the passion for cutting costs can lead to even more costs was recently published in the *Wall Street Journal*. A 6 year-old boy named Shelton who "swallowed lye . . . in his native . . . Guyana" was admitted to the University Hospital of Brooklyn to have his esophagus rebuilt. He has improved and could now go home if he could get "competent in-home nursing care," but instead, he "lives at the hospital," going "on rounds" with the doctors. He cannot be discharged, because as an immigrant, he is eligible under "Emergency Medicaid" for "inpatient hospital care and nothing else." (Lagnado, 2000, p. A1).

Our health care crisis is like the joke about the driver who had to wait at an intersection while a pedestrian was crossing. He became angry because the driver of the car in back of him was loudly and continuously beeping his horn. Finally, tired of the noisy horn, he got out of his car, walked back to the driver of the next car and handed him his car keys. Pointing to the older woman slowly making her way across the intersection, he said to the other driver, "Here, you run her over."

No one really wants to be directly responsible for a patient dying for lack of care. If some distant administrator, operating with a very limited view of human psychology, makes rules that refuse care to patients, the people directly responsible for their care have no choice but to provide the care through some other mechanism. If we pay only for emergency care, more people will be treated as emergencies, and since emergency care is billed at a higher rate, more money will be charged for the same care.

Perhaps at first, there were costs that could be cut without hurting services, but now this has become a kind of 21st-century alchemy. We have allowed ourselves to believe that riches can be created by doing less!

Sometimes the problems that occur as a result of funding cutbacks don't occur in the same place as the cutbacks. They occur somewhere else. Whoever cut the funds claims they have caused no harm, but they have. For example, an article in the *Wall Street Journal* explains that patients are dying in Ghana because, although medical equipment is available, there are no nurses to staff the machines. The reason for this is that recruiters on behalf of countries such as the Netherlands and the United States, where there are nursing shortages, have imported nurses from Africa (Zachary, 2001).

Commenting on the 10–15% nursing shortage in American hospitals and the trend for declining enrollment of nursing students, Sherry Pontious, president and professor of a college of nursing said, "Students and parents are hearing about stagnant salaries and layoffs caused by decreased patient lengths of stay, hospital mergers and work redesign" (Preparing for tomorrow's, 2000, p. 26). Mandatory overtime and 16 hour shifts have led to shortages of nurses willing to work and to deaths of patients treated by unlicensed, unregulated nurse's aides (Poorly trained or overworked nurses, 2000). It is hard to avoid the conclusion that the financial cutbacks leading to nursing shortages create a situation of danger to patients both here and abroad.

A *Chicago Tribune* investigation reported that patients were dying under the care of unlicensed, unregulated nurse's aides and that, under a cost-savings program at two Chicago area hospitals, housekeeping staff were dispensing medication (Poorly trained or overworked, 2000). Loebel, Loebel, Dager, Centerwall, and Reay (1991) report that the fear of living in a nursing home is so great that it was indicated as a precipitant in 44% of a group of elderly suicides.

Contemplating examples like these can strengthen us in our awareness, so that when issues come up in our own health care facilities, we are less apt to give way to unproductive ideas. We have to have the courage to believe that the arrays of financial data really will come out better if we do what makes sense.

Our ideas do not have to be expensive. There are two ways to argue with those who claim that we simply don't have the money to improve health care. The first is to argue that we do have more funds. The second is to argue that we can do a lot more with the funds we have. It doesn't cost any more to turn Billie Press's father so that he isn't facing the wall and to tune his radio and to place him somewhere where he can see a tree or some smiling faces.

The lack of funding hurts us in two ways. First, of course, it limits our resources. But second, and more important, it blocks the process of creative decision making by discouraging mental health professionals from thinking about what they can really do for patients. Many potential discussions end when someone cuts them off by saying "we don't have funds."

Our optimism and critical analyses of the arguments of the advocates are our best tools. I believe that if we engage people in the kinds of friendly discussions in which facts can truly be exchanged, that many more will join us in opposing physician-assisted suicide and in opposing the pessimistic climate of opinion that has led to the desire for physician-assisted suicide.

If indeed mental health professionals became convinced that it is best to avoid physician-assisted suicide, they would become valuable opponents to this practice.

The mental health professionals are the ones who know and care about the Judiths Currens and the Rebecca Badgers who would be hurt by this. We know these kinds of patients and their impulsive ups and downs. We know they do actually enjoy life and make contributions in between their bouts of emotionalism and suicidality. We know they have the potential for continued growth and could achieve much greater happiness unless they impulsively commit suicide.

We are the ones who know how discouragement can distort judgment and how just even a little bit of hope can restore people's desire to live. We are the ones who know how much more can be done for patients than we are currently doing. We are the ones who can see the how superficial the proposed safeguards are—the informed consent procedures, the psychological evaluation, and the second opinion.

It is clear that someone who is willing to risk the lives of Judith Curren and Rebecca Badger to save Billie Press's father pain is not comprehending the value of the lives of Judith Curren and Rebecca Badger.

However, it is perhaps not yet clear that someone who is willing to risk Judith Curren and Rebecca Badger is also misunderstanding Billie Press's father. The advocate of physician-assisted suicide is seeing him in a very limited way. Some of the abstractions that are being used in this debate are oversimplifications of human psychology. One is a kind of sensory man, who maximizes his physical pleasures. Another is homo economicus, who behaves in such a way as to maximize his monetary profit.

Those using a sensory model of man maximizing his physical pleasures are ill equipped to understand why a person in pain would want to prolong his existence. Those who conceptualize man in economic terms are also at a loss to understand why anyone would choose to continue a pained existence. Having lost his earning power, and having lost his ability to act as a consumer, the dying person, according to this model, is simply a burden.

However, the cognitive view of man, which we are finding so useful in mental health today, enables a different conclusion. According to this view, a person is not just a bundle of perceived sensations. Each person, within their own mind, represents all of reality and has developed moral notions of how he would like things to be, not just for himself, but for all the people that he is leaving behind.

Billie Press's father, if he knew the consequences, wouldn't want lethal medication. This is a man who chose to suffer rather than risk his daughter's job. He certainly wouldn't want to kill a few Judith Currens and Rebecca Badgers on his way out!

Far from being a burden, the dying person who chooses to do without lethal medication is, in fact, something of a hero. If he feels useless, or if anyone else regards him as useless, we can explain that by avoiding lethal medications, he is actually saving the lives of hundreds of Judith Currens and Rebecca Badgers. His pain, far from being useless, is actually saving the lives of vulnerable people who would die if he opts to skip the last few days or weeks. He is fortifying our ethical framework and leaving it intact to protect future generations.

Martha Wichorek, the suicidal woman who postulated that there is a stage of "miserable existence" after which you can't help anybody, was simply wrong. By not demanding lethal medication, a dying person can indeed be helpful.

Our attention to the thoughts of our patients and our experience with a wide variety of patients teaches us that even the brain-damaged have a rich subjective existence. As one brain-damaged man wrote, "People living with injuries like mine know intimately that things are awry. . . . This morning, preparing oatmeal for my wife, Beverly, I carefully measured out one-third cup of oats and poured them onto the pan's lid rather than into the bowl" (Skloot, 2000, p. 59). Aware of his awkwardness, he also wrote about people's reaction to his awkwardness: ". . . . I think society at large, medical scientists, insurers, legislators, and the person on the street do feel a kind of contempt for the brain-damaged with their comical way of walking, their odd patterns of speech, their apparent stupidity, their abnormality" (p. 61). Most people, seeing this man walking oddly and doing silly things would be totally surprised by the eloquence and wry sense of humor that reveals itself in his writing.

If we openly discuss these things and if we amplify our model of the mentally healthy to include the kinds of character traits that enable people to sustain themselves even if they become handicapped and to understand and provide for the needs of the vulnerable throughout the life span, we will gradually make the movement for physician-assisted suicide and euthanasia fade in its appeal. The movement thrives only by implying that most people agree, so any opposition that argues from facts and cannot be discounted as irrational emotionalism weakens the position of the advocates of physician-assisted suicide.

Whatever we can inspire our society to do for the sick will help all of us, because each person knows that she will be sick at some time in her life and worries about it.

The young and the old and the sick are part of our world view. Our psychological health depends in part on our confidence in our ability to help them. The ideal of protecting the vulnerable can inspire the doctor, the nurse, the researcher, and the inventor to create and to carry out new and better and more comfortable treatments and to therefore fulfill their own dreams of contributing to the welfare of mankind.

How can we help our culture, which is intoxicated with automated ways of doing things, to take the trouble to notice and care about the subjective suffering of the disabled, to take the trouble to visit them and talk to them and reason with them and befriend them? How can we help our culture, which is intoxicated with quick solutions and with control, to understand that sometimes substantial recuperation or adjustment can occur over a period of time if you just patiently sustain somebody from day to day physically and emotionally. How can we help our culture, which is fascinated with living on the fast track, to slow down enough to maintain a connection with those who can no longer keep up?

Our modern popular psychology envisions each individual as independently developing their own values. It does not acknowledge the human tendency to copy role models and to try to be conventional. I believe that so many people are living on the fast track today because they are following the dictates of what they perceive to be healthy. Encouraged by a popular psychology that emphasizes the self, they feel compelled to focus on certain restricted areas of their lives that they perceived as enhancing their own self-development.

If important mental health leaders take the position that the ideal of mental health is to have the patience to slowly and carefully escort your aged relatives to their daily activities, we would see a change in people's behavior. Can we create a culture in which caregivers are respected and admired and in which services are available to help them so they do not have to fear being exhausted, isolated, and desperate? How can we get our culture to invest more resources in helpful services? Can we train professional caregivers to give skilled emotional support? Can we educate children to value supporting the vulnerable and to have the cognitive and emotional skills to remain hopeful even if they themselves succumb to a chronic disability?

Unfortunately, in our culture at this time, people are not encouraged to step off the fast track for a longer, chronic ailment. Wesley Smith gives examples of people who made the choice to care for their sick relatives. Unfortunately they were sometimes pressured by others who felt that this wasn't appropriate behavior. Lucette Lagnado, caring for her mother in her home, was bothered by the negative reactions of friends who made her feel she was mishandling or wasting her life and a doctor who yelled at her for keeping her mother at home (Smith, 2000, p. 234).

Smith gives another, beautiful example of a friend who was strong enough not to pay attention to conventional trends and who derived tremendous satisfaction from caring for his mother. His friend "walked away from a very successful career in government in Washington, D.C., to care for his dying mother in California" (p. 236). He gave up a lot. The friend said, "I had a girlfriend who I loved. I loved my dog. I was being paid better than I ever had in my life. I had a condominium with a great view of the Capitol" (p. 237).

Why did he do it? He explained, "I had promised my father before he died that I would always take care of my mother . . . my parents always dealt with people who were ill or dying in a very caring and loving manner . . . when my mother took care of her mother . . . it took some of the best years out of her life, and I thought, now that she needs help, what if nobody responded? What an injustice that would be" (p. 237).

How did he feel afterward? He said, "I was blessed to have the opportunity to take care of my mother when she was sick and dying. After it was all over, I felt a peace and enrichment I had never experienced before in my life" (p. 238).

Billie Press's generation has been betrayed by society. Heeding the warnings of Paul Ehrlich (1971) about overpopulation, they focused on helping society rather than on the needs of their own families. They didn't raise big families to take care of themselves and their parents in their old age. Billie Press spent her time and energy teaching the children of others, but society didn't repay her by helping her take care of her father.

Living on the fast track creates a void that, ironically, renders people more vulnerable to the arguments for physician-assisted suicide. The Bill Moyers series on death and dying, shown on public television September 10–13, 2000, showed scenes of dying people talking to their friends about spiritual matters. It seems that once you are clearly dying very soon, our culture allows you to step off the fast track and indulge in these emotional comforts. It is only once you know for sure that your relative is dying very soon that you are allowed by our fast-paced culture to step off the fast track to spend time with them.

Some of the problems of nursing homes may derive from this feature of our culture. In a culture in which living on the fast track is given so much prestige, nursing homes cannot attract enough talented people. Moreover, it is not yet recognized what kind of training nursing home staff should receive. If they do not have the cognitive training to interpret the suffering that they will see in a way that allows them to remain productive, they will begin to suffer the kinds of symptoms that Billie Press is undergoing. It is important for us to do research on these issues and to develop standards of training and supporting nursing home personnel and standards for meeting the psychological needs of patients.

The positive vision of physician-assisted suicide that advocates have been holding up—the peaceful suicide, the family saying a harmonious goodbye, the careful guidelines—does not stand up to examination.

There may be many reasons why has our society been so drawn to this vision, but it is time to reject it. We have all heard about the canary that miners used to take with them into the mine. If the canary fainted, they knew it was time to get out. Our vulnerable patients like Judith Curren and Rebecca Badger are like the canary. A set of beliefs and practices that endangers them is not really good for the rest of us either. If our concern for them impels us to turn away from the idea of assisted suicide, to strengthen our commitment to improve health care, and to connect with and console the vulnerable, we will be saving them and saving ourselves as well.

REFERENCES

APA Board debates pros and cons of breaking ties to AMA's ethics principles. (1998, Apr. 17). *Psychiatric News*, p. 5.

Bach, J.R., Campagnolo, D.I., & Hoeman, S. (1991). Life satisfaction of individuals with Duchenne Muscular Dystrophy using long-term mechanical ventilator support. *American Journal of Physical Medicine and Rehabilitation, 70* (3), 129–135.

Boxer, P.A., Burnett, C., & Swanson, N. (1995). Suicide and occupation: A review of the literature. *Journal of Occupational and Environmental Medicine, 37*, 442–452.

Chevlen, E.M., & Smith, W.J. (2002). *Power over pain: How to get the pain control you need.* Steubenville, OH: International Task Force.

Chochinov, H.M., Wilson, K.G., Enns, M., Mowchun, N., Lander, S., Levitt, M., & Clinch, J.J. (1995). Desire for death in the terminally ill. *American Journal of Psychiatry, 152*(8), 1185–1191.

Christakis, N.A., & Lamont, E.B. (2000). Extent and determinants of error in doctors' prognoses in terminally ill patients: Prospective cohort study. *British Medical Journal, 320,* 469–472.

Colt G.H. (1991). *The enigma of suicide.* New York: Simon & Schuster.

Cundiff, D. (1992). *Euthanasia is not the answer: A hospice physician's view.* Totowa, NJ: Humana Press.

Death without dignity. (1997, May 11). *The Oregonian,* p. E4.

Ehrlich, P.R. (1971). *The population bomb.* New York: Sierra Club/Ballantine Books.

Eisner, R. (1994). *The misunderstood economy: What counts and how to count it.* Boston: Harvard Business School Press.

Ellis, A. (1994). Post-traumatic stress disorder (PTSD): A rational emotive behavioral theory. *Journal of Rational-Emotive and Cognitive-Behavior Therapy, 12,* 3–25.

Emanuel, E.J., Fairclough, D., Clarridge, B.C., Blum, D., Bruera, E., Penley, W.C., Schnipper, L.E., & Mayer, R.J. (2000). Attitudes and practices of U.S. oncologists regarding euthanasia and physician-assisted suicide. *Annals of Internal Medicine, 133,* 527–532.

Fenn, D.S., & Ganzini, L. (1999). Attitudes of Oregon psychologists toward physician-assisted suicide and the Oregon Death with Dignity Act. *Professional Psychology: Research and Practice, 30,* 235–244.

Ganzini, L., Fenn, D.S., Lee, M.A., Heintz, R.T., & Bloom, J.D. (1996). Attitudes of Oregon psychiatrists toward physician-assisted suicide. *American Journal of Psychiatry, 153,* 1469–1475.

Groenewoud, J.H., van der Heide, A., Onwuteaka-Philipsen, B.D., Willems, D.L., van der Maas, P.J., & van der Wal, G. (2000). Clinical problems with the performance of euthanasia and physician-assisted suicide in the Netherlands. *New England Journal of Medicine, 342,* 551–556.

Hamilton, N.G. (2002). Oregon's culture of silence. In K. Foley & H. Hendin (Eds.), *The case against assisted suicide: For the right to end-of-life care,* pp. 175–191). Baltimore, MD: Johns Hopkins University Press.

Hartmann, L., & Meyerson, A. (1998). A debate on physician-assisted suicide. *Psychiatric Services, 49,* 1468–1474.

Hendin, H. (1997). *Seduced by death: Doctors, patients, and the Dutch cure.* New York: W.W. Norton.

Humphry, D. (1991). *Final exit: The practicalities of self-deliverance and assisted suicide for the dying.* Eugene, OR: Hemlock Society.

Kaplan, K.J., & Leonhardi, M. (2000). Kevorkian, Martha Wichorek and us: A personal account. In Kaplan, K.J. (Ed.), *Right to die versus sacredness of life.* (p. 267–270) New York: Baywood Publishing.

Karel, R. (1998, Jan. 2). Oregon DB remains divided as assisted suicide law upheld. *Psychiatric News,* p. 5.

Kassler, J. (1994). *Bitter medicine: Greed and chaos in American health care.* New York: Carol Publishing Group.

Kettler, B. (2000, Jun. 25). A death in the family: "We knew she would do it." *Sunday Mail Tribune* (Medford, OR), pp. 1A, 8A.

Kevorkian, J. (1991). *Prescription—Medicide: The goodness of planned death.* Buffalo, NY: Prometheus Books.

Kirschner, D. (2000, May/June). The epidemic of children who kill: Shouldn't managed care have to share in the blame? *The National Psychologist, 9* (3), 16.

Kleinfeld, A. (1997). Is assisted suicide a right?: A review of legal history. 8th Annual Conference of the Institute for Jewish Medical Ethics.

Lagnado L. (2000, Oct. 18) Rx for misery: Medicaid "Fix" binds immigrants in system many find appalling. *The Wall Street Journal*, p. A1, A16.

Loebel, J.P., Loebel, J.S., Dager, S.R., Centerwall, B.S., & Reay, D.T. (1991). Anticipation of nursing home placement may be a precipitant of suicide among the elderly. *Journal of the American Geriatrics Society, 39*, 407–408.

Loftin, C., McDowall, D., Wiersema, B., & Cottey, T.J. (1991). Effects of restrictive licensing of handguns on homicide and suicide in the District of Columbia. *New England Journal of Medicine, 325*, 1615–1620.

Marker, R. (1993). *Deadly Compassion: The death of Ann Humphry and the truth about euthanasia.* New York, William Morrow and Company.

Marker R. (2000). *Assisted suicide: The debate in the States.* International Anti-Euthanasia Task Force.

Marzuk, P.M., Hirsch, C.S., Leon, A.C., Stajic, M., Hartwell, N., & Portera, L. (1993). Increase in suicide by asphyxiation in New York City after the publication of *Final Exit. New England Journal of Medicine, 329*, 1508–1510.

Marzuk, P.M., Tardiff, K., & Leon, A.C. (1994). Increase in fatal suicidal poisonings and suffocations in the year *Final Exit* was published: A national study. *American Journal of Psychiatry, 151*, 1813–1814.

Massad, L.S. (2000). Missed connections. *Journal of the American Medical Association, 284*, 409–410.

Meyer, P. (1970, Feb.). If Hitler asked you to electrocute a stranger, would you? Probably. *Esquire*. In Rubinstein, J. (Ed.) (1974). *Annual editions: Readings in psychology '74/'75.* (pp. 273–279). Guilford, CT: Dushkin Publishing.

Miller, P.J. (2000). Life after Death with Dignity: The Oregon experience. *Social Work, 45*(3), 263–271.

Phillips, D.M. (2000). JCAHO pain management standards are unveiled. *Journal of the American Medical Association, 284*, 428–429.

Poorly trained or overworked nurses cause thousands of deaths, paper finds. (2000, Sep. 10). *St. Louis Post-Dispatch*, A5.

Preparing for tomorrow's healthcare. (2000, Fall). *Barnes-Jewish Cornerstones, 4*(1), 26–27.

Psychiatrists break from APA stand on physician-assisted suicide. (1997, Mar. 7). *Psychiatric News*, 5,34,35.

Quill, T.E. (1993). *Death and dignity: Making choices and taking charge.* New York: W.W. Norton.

Report, Working Group on Assisted Suicide and End-of-Life Decisions. (2000). American Psychological Association.www.apa.org/pi/aseolf.htm

Rose, K.D., & Rosow, I. (1973). Physicians who kill themselves. *Archives of General Psychiatry, 29*, 800–805.

Schwartz, W.B. (1987). The inevitable failure of current cost-containment strategies: why they can provide only temporary relief. *Journal of the American Medical Association, 257*(2), 220–224.

Shavelson; L. (1995). *A chosen death: The dying confront assisted suicide.* New York: Simon & Schuster.

Skloot, F. (2000, May–June). Me, my brain and I. *Utne Reader*, 59–63, 104.

Smith, W.J. (1997). *Forced exit: The slippery slope from assisted suicide to legalized murder*. New York: Times Books.

Smith, W.J. (1999, Nov. 8). Suicide unlimited in Oregon: The result of legalizing physician-assisted suicide. *The Weekly Standard, 5*(8), 11–14.

Smith, W.J. (2000). *Culture of death: The assault on medical ethics in America*. San Francisco: Encounter Books.

Sullivan, A.D., Hedberg, K., & Hopkins, D. (2001). Legalized physician-assisted suicide in Oregon, 1998–2000. *New England Journal of Medicine, 344*, 605–607.

Thomas, J. (2001). Assisted suicide debate divides APA Council meeting. *The National Psychologist, 10* (2), pp. 1, 3.

Washington v. Glucksberg, 521 U.S. 702 (1997).

Zachary, G.P. (2001, Jan. 24). Shortage of nurses hits hardest where they are needed the most. *The Wall Street Journal*, pp. A1, A12.

Zimbardo, P.G. (1974). Pathology of imprisonment. In *Annual Editions: Readings in Psychology '74/'75* (pp. 280–282). Guilford, CT: Dushkin Publishing Group.

Zoccolillo, M., Murphy, G.E. & Wetzel, R.D. (1986). Depression among medical students. *Journal of Affective Disorders, 11*, 91–96.

Index

About the Author

BARBARA A. OLEVITCH is Clinical Assistant Professor at the Missouri Institute of Mental Health. She is a clinical psychologist specializing in the research and treatment of the chronically mentally ill. She is the author of *Using Cognitive Approaches with the Seriously Mentally Ill: Dialogue Across the Barrier* (Praeger, 1995).